ADVANCES IN TAXATION

Volume 1 · 1987

ADVANCES IN TAXATION

A Research Annual

Editor: SALLY M. JONES
Department of Accounting
University of Texas at Austin

VOLUME 1 · 1987

 JAI PRESS INC.

Greenwich, Connecticut   *London, England*

CONTENTS

v

LIST OF CONTRIBUTORS

William H. Bassichis

Department of Physics
Texas A&M University

Virginia L. Bean

College of Business Administration
University of Nebraska at Omaha

Charles E. Boynton IV

Department of Accounting and
    Information Systems
University of Wisconsin-Madison

D. Larry Crumbley

Department of Accounting
Texas A&M University

William A. Duncan

Accounting Department
Arizona State University

Charles R. Enis

Department of Accounting and
    Management Information
    Systems
Pennsylvania State University

John C. Fellingham

Department of Accounting
University of Iowa

Peggy A. Hite

School of Business
University of Kansas

John J. Hourihan

Bureau of Program and Policy
    Coordination
U.S. Agency for International
Development

Herbert G. Hunt, III

School of Business Administration
University of Vermont

Stephen T. Limberg

Department of Accounting
University of Texas at Austin

Michael L. Moore

School of Accounting
University of Southern California

Michael H. Morris

Department of Accounting
University of Notre Dame

Michael A. O'Dell

Accounting Department
Arizona State University

Richard L. Panich

School of Accounting
University of Southern California

Jack Robison

Accounting Department
California Polytechnic State
University

Justin D. Stolen

College of Business Administration
University of Nebraska at Omaha

Carlton D. Stolle

Department of Accounting
Texas A&M University

William T. Stuart

Department of Anthropology
University of Maryland

Charles W. Swenson

School of Accounting
University of Southern California

Judith E. Watanabe

College of Business Administration
University of Nebraska at Omaha

Patrick J. Wilkie

Department of Accounting
University of Texas at Austin

James L. Wittenbach

Department of Accounting
University of Notre Dame

AIT STATEMENT OF PURPOSE

Advances in Taxation (AIT) is a journal for the publication of academic tax research. We plan to publish articles of interest to a wide range of tax academicians, and therefore, research in all possible subject areas will be considered. Such areas may include the current Federal individual income tax system, and possible alternatives to the system such as a comprehensive base, flat-rate income tax, a consumption base/cash flow tax, or a value-added tax. The Federal corporate income tax is another fruitful area for research, as are the Federal estate, gift and generation-skipping transfer taxes, the Federal employment taxes, and various Federal excise taxes. The Federal tax structure affects not only the domestic economy, but the international economy as well, and the subject of international taxation has become a research area in its own right. Finally, the area of state and local taxation offers opportunities for innovative and useful research.

Submitted research may employ research methodologies ranging from empirical and behavioral to legal analysis. Articles must be readable, relevant, and reliable. To be readable, articles must be understandable and concise. To be relevant, articles must be directly related to problems inherent in systems of taxation. To be reliable, conclusions must follow logically from the evidence and arguments presented. For empirical reports, sound research design and execution are critical. For theoretical reports, reasonable assumptions and logical development are essential.

AIT welcomes all comments from readers.

Editor correspondence pertaining to manuscripts should be sent to:

> Professor Sally M. Jones, *Editor*
> Department of Accounting, CBA 4M.256
> University of Texas at Austin
> Austin, Texas 78712-1172
> (512) 471-5332

EDITORIAL POLICY AND MANUSCRIPT FORM GUIDELINES

1. Manuscripts should be typewritten and double-spaced on 8" × 11" white paper. Only one side of a page should be used. Margins should be set to facilitate editing and duplication except as noted:

    a. tables, figures and exhibits should appear on a separate page. Each should be numbered and have a title.

    b. footnotes should be presented by citing the author's name and the year of publication in the body of the text, e.g., Schwartz [1981]; Reckers and Pany [1980].

2. Manuscripts should include a cover page which indicates the author's name and affilitation.

3. Manuscripts should include on a separate lead page an abstract not exceeding 200 words. The author's name and affiliation should not appear on the abstract.

4. Topical headings and subheadings should be used. Main headings in the manuscript should be centered, secondary headings should be flush with the lefthand margin. (As a guide to usage and style, refer to William Strunk, Jr. and E. B. White. **The Elements of Style.**)

5. Manuscripts must include a list of references which contain only those works actually cited. (As a helpful guide in preparing a list of references, refer to Kate L. Turabian. **A Manual for Writers of Term Papers, Theses, and Dissertations.**)

6. In order to be assured of an anonymous review, authors should not identify themselves directly or indirectly. Reference to unpublished working papers and dissertations should be avoided. If necessary, authors may indicate that the reference is being withheld for the reasons cited above.

7. The author will be provided one complete volume of the **AIT** issue in which his or her manuscript appears and ten off-prints of the article.

8. Manuscripts currently under review by other publications should not be submitted. Complete reports of research presented at a national or regional conference of a professional association (e.g., AAA, AIDS etc.) and "State of the Art" papers are acceptable.

9. **Three** copies of each manuscript should be submitted to the Editor at the University of Texas address. Copies of any and all research instruments also should be included.

10. For additional Information regarding the type of manuscripts that are desired, see **AIT Statement of Purpose.**

POTENTIAL PERSONAL WEALTH REDISTRIBUTION EFFECTS OF STRUCTURAL INCOME TAX REFORM

William A. Duncan, Michael A. O'Dell, and
Richard L. Panich

ABSTRACT

The need for tax revision and the specific form that it should take has been an active subject of debate for the past several years. Although a number of studies have estimated the redistribution of the tax burden occasioned by various proposals for tax reform, none have measured the effect that such change would have on asset values and the resultant redistribution of wealth. The purpose of this study is to develop an indicator of the force and direction of the price change resulting from changes in the tax treatment of various assets under two broad proposals for tax reform, a comprehensive income tax and a consumption-based tax. The research design employed a pretest, posttest analysis of investment asset returns with an intervening tax change as the treatment or event of interest. Discounted after-tax cash flows were recomputed under each new set of tax assumptions and compared to those obtained under current tax law. Changes in each asset's net present value were viewed as a measure of the asset's altered "fair market value" after a change in the tax law had occurred. The results suggest that adoption of either

Advances in Taxation, Volume 1, pages 1–21.
ISBN: 0–89232–782–0

tax alternative would result in a new price structure in which the price of common stock would be higher and the price of owner-occupied residential real estate would be lower. Such tax-induced price changes may, in turn, effect a redistribution of wealth among taxpayers who do not hold a balanced portfolio of affected assets. Serious consideration of such collateral effects is essential if significant tax reform is to be addressed responsibly.

This study employs a series of asset model specifications to illustrate tax-induced changes in market values, a generally ignored consequence of tax legislation. When tax rates are changed for all taxpayers or altered for some income class, little or no effect on asset prices should result. But when substantial changes in the treatment of asset classes occurs, tax-induced alteration of relative after-tax cash flows imply asset price changes.

Prices should change because the fair market value of an asset may be viewed as the net present value of all future cash flows (Copeland and Weston 1980). If tax reform meaningfully alters net cash flows across asset classes, the market value of affected assets should change. The purpose of this study is to illustrate the asset value price vector that may be attributed to substantial tax revision.

A simplified model is employed to represent the relationship between after-tax cash flows and the fair market value of assets. This model is employed to compare stipulated market values under current (1985–1986) provisions with the market values implied by the model when such assets are subject to alternative tax systems.[1]

Two alternative tax systems, a comprehensive tax plan and a consumption tax plan, are compared to the existing system. These alternatives draw upon a landmark study which has long provided theoretical guidance for tax reform advocates (see U.S. Department of the Treasury 1977). The prototypical tax systems developed below incorporate some elements of more recent tax reform proposals where necessary to flesh out the theoretical models (see legislation sponsored by Senator Deconcini, U.S. Congress, Senate 1985a, (S. 321), and Senator Bradley and Representative Gephart, U.S. Congress, Senate 1985b, (S. 409).

The results indicate that tax-induced price adjustments may well cause sizable (but as yet unquantified) price changes and suggest that significant wealth redistribution may be an unintended consequence of tax reform. The study concludes that further analysis of such collateral effects of tax legislation is essential if reform is to be addressed responsibly.

BACKGROUND

Participants in the tax reform debate may be advantageously divided into two camps: those who would use the income tax system to achieve social and economic goals and those who reject the use of taxation for these purposes (see U.S. Department of the Treasury 1982; Pechman and Scholt 1982; and Hoffman 1985).

Those opposing use of the tax system as a tool to alter social or economic decisions contend that special tax treatments accorded certain investment or asset classes are economically inefficient (Shoven 1976; Galper and Zimmerman 1977; Feldstein and Slemrod 1980; Cordes and Sheffrin 1981). The inefficiency arises because the tax-imposed alteration of cash flows will distort market returns across assets, artificially shifting scarce resources between competing investments. Introduction of inefficiencies has a cost in terms of lower outputs associated with an altered mix of goods or services.[2] This group of scholars would support a tax reform which tended toward greater neutrality.

A system based solely on a free-market economy should prefer a neutral tax system (see U.S. Department of the Treasury 1977; Woodworth 1977). A neutral tax system leaves market forces free to allocate resources efficiently. The most efficient allocation of resources maximizes national wealth and, presumably, the well-being of all citizens (Feldstein 1983). But efficiency and wealth maximization may not be the only appropriate criteria. Nonneutral provisions may be defended on the grounds that the social value of the investment or action encouraged exceeds the private value, and that tax benefits granted represent payment by the public for value received.

Whatever the merits, the proliferation of credits and special asset treatments over the last decade suggest that the proponents of neutrality have seldom prevailed. They continue, however, to offer cogent arguments and have remained very influential in the tax reform debate. Moreover, they may well be on the brink of a surprising victory. As this is written, a far-reaching modification of the income tax system is being debated which may see the implementation of a more neutral system.[3] What must be considered, however, is the potential wealth cost to current investors who may be foregoing preferential tax treatment to achieve such neutrality.

METHODOLOGY

The approach employed is intended to develop an indicator of the force and direction of the price change resulting from changes in the tax treatment of various assets. The design employs a pretest, posttest analysis of investment asset returns with an intervening tax change as the treatment or event of interest.

The model is based on the assumption that changes in expected future after-tax cash flows of an asset will affect the value of the asset (Stiglitz 1973; DeAngelo and Masulis 1980). The measure developed, the change in "market value" incident to tax change, is not a point estimate but an indicator of the tax change prior vector; one of many price vectors determining final market value. Nonetheless, it is posited that the marketplace will react to any change in this price vector across asset groups to reestablish equilibrium under any new set of tax assumptions.

The Asset Model

As previously stated, this study seeks to isolate and illustrate the influence of tax legislation on the market price of assets. Risk and other important determinants of value may introduce complexity at the expense of clarity. To achieve isolation, all assets are assumed to be equivalent in all relevant respects other than tax treatment. Hence, all assets are assumed to enter the analysis with the same market price and the same internal rate of return on investment given existing tax levies. Although any rate of return or initial "market" value would surfice, these "assets" were designed to produce a ten percent after-tax internal rate of return on a $100,000 initial value under 1985–1986 tax law.[4] Thus, risk and market factors other than tax policy are assumed to be uniform across asset types.

Individual asset models do differ in the pattern of cash flows, a necessary condition in view of the differences in timing and character of cash flows developed by diverse assets. Although cash flow patterns were developed with reference to historic returns, they were adjusted as necessary to assure an equal internal rate of return for each asset. This was done to isolate the effect on return associated with the preferential tax treatment of certain types of income.

Thus, pretest, we stipulate a risk-free environment in which all investors demand and receive a ten percent after-tax internal rate of return. The event of interest, of course, is the alteration of the tax system. Post-event we assume that all investors continue to demand a ten percent after-tax internal rate of return from all investments and compute the "market price" implied by this rate of return along with an altered tax system and corresponding changes in after-tax cash flows. The "market price" change computed in this manner is an indication of the force and direction of price change associated with an alteration of the current tax system and is labeled the tax-induced price vector.

The researchers recognize that market adjustments to tax changes are by no means as clean and simple. In both the short and the long run, rents and values of properties will change in response to a variety of other factors, including shifts in the bargaining power of the factor provider and purchaser and the availability of additional supplies or substitute goods (Hirshleifer 1980). Nevertheless, this analysis provides an indication, if not a measure, of the initial direction and force of the price vector incident to tax revision.

Asset Selection

The following asset types were selected for study: gold bullion, taxable debt instruments, residential real estate, depreciable personal property used in a trade or business, and corporate common stock. These assets were included in the analysis for two reasons. First, income from such assets is subject to a broad array of those tax provisions that vary across asset types. Second, they are representative of the vast majority of individual wealth holdings (see U.S. Department of Commerce, Bureau of the Census 1982). For example, although gold is not the kind of investment that most investors hold, it is representative of many other assets (gems, coins, stamps, antiques, and so on) exhibiting similar cash flow patterns and tax consequences. Gold appeared to be the proper choice to exemplify this class of asset because it has an active market and value is not affected by variations in condition (as are coins), grade (like gems), or style or history (as with antiques).

Although actual market prices are not used in this article, this study is part of a larger work which does employ such information (Panich, O'Dell, and Duncan 1986). For the purpose of this study, market data is used solely to provide a basis for specifying the timing, character, and amount of asset yield resulting in a prespecified after-tax return of ten percent on an assumed investment of $100,000. Thus, asset yields are derived analytically, but have as their basis historical returns experienced in the marketplace.

Gold

Gold bullion and similar assets generate income or loss only on sale. No other income flow is assumed in the model.

Taxable Debt

Returns on taxable debt usually come from two sources: an annual stream of stated interest and net proceeds at the date of sale or maturity. For purposes of distributing the character of income realized on taxable debt, the model assumes an annual stated interest rate of 12 percent with additional gain realized on sale treated as capital gain.

Rental Housing

Residential real estate held for the production of income produces income from rents and from net proceeds received on disposition. The asset is assumed to appreciate at a rate of five percent per year (the same as owner-occupied housing) and to produce gross rentals of slightly less than one percent of fair market value each year. Both estimates are considered representative of returns experienced in the marketplace in recent years (see U.S. Department of Commerce, Bureau of the Census 1982). The tax benefits from depreciation (Accelerated Cost Recovery System (ACRS) rates assumed) represent additional sources of cash flow and are included in the calculation.

Owner-occupied Housing

The cash flows from owner-occupied housing include net-of-tax expenditures incurred in the normal operation and maintenance of the property and net proceeds at sale. The sales value of the home is based on the assumption that the property appreciates at the rate of five percent per year (the same as rental housing).

In addition, this study includes imputation of annual "rental income" representing the gross rental payments that would otherwise be incurred if the homeowner leased comparable space (Alberts and Kerr 1981). Imputed rental income is included because it represents a true economic return to the homeowner and because imputed rental income must be computed under both the comprehensive tax plan and the savings deduction alternative of the consumption tax plan.

One other factor associated with residential real estate, leverage and associated interest deductions, could have been included. However, returns on investment are considered distinct from each asset's manner of acquisition. As such, each asset is assumed to be acquired entirely with cash to better estimate the influence of a tax law change on only those returns unique to each asset class investigated.

An example of the cash flow and present value computations is presented in Table 1. Note that for this asset group, gain on sale may either be recognized currently or deferred to a later date. Computations are shown only in the instance where the homeowner does not reinvest his sales proceeds in a second home and, consequently, must recognize and pay tax on his gain at time of sale.

Before-tax cash inflows and outflows were estimated by reference to actual asset yields that have been observed in the marketplace. Simplifying assumptions were made as necessary to equate discounted after-tax cash flows to the purchase price paid for each asset. In this instance, imputed rental income is calculated as a fixed annuity over the investor's assumed holding period (five years). The impact of this and any other simplification incorporated into the study is considered to be minor.

Depreciable Personalty

Returns on depreciable personalty used in a trade or business constitute rents or contribution to production of income through use and gain or loss

Table 1. Current Tax Law Calculation of After-Tax Cash Flows
Residential Real Estate—Owner Occupied: Recognition of Gain on Sale

Cash Flow	Year 1	2	3	4	5	6	Total Present Value
Revenues:							
Imputed Rental Income							
Annual Before-Tax "Cash Flow"	10,154	10,154	10,154	10,154	10,154		
Less: Tax Payment	0	0	0	0	0	0	
Annual After-Tax "Cash Flow"	10,154	10,154	10,154	10,154	10,154	0	
Discounted After-Tax "Cash Flow"	9,231	8,392	7,629	6,935	6,305	0	38,492
Sales Proceeds							
Before-Tax Sales Proceeds, Net of Closing Costs	0	0	0	0	116,142	0	
Less: Tax Payment on Gain on Sale	0	0	0	0	0	−3,228	
After-Tax Sales Proceeds	0	0	0	0	116,142	−3,228	
Discounted After-Tax Cash Flow	0	0	0	0	72,115	−1,822	70,293
Expenses:							
Deductible Expenses							
Annual Before-Tax Cash Flow	−1,500	−1,560	−1,622	−1,687	−1,755	0	
Plus: Tax Savings	750	780	811	844	877	0	
Annual After-Tax Cash Flow	−750	−780	−811	−843	−878	0	
Discounted After-Tax Cash Flow	−682	−645	−609	−576	−545	0	−3,057
Nondeductible Expenses							
Annual Before-Tax Cash Flow	−1,300	−1,408	−1,524	−1,650	−1,787	0	
Plus: Tax Savings	0	0	0	0	0	0	
Annual After-Tax Cash Flow	−1,300	−1,408	−1,524	−1,650	−1,787	0	
Discounted After-Tax Cash Flow	−1,182	−1,164	−1,145	−1,127	−1,110	0	−5,728
Total Discounted Present Value							100,000

on disposition. The asset is assumed to be sold in year five at an amount equal to adjusted basis plus five percent of original cost. The resulting $5,000 gain is ordinary income by virtue of Section 1245 depreciation recapture. The balance of the income from the property is comprised of tax savings from the investment credit (at the ten percent maximum rate), depreciation deductions (at current or model tax plan rates) and a level stream of other income required to produce the requisite rate of return. Since all returns are taxed as ordinary income, the assumptions about income affect only the timing and not the character of income.

Corporate Common Stock

Income produced by corporate common stock ownership is comprised of dividends (ordinary income) and appreciation in value (capital gains). For purposes of determining the composition of returns, corporations are assumed to earn a 15 percent annual after-tax return and to pay out 50 percent of after-tax profits annually.[5] The undistributed 50 percent of corporate after-tax income is treated as appreciation in the value of the stock.

Existing Tax Structure

Adoption of one of the alternative tax plans described below would alter or eliminate many provisions of current (1985) tax law. The elements which would be altered and which relate to the assets in this analysis include exclusions, deferrals, conversion, and credits.

Exclusions

Exclusions are items of income that are specifically excluded from the definition of income under current law. An example of such untaxed income is the $125,000 of gain realized on the sale of a principal residence (under certain conditions) and the $100 dividend exclusion available to all individuals.

Deferrals

Deferrals are realized income not recognized until a later tax period. Examples include deferral of recognition when proceeds are reinvested (sales of residences or involuntary conversions) or when the investment is essentially unchanged (like-kind exchanges).

Conversion

Conversion is defined as recoveries of cost taken at ordinary income tax rates coupled with gains recognized at more favorable capital gains tax rates. The latter includes gains on capital assets and Section 1231 trade or business assets. Such conversions are currently limited in part by depreciation and other recapture rules.

Credits

The most prominent of the credits, the investment tax credit, is the only tax credit included in this study (Sommerfeld, Anderson, and Brock 1983).

In addition, there are two reasons why all investment returns are assumed to be taxed at the highest marginal rate (50 percent for ordinary income and 20 percent for long-term capital gain income). First, it is thought that a sizeable number of those individuals who hold investment wealth are in the highest marginal tax bracket (see U.S. Department of Commerce, Bureau of the Census 1982). Second, use of the highest marginal tax rate will give greater clarity to the measurement of the direction of changes in asset prices induced by a change in the tax structure. In a sense, the study captures price changes at their extreme to establish a reference point from which all other mitigating influences may be considered. Use is also made of the highest marginal tax rate under each alternative model plan.

Alternative Tax Systems

During the mid-seventies the U.S. Treasury published *Blueprints for Basic Tax Reform* (U.S. Department of the Treasury 1977). This work broke new ground in the study of the tax base and the theoretical justification of tax alternatives significantly different from the current measure of income subject to tax. It outlined two basic alternatives for tax reform: (1) a comprehensive income tax, and (2) a consumption-based tax. Both alternatives broadened the definition of income subject to tax.

The comprehensive model plan proposes to tax all increments to wealth (consumption plus the change in net worth) not limited by current realization concepts. The consumption tax would levy a tax only when assets are consumed (all unrealized economic appreciation and depreciation would be excluded from the tax base under this alternative).

Blueprints for Basic Tax Reform has provided the theoretical basis for many of the more recent tax reform proposals. Some elements of these recent plans have been incorporated in the prototypical alternatives, however, to flesh out the *Blueprint* outlines where needed (see U.S. Congress, Senate 1985a (S. 321); U.S. Congress, Senate 1985b, (S. 409)).

Comprehensive Income Tax Plan

The comprehensive plan is similar to current law but based on a much broader concept of income. Income in this plan is defined to include both current period consumption and, when practical to do so, net additions to wealth. Thus, the rental value of owner-occupied housing is imputed to the owner and a pro rata share of corporate income is taxable to the shareholder even though it is undistributed. State and local interest would no longer be tax-exempt.

All exclusions, deferrals, conversions, and tax credit provisions would be eliminated under the comprehensive plan. Deductions would be retained, but would generally be limited to business-related expenses such as interest, depreciation, taxes, and other ordinary and necessary expenditures. One new class of deduction, owner-occupied housing–related expenses, would be deductible under the comprehensive plan.

Consumption Tax Plan

Blueprints offered a second plan based on consumption. The consumption tax would adjust income realized during the period for net savings activity to arrive at a measure of current consumption. Two different methods of measuring consumption, the savings deduction method or the tax prepayment method, would be available. Taxpayers would be able to select the method to be applied on a transaction-by-transaction basis.

The savings deduction method would use a "qualified account" to measure investments. Here the tax base would be equal to income less additions to the qualified account: the difference would be the amount of income consumed during the period. By the same token, withdrawals from the qualified account would be added to current period income to arrive at a measure of consumption. Thus, taxation would generally be deferred until the taxpayer chose to consume and pay the tax due.

The tax prepayment method takes the opposite tack. All investment activity is treated as a form of personal consumption so all income is treated as currently taxable. This definition of income, however, does not include receipts related to investments acquired with after-tax dollars. In other words, although no deduction is allowed for the initial investment, subsequent depreciation, or any operating expenditure, investment returns (rents, gains or recoveries of capital) are treated as tax-paid and escape taxation when received.

Modification Of The Model Plans

Because some parts of the *Blueprints* model plans were incomplete or open-ended, this study incorporates several features of recent tax reform proposals to complete the specification of each tax model. The three most important adaptations are tax rates, depreciation, and imputed rental income.

Tax Rates

The *Blueprints* plan supported adoption of generally lower tax rates. No specific rates were suggested.

For the Comprehensive plan this study assumes the progressive tax rate structure offered for individual taxpayers in the Bradley-Gephart "Fair Tax Act" proposal (U.S. Congress 1985b, S.409). Thus, for single returns, taxable income below $25,000 is subject to a 14 percent "base rate." Taxable income above this amount is subject to rates of 26 percent (from $25,000 to $37,500) and 30 percent (for income over $37,500). For purposes of this study, only the highest marginal tax rate (30 percent) is used.

A flat tax rate of 19 percent is assumed for the consumption tax plan. This was a rate proposed by Senator DeConcini (D-Arizona) in an initiative theoretically similar to the consumption tax model (U.S. Congress 1985a, S. 321).

Depreciation

No depreciation deduction is allowed under the consumption plan since all investments are treated as either consumption (tax prepaid) or tax deferred (deductible as made). The *Blueprints* proposal supports a periodic depreciation charge with respect to the comprehensive plan but does not provide a suggested schedule or rate for cost recovery. This study assumes the Bradley-Gephart cost recovery system in conjunction with the latter plan.

Bradley-Gephart proposes that assets be divided into six classes based on their Class Life Asset Depreciation Range (CLADR) midpoint lives. The lives range from four to 40 years and depreciation is computed using the 250 percent declining balance method. Like ACRS, a half-year convention is employed only for personalty and no depreciation is allowed in the year of disposition. The assets employed in this study fall into one of two classes: ten-year personalty (Class 3) or real estate with a 40-year life (Class 6).

Imputed Rental Income

The U.S. Treasury did not specify in *Blueprints* the means by which imputed rental income would be computed (this is required for owner-occupied housing). A monthly one percent of fair market value "rule of thumb" rental rate has long been employed by the real estate industry.[6] This estimator began to lose relevance with market changes in the late 1970s. Thus, post-1978 imputed rental rates were estimated by reducing the one-percent rule of thumb by a percentage computed with reference to Consumer Price Index data (see U.S. Department of Commerce, Bureau of the Census, 1982). The reduction percentage represents the annual change in the relationship between the "residential rent CPI" and the "home purchase CPI."

Revised Cash Flow and Present Value Computations

Tables 2, 3 and 4 illustrate the potential effects of an intervening tax change on asset yields for investments in owner-occupied housing where gain on sale is currently recognized and taxed. In each case, discounted after-tax cash flows are recomputed under each new set of tax assumptions (the savings deduction plan, the tax prepayment plan and the comprehensive plan) and summed. Each new net present value can be viewed as a measure of the asset's altered fair market value after a change in the tax law has occurred. As referenced earlier, this assumes that the fair market value of an asset is equivalent to the net present value of all future cash flows, inclusive of tax effects.

Of course, these estimates are best thought of as surrogates of the price vectors (that is, the direction of change in asset values) associated with a change in national tax policy. Their value as rigid point estimates is severely constrained because there was no consideration of changes in other key macroeconomic variables concurrent with a change in asset yields induced by a change in tax structure. Nonetheless, the approach is useful to identify price change tendencies for each of the target asset groups that may be of particular significance in the short run (Hirshleifer 1980).

RESULTS

Table 5 and Figure 1 present the results as revised market price estimates for all assets investigated. Only dollar values are listed in Table 5; these same amounts are plotted on a graph in Figure 1.

The Comprehensive Income Tax Plan

Holders of most investment asset groups would appear to experience a wealth gain upon enactment of this tax alternative. Those who own and occupy their own homes or who have made investments in gold bullion (as representative of a larger class of similarly taxed assets), however, may sustain wealth losses. This is so if investors continue to demand the same after-tax rate of return (assumed to be ten percent in this study) once the tax laws have been changed. Thus, holders of those assets with higher after-tax cash flows should be able to command correspondingly higher prices in the marketplace, as suggested by the direction of the price vector for corporate

Table 2. Savings Deduction Plan Calculation of After-Tax Cash Flows Residential Real Estate—Owner Occupied: Recognition of Gain on Sale

Cash Flow	Year 1	2	3	4	5	6	Total Present Value
Revenues:							
Imputed Rental Income							
Annual Before-Tax "Cash Flow"	10,154	10,154	10,154	10,154	10,154	0	
Less: Tax Payment	−1,929	−1,929	−1,929	−1,929	−1,929	0	
Annual After-Tax "Cash Flow"	8,225	8,225	8,225	8,225	8,225	0	
Discounted After-Tax "Cash Flow"	7,477	6,798	6,180	5,618	5,107	0	31,180
Tax Savings on Direct Expensing in Year of Acquisition	19,000	0	0	0	0	0	
Discounted Tax Savings	17,273	0	0	0	0	0	17,273
Sales Proceeds							
Before-Tax Sales Proceeds, Net of Closing Costs	0	0	0	0	116,142	0	
Less: Tax Payment on Net Sales Proceeds	0	0	0	0	0	−22,067	
After-Tax Sales Proceeds	0	0	0	0	116,142	−22,067	
Discounted After-Tax Cash Flow	0	0	0	0	72,115	−12,456	59,659
Expenses:							
Deductible Expenses							
Annual Before-Tax Cash Flow	−2,800	−2,968	−3,146	−3,337	−3,542	0	
Plus: Tax Savings	532	564	598	634	673	0	
Annual After-Tax Cash Flow	−2,268	−2,404	−2,548	−2,703	−2,869	0	
Discounted After-Tax Cash Flow	−2,062	−1,987	−1,915	−1,846	−1,782	0	−9,592
Total Discounted Present Value							98,520

Table 3.   Tax Prepayment Plan Calculation of After-Tax Cash Flows
Residential Real Estate—Owner Occupied: Recognition of Gain on Sale

	Year						Total Present Value
Cash Flow	1	2	3	4	5	6	
Revenues:							
Imputed Rental Income							
Annual Before-Tax							
"Cash Flow"	10,154	10,154	10,154	10,154	10,154	0	
Less: Tax Payment	0	0	0	0	0	0	
Annual After-Tax							
"Cash Flow"	10,154	10,154	10,154	10,154	10,154	0	
Discounted After-Tax							
"Cash Flow"	9,231	8,392	7,629	6,935	6,305	0	38,492
Sales Proceeds							
Before-Tax Sales							
Proceeds, Net of							
Closing Costs	0	0	0	0	116,142	0	
Less: Tax Payment	0	0	0	0	0	0	
After-Tax Sales							
Proceeds	0	0	0	0	116,142	0	
Discounted After-Tax							
Cash Flow	0	0	0	0	72,115	0	72,115
Expenses:							
Nondeductible Expenses							
Annual Before-Tax							
Cash Flow	−2,800	−2,968	−3,146	−3,337	−3,542	0	
Plus: Tax Savings	0	0	0	0	0	0	
Annual After-Tax Cash							
Flow	−2,800	−2,968	−3,146	−3,337	−3,542	0	
Discounted After-Tax							
Cash Flow	−2,545	−2,453	−2,364	−2,280	−2,199	0	−11,841
Total Discounted Present Value							98,766

Table 4. Comprehensive Plan Calculation of After-Tax Cash Flows
Residential Real Estate—Owner Occupied: Recognition of Gain on Sale

Cash Flow	Year 1	2	3	4	5	6	Total Present Value
Revenues:							
Imputed Rental Income							
Annual Before-Tax "Cash Flow"	10,154	10,154	10,154	10,154	10,154	0	
Less: Tax Payment	−3,046	−3,046	−3,046	−3,046	−3,046	0	
Annual After-Tax "Cash Flow"	7,108	7,108	7,108	7,108	7,108	0	
Discounted After-Tax "Cash Flow"	6,462	5,874	5,340	4,855	4,413	0	26,944
Tax Savings on Annual Depreciation							
Deductions	1,875	1,758	1,648	1,545	1,448	0	
Discounted Tax Savings	1,705	1,453	1,238	1,055	899	0	6,350
Sales Proceeds							
Before-Tax Sales Proceeds, Net of Closing Costs	0	0	0	0	116,142	0	
Less: Tax Payment on Gain of Sale	0	0	0	0	0	−13,117	
After-Tax Sales Proceeds	0	0	0	0	116,142	−13,117	
Discounted After-Tax Cash Flow	0	0	0	0	72,115	−7,404	64,711
Expenses:							
Deductible Expenses							
Annual Before-Tax Cash Flow	−2,800	−2,968	−3,146	−3,337	−3,542	0	
Plus: Tax Savings	840	890	944	1,001	1,063	0	
Annual After-Tax Cash Flow	−1,960	−2,078	−2,202	−2,336	−2,479	0	
Discounted After-Tax Cash Flow	−1,782	−1,717	−1,654	−1,596	−1,538	0	−8,287
Total Discounted Present Value							89,718

Table 5.   Revised Price Estimates (in dollars)

| Investment Asset Group | Current Tax Assumptions | Revised Market Prices | | Comprehensive Income Tax |
| | | Consumption Tax | | |
	50% Marginal Tax Rate	Savings Deduction Method	Tax Prepayment Method	30% Marginal Tax Rate
Gold Bullion	100,000	106,973	108,428	95,791
Taxable Debt	100,000	121,433	128,593	108,642
Residential Real Estate— Owner Occupied:				
Recognition of Gain on Sale	100,000	98,520	98,766	89,718
Deferral of Gain on Sale	100,000	97,042	96,943	88,439
Held for the Production of Income	100,000	111,402	114,669	100,848
Depreciable Personal Property Usedin a Trade or Business	100,000	118,329	124,394	109,004
Corporate Common Stock	100,000	359,909	379,681	154,171

common stock, depreciable personalty, taxable debt, and rental property. Holders of owner-occupied housing and gold, however, may be forced to absorb a loss in market value because of lower after-tax cash flows projected under this model plan.

Most asset returns are substantially improved because of the reduction in marginal tax rates from 50 to 30 percent. In addition, investments in corporate common stock display a large and positive price vector that is unmatched by any other asset class. This may be attributed to the elimination of a separate income tax at the corporate level, thereby freeing large amounts of income for distribution to shareholders or retention and reinvestment.

Other assets, however, experience a deterioration in returns because of the loss of the 20 percent capital gains rate and the imposition of full marginal rates (30 percent in this study) in its stead. This is particularly true of investments in gold bullion, where all returns are considered capital in nature and subject to tax at no more than 20 percent. Those who own and occupy their own homes fare worse for an additional reason. Imputed rental income, considered to be economic or real income but nontaxable under current law, is subject to tax as though such income were realized in cash.

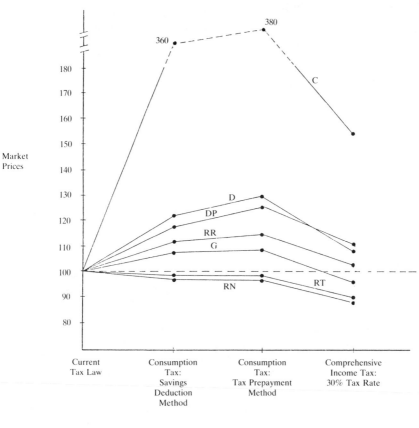

Figure 1.   Revised Market Prices
(In Thousands Of Dollars)

The Consumption Tax Plan

Similar results obtain under both variations of this model plan (the savings deduction method and the tax prepayment method), with one exception. Asset returns for investments in gold bullion improve because the marginal tax rate assumed (a flat rate of 19 percent) is less than the 20 percent capital gains rate evoked under current law.

All asset yields (with the exception of owner-occupied housing) benefit from the reduction in marginal tax rates from 50 to 19 percent. As before, investments in corporate common stock display a very large and positive price vector, attributable in large measure to the elimination of a separate income tax at the corporate level.

Price vectors for owner-occupied housing remain moderately negative for two reasons. Yields are driven down if the savings deduction method is elected because imputed rental income is subject to tax. Ironically, yields are also lowered under the tax prepayment method, but for a different reason. In this instance, yields fall because the deduction for property tax expense is no longer available as an offset to other reported income.

LIMITATIONS

This model may be expected to overstate the influence of tax policy on the valuation of common stock and taxable debt because tax changes do not affect all market participants equally. First, a large part of the market for debt and equity securities is comprised of tax exempt entities (that is, pension and profit sharing plans and similar investors). Second, a significant part of the market may be expected to be comprised of taxpayers subject to substantially less than maximum tax rates (middle-class taxpayers, retired persons, and banks). Finally, participation in the market by nonresident aliens who live outside the boundaries of our tax system has not been considered. Each of these factors reduces the extent to which changes in national tax policy will affect investor cash flows and, of course, the resultant price movements.

In addition, this study has stressed internal validity at the expense of external validity. Different assets do not actually have identical rates of return, and risk is a significant determinant of market price. In addition, many other factors needed to capture the richness of the real world are omitted from the analysis. Finally, some asset prices are set in international markets, and some market participants are not taxable: in either case national tax policy may have little influence.

The authors justify acceptance of these limitations on the grounds that research is an iterative task and a basic understanding of phenomena is a necessary precursor to the design of empirical work. Future work should first focus on an expansion and refinement of this theoretical approach to capture a broader array of market participants. For example, the assumption of maximum tax rates ignores the significant participation of nontaxable entities (such as pension funds) and of lower-rate taxpayers in the stock, debt, and real estate markets. Inclusion of these participants should reduce the estimate of these asset tax price vectors. Leverage, its availability, level of utilization, and tax deductibility may further alter results.

The design of an empirical study must await significant tax revision to validate, extend, or reject these results. As this is written, such tax revision appears imminent and offers an unparalleled opportunity for the researcher to implement these suggestions in the foreseeable future.[3]

CONCLUSIONS

This study points up a generally ignored consequence of tax reform; tax-induced changes in asset market values. The results suggest that, with all other factors held constant, adoption of one of the model tax plans examined herein would result in a new price structure in which the price of common stock is higher and the price of owner-occupied residential real estate is lower. Whether such a result is acceptable is a matter to be resolved in the political arena.

The recognition of the potential for asset price changes incident to tax reform appears essential. But more precise estimates of price changes and the distributional consequences to those holding unbalanced portfolios are needed if the political process by which tax burdens are allocated is to work properly.

NOTES

1. The model was developed to complement a more empirically based study submitted to *Advances in Taxation*.

2. See Jane G. Gravelle, "The Social Cost of Nonneutral Taxation: Estimates for Nonresidential Capital," in *Depreciation, Inflation and The Taxation of Income from Capital*; edited, by Charles R. Hulter (Washington, D.C.: The Urban Institute Press, 1981), pp. 239–248. Gravelle estimates the welfare loss from nonneutrality at $2.5 billion for the year 1978.

3. The tax reform debate has culminated with the passage of the Tax Reform Act of 1986 on October 22, 1986.

4. A sensitivity analysis indicates that changes in the IRR assumption did not materially affect results across asset groups.

5. These values represent average per-share data compiled by Standard and Poor's Corporation for 500 stocks from 1973–1982.

6. This estimate was provided by Russ Lyon Realty and Wagner Realty, both of Phoenix, Arizona.

REFERENCES

Alberts, W., and H. Kerr (1981), "The Rate of Return from Investing in Single-Family Housing," *Land Economics* (May 1981), pp. 230–242.

Bradford, D. (1982), "The Choice Between Income and Consumption Taxes," *Tax Notes* (August 23, 1982), pp. 715–723.

Brennan, G., and D. Nellor (1982), "Wealth, Consumption and Tax Neutrality," *National Tax Journal* (December 1982), pp. 427–436.

Copeland, T. E., and J. F. Weston (1980), *Financial Theory and Corporate Policy* (Addison-Wesley Publishing Co., 1980).

Cordes, J., and S. Sheffrin (1981), "Taxation and the Sectoral Allocation of Capital in the U.S.," *National Tax Journal* (December 1981), pp. 419–432.

DeAngelo, H., and R. Masulis (1980), "Optimal Capital Structure Under Corporate and Personal Taxation," *Journal of Financial Economies*, pp. 3–30.

Diewert, W. E. (1981), "On Measuring the Loss of Output Due to Nonneutral Business Taxation," in *Depreciation, Inflation, and the Taxation of Income From Capital* (Urban Institute Press, 1981), p. 57.

Esenwein, G. (1982), "An Overview of the Issues Concerning a Flat-Rate Income Tax," *Tax Notes* (June 21, 1982), pp. 947–950.

Feldstein, M. (1983), "Tax Reform and Capital Formation," an address given to the Council of Economic Advisers to the American Council for Capital Formation (Washington, D.C., January 19, 1983).

Feldstein, M., and J. Slemrod (1980), "Personal Taxation, Portfolio Choice and the Effect of the Corporate Income Tax," *Journal of Political Economy* (1980), pp. 854–866.

Franz, Pick (1980), *Pick's Currency Yearbook* (Pick Publishing Corporation, 1980).

Galper, H. (1983), "The Coming Reexamination of Tax Policy," *Tax Notes* (May 2, 1983), pp. 379–391.

Galper, H., and D. Zimmerman (1977), "Preferential Taxation and Portfolio Choice: Some Empirical Evidence," *National Tax Journal* (1977), pp. 387–394.

Gensheimer, C. (1983), "Revising the Individual Income Tax," *Tax Notes* (August 8, 1983), pp. 427–432.

Gravelle, J. (1981), "The Social Cost of Nonneutral Taxation: Estimates for Nonresidential Capital," in *Depreciation, Inflation and the Taxation of Income From Capital* (Urban Institute Press, 1981), pp. 239–248.

Hall, R. E., and A. Rabushka (1983), "A Proposal for a Flat-Rate Consumption Tax," a paper prepared for the American Council for Capital Formation: Center for Policy Research (Washington, D.C., January 19–21, 1983).

Hirshleifer, J. (1980), *Price Theory and Applications* (Prentice-Hall, Inc., 1980).

Hoffman, W. H. (1985), *West's Federal Taxation: Corporations, Partnerships, Estates, and Trusts* (West Publishing Co., 1985).

Panich, R. L., M. A. O'Dell, and W. A. Duncan (1986), "Federal Tax Policy: The Perceived Effect of Major Tax Changes on Asset Prices and the Distribution of Wealth," unpublished working paper (Arizona State University, 1986).

Pechman, J. A., and J. K. Scholt (1982), "Comprehensive Income Taxation and Rate Reduction," a statement prepared for the Senate Finance Committee (Brookings Institution, Economic Studies Program, September 30, 1982).

Salomon Brothers (1982), *Analytical Record of Yields and Yield Sources* (Salomon Brothers, Inc., April 1982).

Shoven, J. B. (1976), "The Incidence and Efficiency of Taxes on Income from Capital," *Journal of Political Economy* (1976), pp. 1261–83.

Sommerfeld, R. M., H. M. Anderson, and H. R. Brock (1983), *An Introduction to Taxation* (Harcourt Brace Jovanovich, Inc., 1983).

Standard & Poor's (1983), "Security Price Index Record," *Standard & Poor's Statistical Service* (Standard & Poor's Corporation, 1983).

Stiglitz, J. E. (1973), "Taxation, Corporate Financial Policy and the Cost of Capital," *Journal of Public Economics* (1973), pp. 1–34.

Surrey, S. (1980), "Our Troubled Tax Policy: False Routes and Proper Paths to Change," a presidential address given at the Seventy-Third Annual Meeting of the National Tax Association (New Orleans, La., November 17, 1980).

U.S. Congress, Senate (1985a), *Flat Rate Tax System* (S. 321), 99th Cong., 1st Sess., (January 31, 1985).

_____ (1985b), *Fair Tax Act of 1985* (S. 409), 99th Cong., 1st Sess., (February 6, 1985).

U.S. Department of Commerce, Bureau of the Census (1982), *Statistical Abstract of the United States: 1982–1983* (U.S. Government Printing Office, 1982).

U.S. Department of Housing and Urban Development (1983), *Characteristics of FHA Single-Family Mortgages: Calendar Year 1982* (U.S. Government Printing Office, 1983).

U.S. Department of the Treasury (1977), *Blueprints for Basic Tax Reform* (U.S. Government Printing Office, January, 1977).

_____ (1981), *1980 Statistics of Income: Corporate Income Tax Returns* (U.S. Government Printing Office, 1981).

_____ (1982), "Statement of the Honorable John E. Chapoton, Assistant Secretary of the Treasury for Tax Policy Before the Senate Finance Committee," (September 28, 1982).

U.S. Federal Home Loan Bank Board (1983), "Mortgage Markets," *Federal Home Loan Bank Board Journal* (U.S. Government Printing Office, November 1983).

Wildavsky, A. (1981), "A Uniform Income Tax," *Tax Notes* (March 23, 1981), pp. 611–612.

Woodworth, L. (1977), "General Policy Considerations Affecting the Choice of a Particular Tax Base," *National Tax Journal* (September 1977), pp. 231–235.

TAX RATES, TAX SHELTERS AND OPTIMAL PORTFOLIOS

John C. Fellingham, Stephen T. Limberg, and Patrick J. Wilkie

ABSTRACT

This paper shows optimal portfolios will be diversified and investor-specific solely because of two fundamental features of the extant tax law; progressive tax rates and dissimilar tax treatment of investment cash flows. The presence of uncertain investment returns and investor risk aversion is not necessary for this result to be obtained.

The setting here includes perfect certainty and a simplified version of the current tax system. Each investment's pre-tax return is fixed, but its after-tax return is shown to be variable, dependent upon:

1. the progressivity of the tax rate structure,
2. the investor's initial, noninvestment (exogenous) tax attributes (that is, amount of other taxable income),
3. the manner in which investment cash flows are translated into taxable income,

Advances in Taxation, Volume 1, pages 23–47.
Copyright © 1987 JAI Press Inc.
All rights of reproduction in any form reserved.
ISBN: 0–89232–782–0

4. the time-pattern exhibited by such cash flows, and
5. the amount of each investment included in the portfolio.

It is also shown that these factors interact in such a manner that investments with similar pre-tax rates of return will, in general, experience lower and dissimilar after-tax returns. Further, it is demonstrated that as investing takes place, the after-tax rate of return declines to different degrees across investments. Thus, the relative attractiveness of investments changes as investing occurs and diversified, investor-specific optimal portfolios result.

INTRODUCTION

A diverse set of investments is available in current markets. The richness of this set provides investors with the opportunity to construct investment portfolios which are tailored to their individual preferences and attributes. The process of identifying optimal portfolios, however, is not easy or without cost, even in a setting with complete certainty. Specifically, solving the optimization problem requires accounting for both the direct (pre-tax) and indirect (tax-induced) cash flow for each potential portfolio.

The direct cash flows of an investment are those associated with its acquisition (downpayment), operation (operating revenues and expenses) and disposal (sales proceeds). In a certainty setting the analysis of these cash flows across portfolios is relatively straightforward; such flows are assumed to be known and independent across investments.

The indirect or tax-induced cash flows of an investment are the changes in the investor's tax payments that result from the investment's acquisition, operation, and disposal. Unlike the case with direct cash flows, however, analyzing the indirect cash flows of an investment is complex and potentially costly. The analysis is complex because the tax effects of an investment are not independent of the investor or of the other investments in the portfolio.

The tax effect of an investment depends first on the tax attributes of the investors; the capacity they possess to exploit particular tax features of an investment. For example, in each year an investor will possess some combination of tax attributes; a net-operating-loss carryforward, a capital loss carryforward, a certain amount of ordinary income, deductions, exemptions and credits, and a resulting marginal tax rate. The initial values for these attributes in each year can be assumed to be determined exogenously, without regard for the composition of the investment portfolio. During each year, however, values may change as investments are undertaken, with the result that the relative and absolute attractiveness of successive investments may be changed as well. For instance, the attractiveness of the marginal unit of a leveraged real estate shelter will decline as the investor's marginal tax rate falls, the investment interest limitation is reached, or the alternative minimum tax comes into play.

The second aspect of this complexity is that the available tax features of a portfolio of investments are not simply additive across investments, as is the case with direct cash flows. Some tax features can act to offset one another, such as with long-term capital gains and short-term capital losses, while others are limited or restricted in magnitude. Examples of the latter include interest deductions and the investment interest limitation, investment credits and the limitation of investment credits, losses and the at risk rules, and preference deductions and the alternative minimum tax.

Traditionally, the rationale for portfolio strategies has depended on uncertain security returns and investor risk aversion. See, for example, the classic works of Markowitz (1952) and Sharpe (1963).[1] Recently, however, Fellingham and Wolfson (1978) have shown that such conditions are not necessary for one to seek diversification in forming optimal portfolios. Specifically, they found that the existence of a progressive tax rate structure will cause a risk-neutral individual to diversify due to the "concavification" of a linear preference function. Their findings hold when progressivity refers to a marginal, rather than average tax rate that rises with income (Schneider 1980; Fellingham and Wolfson 1984).

This study expands upon the work of Fellingham and Wolfson by showing that in a setting with certainty and a progressive tax rate schedule, diversification of investments will occur because of declining after-tax returns to scale. Such declines in after-tax rates of return result because the very act of investing causes intra-temporal tax bracket variation.

The purpose of this paper is to develop a method for identifying investor-specific, optimal portfolios of investments. The setting here includes perfect certainty and a simplified version of the extant tax law; one class of income with a progressive tax rate structure. The task is to allocate a given amount of resources at period zero across "m" investment alternatives for "n" future periods so that after-tax wealth at the end of period n is maximized.

The remainder of the paper is organized in the following manner. In the second section a unique expression for mapping pre-tax cash flows to taxable income is specified. This expression contributes to the model by providing a scale-independent measure which relates the direct cash flows of an investment to their effects on taxable income. The third section formulates and illustrates a two-date model as a simplified basis for further analysis. In the fourth section this model is used to show that differential initial tax rates across investors and inter-temporal changes in such rates necessitate investor-specific portfolio decisions. Clientele effects in the buying and selling of tax shelters are predicted with the potential for empirical verification. In the fifth section intra-temporal tax rate changes are shown to induce declining after-tax returns to scale in certain investments. It is shown that a portfolio investment strategy will produce results that are at least as good as those obtained from a single-investment, plunging strategy. The sixth section expands the model by illustrating optimal portfolio selection in a more realistic multiple-period and multiple-investment setting.

ACCOUNTING RELATIONSHIPS

The analysis of portfolio decisions is facilitated by identifying the direct (pre-tax) cash flows of an investment and then mapping them into taxable income. The accounting relationship, p, between direct cash flows and taxable income in year j can be expressed as follows:

$$p_j = \frac{x_j}{c_j}.$$

where x_j = the investor's taxable income (or loss) from the investment in year j, and c_j = the investor's direct cash flow from the investment in year j.

For convenience we refer to this function as the accounting ratio of an investment. To the extent that there are k different types of income (or deduction) for tax purposes, there are k unique accounting characteristics. However, at this point we assume that there is only one class of income, so-called ordinary income.

The accounting ratio of an investment is scale-independent; the accounting relationship between direct cash flows and taxable income is assumed to be proportional for any specific investment and year. For example, doubling the amount of an investment will usually double the investor's taxable income (or loss) from the investment.[2]

For any specific investment, however, it is unlikely that p_j will be the same for each of the years in the investment's useful life. For instance, upon purchasing a $1,000, three-year ten-percent taxable bond, p_0 is 0.00 (x_0/c_0 = 0/ − 1,000). Yet, $p_1 = p_2 = 1.00$, as the entire amount of each year's direct cash flow ($100 of interest) is fully taxable. In year three, p_3 = 0.09, as only the $100 interest portion of the $1,100 received is subject to taxation.

The range of attainable values for the accounting ratio is unbounded; any real number is feasible.[3] However, because the ratio's value is a ratio of two numbers, positive and negative values have distinctly different meanings. Specifically, the sign of the value does not indicate the presence of cash inflows or outflows. Rather, positive ratio values reflect agreement between cash inflows and increases (or outflows and decreases) in taxable income, while negative ratio values signify disagreement between the two.

For example, a positive value for the accounting ratio at the time of the initial investment indicates a large write-off of the investment (or decline in taxable income) associated with the initial cash outlay. Both x_0 and c_0 are negative. A positive value at liquidation, however, refers to the exist-

Table 1. Accounting Ratios for a Hypothetical Oil and Gas Venture

Year	x_j	c_j	p_j
	$	$	
0	(7,500)	(10,000)	0.75
1	2,900	4,000	0.73
2	2,600	3,500	0.74
3	4,000	4,500	0.88
	2,000	2,000	

ence of a large gain on disposition (increase in taxable income) upon the receipt of the liquidation proceeds. Here, x_n and c_n are positive. In contrast, a negative value indicates either a decrease in taxable income coupled with a positive cash flow (x_j is negative and c_j is positive), as occurs when depreciation or depletion deductions shelter operating revenues, or an increase in taxable income in conjunction with a cash outflow (x_j is positive and c_j is negative), so-called phantom gain, which occurs when liquidation proceeds are sufficient to generate a taxable gain, but are not enough to extinguish the outstanding debt.

To illustrate, consider a hypothetical oil and gas tax shelter. In the initial year of the project intangible drilling and development costs (IDC) are typically deductible. A partnership agreement constructed to exploit this provision will allocate a major portion of the IDC to the limited partners, usually creating a write-off of 60 to 90 percent of the initial cash investment.[4] In subsequent years specially allocated depletion allowances may reduce taxable income below cash inflows. Therefore, the accounting ratios for a $10,000 unit in such an oil and gas venture might appear as shown in Table 1.

The term c_0 represents the investor's $10,000 cash investment in the shelter, while the $7,500 deduction in the initial year, x_0, might be attributable to IDC. Depletion deductions could result in taxable income, x_1 and x_2, that is less than direct cash inflows from operations in years one and two. In year three, direct cash inflows may occur from operations and disposal of the venture. Thus, x_3 might reflect taxable gains from disposition, net of the operating results in that period. The values of the accounting ratio capture these relationships for each year.

Notice in this example that, compared to the investment in taxable bonds, the time-pattern of accounting ratios for the oil and gas tax shelter is distinctly different. In particular, it has relatively higher ratio values for the initial and final years and relatively lower values in years one and two. This time-pattern of the accounting ratios is the trademark of a tax shelter: early period write-offs of the initial investment, tax-preferred or sheltered

Table 2.   Accounting Ratios for a Hypothetical Leveraged Oil and Gas Venture

Year	x_j	c_j	p_j
	$	$	
0	(7,500)	(1,000)	7.50
1	2,000	3,100	0.65
2	1,700	2,600	0.65
3	3,100	(5,400)	−0.57
	(700)	(700)	

operating income and finally, the "day -of -reckoning," with relatively large increments to gross income, if not taxable income, at liquidation.

To demonstrate the range of feasible ratio values, reconsider the previous example with leverage. Assume that the investor uses recourse debt with a 10 percent simple interest rate to finance 90 percent of the $10,000 investment. The accounting ratios in this case are shown in Table 2.

In this instance the values of the accounting ratio vary more widely than in the unlevered case; ranging from 7.50 at the time of investment to −0.57 at liquidation. The values for p_1 and p_2 are slightly different too, due to the annual interest payments on the loan of $900 per year. Here, the investor receives write-offs of 7.5 to 1 for his initial investment, but also experiences phantom gain as the proceeds from liquidation are sufficient to generate taxable gain, but not enough to repay the outstanding liability. The investor must contribute $5,400 from other sources to pay off the debt.[5]

To summarize, the examples shown above demonstrate that the accounting ratio is a useful means of describing the relationships that exist between the annual cash flows of an investment and their effects on taxable income. The p_js are assumed to be constant for any level of a specific investment in a given year. However, it is unlikely that their values will be the same for each year throughout an investment's useful life because of inter-period changes in the relationship between direct cash flows and taxable income. Further, the range of attainable values for the accounting ratio is unbounded, and the interpretation of each value is complex, depending on the sign of both the numerator (change in taxable income) and the denominator (direct cash flow).

A TWO-DATE MODEL

Optimal investment strategy in the two-date model is a function of both the accounting ratios of an investment and the tax attributes of the investor. Of particular importance is the investor's marginal tax rate, t_j, which in a

progressive tax rate setting depends upon the investor's other, noninvestment (and exogenous) income. The interaction between the investment's
accounting ratios and the investor's marginal tax rate can be demonstrated
through the use of a simplified two-date model.

   Consider a two-date, certainty setting in which a pre-tax investment, I, is
made in the year 0 and a direct cash flow, $(1+s)I$, is received in year one.
Here s is the pre-tax rate of return. Appending a tax credit, i (stated as a
percent of the investment), and a tax rate, t, allows for the specification of
the amount of the after-tax investment, a, as a function of the pre-tax
investment:

$$a = I(1 - p_0 t_0) - iI,$$

which implies

$$I = \frac{a}{1 - p_0 t_0 - i},$$

and

$$TW = \frac{(1 + s)\, a\, (1 - p_1 t_1)}{(1 - p_0 t_0 - i)}. \tag{1}$$

Here, TW is the after-tax terminal wealth in period 1 expressed as a function
of the after-tax investment, a. When $t_0 = t_1 = t$, equation one reduces to:

$$TW = \frac{(1 + s)\, a\, (1 - p_1 t_1)}{(1 - p_0 t_0 - i)}. \tag{1'}$$

   The notation for the two-date model is as follows:

I = pre-tax investment in year 0,
s = pre-tax rate of return on I,
p_j = accounting ratio for an investment in period j,
t_j = marginal tax rate in period j,
a = after-tax investment in year 0, and
i = investment tax credit expressed as a percent of investment, I.

   To demonstrate the use of this model, consider the following hypothetical
example. Assume that an investor invests \$20,000, I, in an investment that
has a pre-tax rate of return of 10 percent ($s = 0.10$). The investor's marginal
tax rate is 50 percent for each period ($t_0 = t_1 = 0.50$). The investment allows
for a 10 percent investment tax credit ($i = 0.10$) and has accounting ratios
of 70 percent in period zero and 77 percent in period one ($p_0 = 0.70$, $p_1 =
0.77$). Table 3 uses the two-date model to compute the after-tax rates of
return.

   Notice that the initial investment of \$20,000 overstates the actual outlay

Table 3.   The Two-date Model—a Numerical Example

Assumptions:

$I = \$20,000$ $\qquad i = 0.10$
$s = 0.10$ $\qquad p_0 = 0.70$
$t_0 = t_1 = 0.50$ $\qquad p_1 = 0.77$

Calculations:

$$a = I(1 - p_0 t_0) - iI \rightarrow \$20,000(1 - (0.70)(0.50) - (0.10)(\$20,000)) = \$11,000$$

$$TW = \frac{(1 + s)\, a\, (1 - p_1 t_1)}{(1 - p_0 t_0 - i)} \rightarrow \frac{(1 + 0.10)\,\$11,000\,(1 - (0.77)(0.50))}{(1 - (0.70)(0.50) - 0.10)} = \$13,530$$

$$\text{After-tax rate of return} = \frac{(\$13,530 - \$11,000)}{\$11,000} = \frac{\$\,2,530}{\$11,000} = 0.23$$

because of the tax benefits available to the investor. These benefits include the investment tax credit of \$2,000 (\$20,000i) and a \$14,000 (\$20,000p_0) tax deduction, which produces \$7,000 (\$14,000t_0) of tax savings. Together, they reduce the amount actually invested from \$20,000 to \$11,000.

In year one, a direct cash flow of \$22,000 (\$20,000(1 + s)) is received. However, there is \$16,940 (\$22,000p_1) of taxable income associated with this inflow that produces a tax cost of \$8,470 (\$16,940t_1). The result is that after-tax terminal wealth equals \$13,530 (\$22,000 − \$8,470) and the after-tax rate of return is 23 percent (\$2,530/\$11,000); an amount substantially greater than the pre-tax rate of return of 10 percent. Thus, the importance of accounting for both the direct and indirect cash flows of an investment in determining the actual rate of return is apparent.

INTER-TEMPORAL VARIATION OF ACCOUNTING RATIOS AND TAX RATES

The effect that the inter-temporal variation of accounting ratios and tax rates has on terminal wealth can be demonstrated by using the two-date model developed in the previous section with various inter-temporal combinations of p_j and t_j.

In Table 4, one aspect of this effect is demonstrated as the terminal wealth associated with various time-patterns of p_j and a constant tax rate (that is, $t_0 = t_1 = t$) are shown. The sensitivity of this effect to the level of the tax rate is also illustrated by recomputing the terminal wealth values under a second, but still constant tax rate. The terminal wealth values are computed under the assumptions that the after-tax investment, a, is \$10,000 and there is no investment return or investment credit ($s = i = 0.0$). Thus, the

Table 4. Terminal Wealth for Different Time-patterns of Accounting Ratios With a Constant Tax Rate

	Example One: t = 33 percent				*Example Two: t = 50 percent*			
p_0	0.60	0.70	0.80	0.90	0.60	0.70	0.80	0.90
p_1								
0.60	$10,000	$10,429	$10,897	$11,408	$10,000	$10,769	$11,667	$12,727
0.70	9,587	10,000	10,448	10,939	9,286	10,000	10,833	11,818
0.80	9,177	9,571	10,000	10,469	8,571	9,231	10,000	10,909
0.90	8,766	9,142	9,552	10,000	7,857	8,464	9,167	10,000

differences in terminal wealth values within the examples in the table result solely from the time pattern of the p_js.[6]

Two observations about the values of terminal wealth are noteworthy. First, the amounts along the $p_0 = p_1$ diagonal for both examples are constant and equal to $10,000; the after-tax investment amount. This occurs because with no investment tax credit ($i = 0.00$) Eq. (1) reduces to:

$$TW = a(1 + s); \text{ if } p_0 = p_1 \text{ and } t_0 = t_1.$$

In this case terminal wealth is unaffected by the investor's tax rate, t_j. Consequently, after-tax return, $(TW - a)/a$, equals pre-tax return, s, as in this example where they are both equal to zero.

The second observation is that, for any given p_0, a 10 percentage-point decrement in p_1 (moving up the columns) increases terminal wealth by a constant amount. For example, in example one, when p_0 is 0.60 every decrement of 10 percentage points in p_1 increases terminal wealth by $380, whereas a similar increment results in a $380 decrease in terminal wealth.[7]

The critical observation, however, involves comparisons of the terminal wealth values between examples one and two. Specifically, terminal wealth is more spread out in example two, where the tax rate is higher (50 percent instead of 33 percent). For example, with p_1 fixed at 0.70, a decrease in p_0 from 0.70 to 0.60 causes a greater reduction in terminal wealth for a tax-payer in the 50-percent tax bracket ($10,729 - $10,000 = $729) compared to a taxpayer in the 33 percent bracket ($10,429 - $10,000 = $429). This indicates that high-bracket taxpayers will be more sensitive to any given change in the time pattern of p_js than taxpayers in lower tax brackets. This finding can be expressed more formally by differentiating Eq. (1) with respect to tax rates:

$$\frac{\partial TW}{\partial t} \gtreqless 0 <==> p_0 \gtreqless p_1 \text{ (for } i = 0). \tag{2}$$

In addition, notice that the absolute value of the difference between the amounts in examples one and two increases as p_0 increases and p_1 decreases. Intuitively, as p_0 increases and p_1 decreases taxable income is reduced. Thus, taxpayers with higher tax rates will benefit most from such reductions in taxable income. Once again, this finding can be expressed more formally by differentiating Eq. (2) with respect to p_0 and p_1:

$$\frac{\partial^2 TW}{\partial p_0 \partial t} > 0; \frac{\partial^2 TW}{\partial p_1 \partial t} < 0. \tag{3}$$

In summary, any given set of accounting ratios, p_0 and p_1, will have a greater impact on the terminal wealth of high-bracket taxpayers relative to those in lower tax brackets. Further, for any given tax rate, the effect on terminal wealth of differences between the accounting ratio values is directly related to the magnitude of the difference in such values.

This analysis of the relationship between terminal wealth, the investment's accounting ratios and the investor's tax rates can be extended still further, however, by allowing the tax rates to vary over the useful life of the investment. Specifically, Table 5 illustrates the effect that inter-temporal tax rate variation has on the relative and absolute attractiveness of two alternative investments and thus, on terminal wealth.

In this table there are two investment alternatives and two time-patterns of tax rates. The first investment alternative is a tax shelter with a pre-tax rate of return of 8 percent and accounting ratios of 70 percent and 65 percent for years zero and one, respectively. The second investment is a tax-free bond with a pre-tax and after-tax rate of return of 10 percent. The accounting ratios for the tax-free bond are zero for both years. Both investments require after-tax investments of $10,000. In the first setting, the tax rate is fixed over time with $t_0 = t_1 = 0.45$. In the second setting, however, the tax rate increases by four percentage points over the useful life of the investment so that $t_0 = 0.45$ and $t_1 = 0.49$.

In the first tax-rate setting, the tax shelter is the superior investment because it produces a greater amount of terminal wealth ($TW = \$11,155$) than the tax-free bond ($TW = \$11,000$). Here, the tax rate is constant over time; $t_0 = t_1 = 0.45$. In the second setting, however, it is the tax-free bond that is the superior investment, as the terminal wealth associated with the tax shelter investment falls to $10,745, while that of the tax-free bond remains unchanged. Here, the tax rate varies over time with $t_0 = 0.45$ and $t_1 = 0.49$: a four percentage point increase in the tax rate for year one.

This extension of the analysis can also be demonstrated more formally by referring to Eq. (1) and differentiating with respect to the tax rates, t_0 and t_1:

Table 5. Terminal Wealth under Differing Inter-temporal Tax Rates

	Variable	Tax Shelter	Tax-free (muni) Bond
Assumptions:	s	0.08	0.10
	i	0	0
	p_0	0.70	0
	p_1	0.65	0
	a	$10,000	$10,000
Setting 1: $t_0 = t_1 = .45$			
	TW	$11,155	$11,000
	ROR	11.6%	10.0%
Setting 2: $t_0 = 0.45, t_1 = 0.49$			
	TW	$10,745	$11,000
	ROR	7.5%	10.0%

$$\frac{\partial TW}{\partial t_0} > 0 \text{ for } p_0 > 0; \text{ and}$$

$$\frac{\partial TW}{\partial t_1} < 0 \text{ for } p_1 > 0. \tag{4}$$

In words, for positive values of p_0 and p_1, changes in terminal wealth are directly related to changes in t_0, and inversely related to changes in t_1.

Thus, the analysis here demonstrates that the terminal wealth associated with an investment depends upon the level and the inter-temporal variation of both the investment's accounting ratios and the investor's tax rates. Specifically, terminal wealth increases when p_j and t_j are larger, given that $p_0 > p_1$ and $t_0 > t_1$.

This can be stated more formally by differentiating Eq.(1) with respect to both the accounting ratio and the tax rate

$$\frac{\partial^2 TW}{\partial t_0 \partial p_0} > 0; \frac{\partial^2 TW}{\partial t_1 \partial p_1} < 0. \tag{5}$$

In other words, the magnitude of the increase in terminal wealth associated with changes in the accounting ratio and the tax rate grows as the initial accounting ratio and tax rate rise and as the final accounting ratio and tax rate fall. Specifically there is an interaction between the tax rate and the accounting ratios of the tax shelter. A good shelter (in the sense of higher p_0 or lower p_1) improves faster as p_0 and t_0 increase and as p_1 and t_1 decrease.

An empirical result of the relationship between terminal wealth, the investment's accounting ratios and the investor's tax rates should be observed in the behavior of tax-shelter investors and promoters. In particular, the fact that a given set of accounting ratios, p_0 and p_1, has a greater impact on the terminal wealth of high or decreasing tax-rate taxpayers compared to those in low or increasing tax brackets, should affect the types of investments investors make and the types of investors to whom promoters market investments.

Thus, an "investor effect" should be that high or decreasing tax bracket taxpayers will be willing to incur more costs to seek out a tax shelter with a favorable time-pattern of accounting ratios than their low or increasing bracket counterparts. Under an analogous "promoter (or clientele) effect," organizers of favorable tax shelters should be expected to market their product to a clientele comprised of high or decreasing tax bracket taxpayers; whereas, one would expect unfavorable tax shelters to be marketed to persons in low or increasing tax brackets.[8] For example, the optimal portfolio for a high- or decreasing-bracket taxpayer is likely to include investments with relatively low pre-tax returns, but with favorable time-patterns of accounting ratios. In contrast, taxpayers in low or increasing tax brackets are likely to concentrate their resources on investments with high pre-tax returns, regardless of their accounting ratios.

OPTIMAL PORTFOLIOS IN A TWO-DATE SETTING

In the previous section, the effect of the investment's inter-period accounting ratios and the investor's inter-period tax rates on terminal wealth was developed. Here that analysis is expanded by examining the effect that successive investments have on the intra-temporal marginal tax rate of the investor, and thus on terminal wealth.

Investment-induced bracket shifts (intra-temporal rate variation) create declining after-tax returns to scale for successive investments in a favorable tax shelter. Such declines in after-tax rates of return occur because, in the presence of a progressive tax rate structure, a given set of accounting ratios will yield decreasing tax benefits, and/or increasing tax costs as the investor's marginal tax rate is affected by previous investments. Therefore, such declining returns to scale create a circular, investor-specific decision problem, since tax brackets determine the investment strategy while the investment determines the tax brackets. In particular, investments with different accounting ratios may affect an investor's marginal tax rate differently, and thus, experience different rates of decline in their after-tax rates of return. This phenomenon suggests that a portfolio or multiple asset investment strategy will be at least weakly preferred to a plunging or single asset investment strategy, which is optimal in a no-tax, certainty setting.

Table 6. The Effect of Intra-temporal Variations on Terminal Wealth

	Intra-temporal Tax Rate Variation						
(1)	*(2)*	*(3)*	*(4)*	*(5)*	*(6) Portfolio*		
Variable	*Shelter Investment*	*Shelter Investment*	*Shelter Investment*	*Shelter Investment*	*Shelter*	*Muni*	*Total*
a	\$10,000	\$10,000	\$10,000	\$40,000	\$21,920	\$18,080	\$40,000
$t_0 = t_1 = t$	45%	(a)	(a)	(a)	(a)	0%	(a)
OI Yr. 0[(b)]	n/a	\$108,000	\$108,000	\$108,000	⟵	\$108,000	⟶
OI Yr. 1	n/a	108,000	85,000	85,000	⟵	85,000	⟶
TW	\$11,155	\$10,801	\$11,173	\$43,397	\$24,469	\$19,888	\$44,357
ROR	11.6%	8.0%	11.7%	8.5%	11.6%	10.0%	10.9%

Notes:
n/a = not applicable, other income is not relevant; the tax rates are exogenously given.
a = the tax rate depends on the amount of other income. Using the 1984, married–filing-jointly rate schedule, \$108,000 of other income is in the 45% bracket, while \$85,000 is in the 42% bracket.
b = OI refers to the taxpayer's "other" (exogenous) income.

The impact of intra-temporal tax rate variation on investment decisions, and thus, on terminal wealth, is demonstrated in Table 6. Here the investor has the same investment choices as in Table 5; a tax-free bond with a pre-tax and after-tax rate of return of 10 percent and a tax shelter investment with a pre-tax rate of return of 8 percent and accounting ratios of 70 and 65 percent for years zero and one, respectively. In this example, however, the investor's marginal tax rates are allowed to vary from their initial, exogenous values as the taxable income or loss produced by an investment is realized.

The first column of Table 6 identifies the rows in the exhibit:

1. the amount of after-tax investment, *a*
2. the tax rates for the constant rate example, $t_0 = t_1 = t$,
3. the amount of other, noninvestment (and exogenous) income, OI
4. the terminal wealth associated with each investment strategy, TW, and
5. the rate of return for each investment strategy, ROR.

Column two of Table 6 is the "constant tax rate" setting of Table 5 where the investor's marginal tax rate is assumed to be unaffected by the nature of the investment undertaken: the tax rates are 45 percent for both years.

In columns three through six the investor's initial marginal tax rate for each year is determined by applying the 1984 joint return rate schedule to the other income that the investor is endowed with. The marginal tax rate for \$108,000 is 45 percent, and for \$85,000 the rate is 42 percent.

Finally, in column five and six the amount of after-tax investment is increased from $10,000 to $40,000. Within column six, the portion of the $40,000 invested in the tax shelter and the tax-free bond (or muni) is shown.

The impact of intra-temporal tax rate variation on after-tax returns, and thus on investment decisions, is dramatic. This is demonstrated in Table 6 in four steps. First, in column two, the result obtained from the constant tax rate analysis of Table 5 is carried forward to act as a benchmark[9]. In that setting the tax shelter investment is superior to the tax-free bond as it produces an 11.6 percent rate of return. In column three, however, the tax shelter investment is analyzed in the context of intra-temporal tax rate variation. In this case, the marginal tax rate is initially established at 45 percent (other income is set at $108,000), as in the constant rate case, but here it is allowed to vary as taxable income or loss from the tax shelter is realized. Specifically, as deductions generated by the tax shelter are realized, the tax rate falls such that the tax savings produced by additional deductions are smaller. Similarly, as tax shelter income is realized, the tax rate rises and tax costs produced by additional income are greater. The net result is that because of the induced tax bracket shift, the tax shelter experiences declining after-tax returns to scale. As such, its after-tax rate of return drops from 11.6 percent to 8 percent, below the 10 percent return available from the tax-free bond.

Second, in column four, the effect of intra-temporal rate variation is recomputed when the amount of other income in year one is reduced from $108,000 to $85,000. This effectively lowers the initial marginal tax rate in year one to 42 percent. In this case, the rate of return on the tax shelter investment is 11.7 percent, a return greater than that realized in either of the first two cases. This demonstrates not only the importance of intra-temporal tax rate variation, but also the effect of the time-pattern of other income and the width and progressivity of the tax brackets on the attractiveness of the tax shelter investment.

Third, in column five, the amount invested in the tax-shelter is increased from $10,000 to $40,000, with other income remaining at $108,000 in year zero and $85,000 in year one. In this case the rate of return on the $40,000 investment in the tax shelter, the so-called plunging or no diversification strategy, falls to 8.5 percent. Obviously, while the first $10,000 of investment in the tax shelter produced an 11.7 percent return, additional dollars of investment generated successively smaller returns such that the overall rate of return on the tax shelter was below that of the tax-free bond. This occurred because the deductions generated by the tax shelter were tax-effected at successively lower tax rates, while the income thrown off by the shelter was taxed at successively higher tax rates.

In the final step, column six, $40,000 is again invested, but in this case it can be allocated between the tax shelter and the tax-free bond: the portfolio strategy. Specifically, the investment procedure here is to invest in the tax shelter as long as the after-tax rate of return earned on the next dollar invested exceeds that of the tax-free bond (that is, 10 percent). The result obtained by using this procedure is that the first $21,920 is invested in the tax shelter and the remaining $18,080 is invested in the tax-free bond so that the overall rate of return rises to 10.9 percent. This return is greater than when the $40,000 is invested under the plunging strategy where it generates either the 10.0 percent available from the tax-free bond or the 8.5 percent from the tax shelter.

The results displayed in Table 6 indicate that the optimal investment decisions will ultimately depend on the level of the accounting ratios and tax rates, their inter-temporal variation, and the intra-temporal variation of the tax rate. Further, the interaction of these three factors is sufficiently complex that intuition is confounded: convenient generalizations of the previous section, such as the statement that shelters are best for high or increasing tax-bracket taxpayers, are lost. Thus, the investment decision is a problematic one in which the optimal portfolio can only be identified consistently by employing a portfolio strategy.

OPTIMAL PORTFOLIOS IN A MULTIPLE-PERIOD, MULTIPLE-INVESTMENT SETTING

The analysis conducted in the previous sections identifies the optimal portfolio in a two-date setting. Here, the analysis is extended to cover multiple periods and multiple investments.

To identify the optimal portfolio in a multiple period setting, an analog of equation 1 is required.

$$TW = \frac{a}{1 - p_0 t_0 - i} \sum_{j=1}^{n} s_j \, (1 - p_j t_j) \, (1 + q)^{n - j}. \tag{1''}$$

Here, it is assumed that an investment is held for n periods and that intermediate cash flows are invested at a tax-free rate, q. This obviates the need to solve the second-order problem of optimally investing cash flows from earlier investments. An optimization programming routine uses this formulation to identify the optimal portfolio.

The basic effects noted in the two-date model carry through in this setting. In particular, the tax effects

$$\frac{\partial TW}{\partial t_0} > 0; \frac{\partial TW}{\partial t_j} < 0;$$

Table 7.   Identifying the Optimal Portfolio in a Multiple-Period, Multiple-Investment Setting

Investment Attributes:

There are four hypothetical investment alternatives: two oil and gas tax shelters (Shelter 1 and Shelter 2), a 12-percent taxable bond (Bond) and a 7-percent tax-free bond (Muni). The accounting ratios and pre-tax rates of return for these four investments are as follows:[10]

Accounting Ratios

	p_0	p_1	p_2	p_3	p_4	i
Shelter 1	0.75	0.82	0.80	0.79	0.77	0.000
Shelter 2	0.75	0.66	0.64	0.61	0.59	0.025
Bond	0.00	1.00	1.00	1.00	0.11	0.000
Muni	0.00	0.00	0.00	0.00	0.00	0.000

Pre-tax Rates of Return

	s_1	s_2	s_3	s_4
Shelter 1	0.44	0.35	0.30	0.20
Shelter 2	0.38	0.28	0.24	0.21
Bond	0.12	0.12	0.12	1.12
Muni	0.07	0.07	0.07	1.07

Investor Attributes:

Three different time-patterns or cases of other income exist. The marginal tax rates associated with the two income levels are 38 percent ($50,000) and 45 percent ($100,000).

Other Income Time-pattern

	Year 0	Year 1	Year 2	Year 3	Year 4
			$		
Case 1	50,000	50,000	50,000	50,000	50,000
Case 2	100,000	100,000	100,000	100,000	100,000
Case 3	100,000	50,000	50,000	50,000	50,000

Results:

The optimal portfolios for the three investor settings are as follows:

(*continued*)

Table 7 (continued)

| | Optimal Portfolios | | |
	Case 1	Case 2	Case 3
		$	
Shelter 1	19,733	26,053	58,786
Shelter 2	0	11,748	0
Bonds	25,361	0	0
Munis	0	14,832	0
Pre-tax			
Investment[a]	45,094	52,633	58,786
TW	53,310	53,500	57,705

Note:
[a] = The amounts shown are the pre-tax investments in each of the four alternatives. In total these
amounts relate to $40,000 of after-tax investment.

the accounting effects

$$\frac{\partial TW}{\partial p_0} > 0; \quad \frac{\partial TW}{\partial p_j} < 0;$$

and the interaction effects

$$\frac{\partial^2 TW}{\partial p_0 \partial t_0} > 0; \quad \frac{\partial^2 TW}{\partial p_j \partial t_j} < 0.$$

For the case of $t_0 = t_j = t$ for all j, the sign of $\frac{\partial TW}{\partial t}$ is not as crisp as in the

two-date case. However, if $p_0 > p_j$ for all j and $i > 0$, then $\frac{\partial TW}{\partial t} > 0.$

Conversely, if $p_j > p_0$ for all j and $i = 0$, then $\frac{\partial TW}{\partial t} < 0.$

To demonstrate the use of this model and illustrate the effect that a
multi-period, multi-investment setting has on the composition of the optimal portfolio, consider the example in Table 7. In this example there are
four investment alternatives and three time patterns of other income. All
the investments take place in year zero and are liquidated in year four.
Intermediate cash flows are reinvested at a 6 percent tax-free rate. The
amount of after-tax investment in year zero is set equal to $40,000.

The investment strategy is to examine each of the four investment alternatives and identify the one that adds the most to terminal wealth for a
one-dollar, after-tax investment in year zero. This one dollar of the most
efficient investment is added to the portfolio and the search process is
continued until the entire $40,000 is invested.

The results in the first case of Table 7 are consistent with those obtained in the two-date world. Here, the return characteristics of Shelter 1 make it the most attractive alternative for the first (after-tax) dollar invested. It exhibits declining after-tax returns to scale, however, and before the $40,000 is entirely invested, bonds (which, because of their lower p_0 and p_4 values, are less sensitive to bracket shift) become more attractive. In this case, taxable bonds are preferred to tax-free municipals because, at the tax-rate bracket in which Shelter 1 "burns out," their after-tax rate of return is higher.

In case two, a higher initial tax rate exists for each of the four years. Because the terminal wealth associated with an investment in Shelter 1 decreases as the tax rate rises, Shelter 1 is less attractive here than in the previous case. Stated more formally, $\dfrac{\partial TW}{\partial t} < 0$ for Shelter 1 and $\dfrac{\partial TW}{\partial t} > 0$ for Shelter 2.

Yet, despite the increase in tax rate, Shelter 1 is still the more efficient investment initially. However, because of the interaction of accounting ratios, initial tax rates, and intra-temporal rate variation, it is also more susceptible to bracket shift. Thus, as investments are made in Shelter 1, it becomes progressively less attractive until eventually Shelter 2 becomes the more efficient investment.

This phenomenon can be depicted more formally in the following manner:

$$\frac{\partial^2 TW}{\partial t_0 \partial p_0} > 0; \frac{\partial^2 TW}{\partial t_j \partial p_j} < 0.$$

Specifically, while p_0 is the same for both shelters, the remaining p_js for Shelter 1 exceed those for Shelter 2. Thus, Shelter 1 is more sensitive to bracket shift. As this occurs, Shelter 2 becomes the more attractive investment.

Shelter 2, however, also experiences declining after-tax returns to scale. Thus, before the $40,000 has been entirely invested, municipal bonds (with constant after-tax returns) become the most efficient investment and are used to complete the portfolio. In this case, the optimal portfolio consists of three different investments.

For case three the relevant comparison is with case two; the tax rate is initially the same but declines in the years subsequent to the investment. Again the relevant relationship is

$$\frac{\partial^2 TW}{\partial p_j \partial t_j} < 0.$$

Since Shelter 1 has the highest p_js, it is the most attractive investment in this case. In fact, the entire $40,000 can be invested in Shelter 1 before its after-tax rate of return declines below that of the other investment alternatives. Thus, in this case, the optimal portfolio consists of a single investment, Shelter 1.

In summary, when the analysis developed in the previous sections is applied here in a multi-investment, multi-period setting, the results obtained confirm the notion that portfolios identified through the use of the portfolio investment strategy have after-tax rates of return that are at least as high as those identified with the plunging strategy.

CONCLUSIONS

This study extends previous analyses of optimal portfolios by considering both the direct and indirect cash flows of investments in a setting with perfect certainty and a simplified version of the extant tax law. It explains the existence of diversified, investor-specific investment portfolios without referring to investment return uncertainty or investor risk preferences. Specifically, this study demonstrates that such portfolios exist because intra-temporal rate variation causes investments to experience declining after-tax returns to scale.

The study begins by developing a scale-independent measure that relates the direct cash flows of an investment to their effects on the investor's taxable income. This measure, the investment's accounting ratio, is used in conjunction with the investor's marginal tax rate to compute the terminal wealth associated with various investments and then to identify the optimal portfolio.

Three important findings emerge from this analysis. First, the impact on terminal wealth associated with an investment's accounting ratios is directly related to the investor's tax bracket. Consequently, potentially testable clientele effects are anticipated, wherein promoters of favorable tax shelters will, in general, seek out investors with distinctly different time patterns of tax rates compared to those marketing investments with unfavorable accounting ratios.

Second, the analysis shows that the terminal wealth associated with a given investment depends upon the level of the investment's accounting ratios and the investor's tax rates; the inter-temporal variation of these factors; and the intra-temporal variation of the marginal tax rate. In short, it depends highly on the nature of the tax system.

Third, the study demonstrates that certain fundamental features of the extant tax system cause optimal portfolios to be diversified and investor-specific. It shows that investments will experience declining after-tax returns to scale when the tax rate structure is progressive, and when all direct cash flows do not have the same effect on taxable income, that is, the accounting ratios are not the same across investments or over time. Specifically, the analysis shows that when different investments possess different levels and time patterns of accounting ratios they will experience different rates of decline in after-tax return. Such differences across investments require that the optimal portfolio be comprised of multiple investments if the after-tax rate of return is to be maximized. Further, the study shows that, to the extent that investors possess different levels and time patterns of tax rates, the optimal portfolio will be diversified in a different way for each investor: it will be investor-specific.

While the setting employed in this study involved a simplified version of the extant tax law, the findings obtained here would remain intact even if a richer tax environment were used. In fact, the introduction of such refinements as the at risk rules, the investment interest limitation, or the alternative minimum tax would only accentuate the findings obtained here since, by their very nature, such provisions cause investments to experience declining after-tax rates of return even when the marginal tax rate is held constant. Other special provisions would be likely to have the same effect.

In addition, the model used here can also accommodate nontax refinements, such as declining returns to scale for technology. Further, some refinements as, for example, noncontinuous investment constraints, may actually simplify the model. Finally, extensions of the approach developed here may ultimately incorporate investment return uncertainty and investor risk preference, the traditional factors used to explain portfolio composition, so that a "complete" model of investment choice would be available.

ACKNOWLEDGMENTS

The authors are grateful for financial support provided by the Arthur Young Foundation. In addition, we acknowledge helpful comments from Paul Newman (University of Texas at Austin), Mark Wolfson (Stanford University) and participants in the accounting workshop at the University of Texas at Austin.

NOTES

1. Subsequent works have analyzed and extended these findings by showing that optimal portfolios change with alterations in the uncertainty associated with returns. See, for example, Samuelson (1967), Hakansson (1971a, 1971b), and Ekern (1971). In addition, Halperin (1983) has identified conditions under which the owner-manager of a closely held corporation will modify his consumption-investment decisions based on an increase in his perceived instability of the tax laws.

2. Proportionality also applies to a leveraged investment assuming the financing percentage and interest rate do not vary across the amount invested. Consider, for example, the purchase of two $50,000 units in a leveraged real estate tax shelter. Since the financing percentage and interest rate are usually the same for both units, the direct cash flows and tax effects for two units are exactly twice that of a single unit.

Detail to Table 6, Column 3
(Same assumptions as Table 5, except pre-inventory other
income = $108,000)

Year 0:			
I (10,000/(1 − (0.7) (0.45))			$14,599
Other income	$108,000		
Tax on other income		$36,000	
Tax deduction from I			
(14,599 × 0.70)	(10,219)		
Taxable income (TI)	$97,781		
Tax on TI		(31,401)	
Tax benefit from I			(4,599)
a			$10,000
Year 1:			
Pre-tax cash flow (CF) from I			
(14,599 × (1 + .08))			$15,767
Other income	$108,000		
TI from I (15,767 x .65)	10,249		
TI	$118,249		
Tax on TI		$40,966	
Tax on other income (same as			
year 0)		(36,000)	
Tax cost from I			(4,966)
TW			$10,801
ROR			8.0%

3.   In limited cases, p_j may not be an effective mapping of pre-tax cash flows into taxable income (or loss), as for example, when c_j = 0. In these cases the portfolio optimization problem may be solved by using an additive mapping of an investment's accounting ratios.
4.   See, for example, Price Waterhouse (1983).
5.   Aside from demonstrating the range of feasible values for the accounting ratio, borrowing is not considered in this paper. Expanding the analysis to include borrowing would be technically straightforward, but it would not add to the findings obtained with the more basic setting.
6.   The accounting ratios of an investment are likely to vary over time because of the existence of liquidation gains or losses or the existence of special provisions in the tax law that treat certain direct cash flows differently than others. The marginal tax rates for an investor can change over time as other income varies or the tax rate structure is altered.
7.   Stated more formally, partial differentiation of (1) with respect to p_0 and p_1 when $t_0 = t_1 = t$ results in the following:

$$\frac{\partial TW}{\partial p_0} > 0; \frac{\partial TW}{\partial p_1} < 0.$$

The first inequality is true when $(1 - p_1 t) > 0$; the second is true when $(1 - p_0 t - i) > 0$. Both will be assumed throughout. (All derivations are presented in the Appendix.) These two inequalities indicate that a tax shelter becomes more appealing (TW increases) as p_0 becomes larger, p_1 becomes smaller, or both.

The dollar effects of incremental p_0 are below the effects of decremental p_1 when p_1 exceeds p_0 and vice versa.

$$\left|\frac{\partial TW}{\partial p_0}\right| \gtreqless \left|\frac{\partial TW}{\partial p_1}\right| \quad <==> \quad p_0 \gtreqless p_1 \quad \text{when } i = 0$$

This suggests that a tax-rational strategy relative to the accounting ratios of a tax shelter is to concentrate on maximizing p_0 when p_0 exceeds p_1, and minimize p_1 when the converse is true.

8. For examples of clientele effects in auditing see DeAngelo (1981) and Rhodes, Whitsell, and Kelsey (1974).

9. The calculations pertaining to Table 6, column 3, are detailed on page 43. The calculations for the investments in the other columns of the exhibit are performed in a similar manner.

10. Shelter 1 is based on prospectus projections from the Walker Drilling Program 1983-A, Ltd. Shelter 2 is based on a prototype oil and gas investment presented in Price Waterhouse (1983.) The accounting relationships formulated from these ventures assume no cash flow or taxable gain or loss from the disposition of the shelters.

REFERENCES

DeAngelo, L. E., *The Auditor-Client Contractual Relationship, An Economic Analysis* (UMI Research Press, 1981).

Ekern, S. (November 1971), "Taxation: Political Risk and Portfolio Selection," *Economica* (vol. XXXVIII, no. 152) pp. 421–430.

Fellingham, J. C., and Wolfson, M. A. (December 1978), "The Effects of Alternative Income Tax Structures on Risk Taking in Capital Markets," *National Tax Journal* (vol. XXXI, no. 4) pp. 339–347.

Fellingham, J. C., and Wolfson, M. A. (March 1984), "Progressive Income Taxes and the Demand for Risky Assets," *National Tax Journal* (vol. XXXVII, no. 1) pp. 127–129.

Hakansson, N. (January 1971a), "Capital Growth and the Mean-Variance Approach to Portfolio Selection," *Journal of Financial and Quantitative Analysis*, (vol. VI, no. 1) pp. 517–557.

Hakansson, N. (September 1971b), "Multi-Period Mean-Variance Analysis Toward a General Theory of Portfolio Choice," *Journal of Finance*, (vol. XXVI, no. 4) pp. 857–884.

Halperin, R. (Winter 1983), "The Perceived Instability of Tax Legislation and Its Effect on Consumption-Investment Decisions." *Journal of Accounting and Public Policy* (vol. 2, no. 4) pp. 239–262.

Markowitz, H. M. (March 1952), "Portfolio Selection," *Journal of Finance* (vol. VII, no. 1) 77–91.

Price Waterhouse, *Tax Information Planning Service—Current Tax Aspects of Investing in Public Oil and Gas Drilling Programs* (Price Waterhouse, New York, N.Y., November 1983).

Rhodes, J. G., G. M. Whitsell, and R. L. Kelsey (October 1974), "Client-Industry Concentrations," *The Accounting Review* (vol. XLIX, no. 4) pp. 772–787.

Samuelson, P. (March 1967), "General Proof that Diversification Pays," *Journal of Financial and Quantitative Analysis* (vol. II, No. 1) pp. 1–12.

Schneider, D. (March 1980), "The Effects of Progressive and Proportional Income Taxation on Risk Taking," *National Tax Journal* (vol. XXXIII, no. 1) pp. 67–95.

Sharpe, W. F. (January 1963), "A Simplified Model for Portfolio Analysis." *Management Science* (vol. IX, no. 2) pp. 277–293.

Walker Drilling Program 1983-A, Ltd.

APPENDIX

(1) $TW = a - I(1 - p_0 t_0 - i) + I(1 + s)(1 - p_1 t_1)$

$$TW = a - a + \frac{a(1 + s)(1 - p_1 t_1)}{(1 - p_0 t_0 - i)}$$

$$TW = \frac{(1 + s) \, a \, (1 - p_1 t_1)}{(1 - p_0 t_0 - i)}$$

(1') $$TW = \frac{(1 + s) \, a \, (1 - p_1 t)}{(1 - p_0 t - i)}$$

$$\frac{\partial TW}{\partial p_0} = \frac{(1 + s) \, a \, (1 - p_1 t) \, t}{(1 - p_0 t - i)^2} > 0, \text{ when } 1 - p_1 t > 0$$

$$\frac{\partial TW}{\partial p_1} = \frac{(1 + s) \, a \, (-t)}{1 - p_0 t - i} < 0, \text{ when } 1 - p_0 t - i > 0$$

$$\frac{\partial^2 TW}{\partial p_0 2} = \frac{(1 + s) \, a \, (1 - p_1 t) t^2}{(1 - p_0 t - i)^3} > 0$$

$$\frac{\partial^2 TW}{\partial p_1^2} = 0$$

$$\left| \frac{\partial TW}{\partial p_0} \right| = \frac{(1 + s) \, at \, (1 - p_1 t)}{(1 - p_0 t - i)^2}$$

$$\left| \frac{\partial TW}{\partial p_1} \right| = \frac{(1 + s) \, at}{1 - p_0 t - i}$$

$$= \frac{(1 + s) \, at \, (1 - p_0 t - i)}{(1 - p_0 t - i)^3}$$

$$\left| \frac{\partial TW}{\partial p_0} \right| = \left| \frac{\partial TW}{\partial p_1} \right| \left(\frac{1 - p_1 t}{1 - p_0 t} \right) \text{ when } i = 0$$

$$\frac{\partial TW}{\partial t} = (1 + s)a \left[\frac{-p_1}{1 - p_0 t - i} + \frac{(1 - p_1 t)p_0}{(1 - p_0 t - i)^2} \right]$$

(2) $$\frac{\partial TW}{\partial t} = \frac{(1 + s) \, a \, (p_0 + p_1 i - p_1)}{(1 - p_0 t - i)^2} \begin{array}{l} > 0 \text{ when } p_0 > p_1 \\ < 0 \text{ when } p_1 > p_0 \text{ and } i = 0 \end{array}$$

$$\frac{\partial^2 TW}{\partial t \partial p_0} = (1 + s)a \left[\frac{(p_0 + p_1 i - p_1)2t}{(1 - p_0 t - i)^3} + \frac{1}{(1 - p_0 t - i)^2} \right]$$

$$= \frac{(1 + s)a}{(1 - p_0 t - i)^3} \ [2p_0 t + 2p_1 ti - 2p_1 t + 1 - p_0 t - i]$$

(3) $\dfrac{\partial^2 TW}{\partial t \partial p_0} = \dfrac{(1 - s) \ a \ [p_0 t + (1 - i) \ (1 - 2p_1 t)]}{(1 - p_0 t - i)^3} > 0$ if $1 - p_0 t - i > 0$ and $t < 0.5$

$$\frac{\partial^2 TW}{\partial t \partial p_1} = \frac{(1 + s) \ a \ (i - 1)}{(1 - p_0 t - i)^2} < 0$$

(1) $\quad TW = \dfrac{(1 + s) \ a \ (1 - p_1 t_1)}{(1 - p_0 t_0 - i)}$

(4) $\quad \dfrac{\partial TW}{\partial t_0} = \dfrac{(1 + s) \ a \ (1 - p_1 t_1) p_0}{(1 - p_0 t_0 - i)^2} > 0$

$$\frac{\partial TW}{\partial t_1} = \frac{(1 + s) \ a \ (-p_1)}{(1 - p_0 t_0 - i)} < 0$$

$$\frac{\partial^2 TW}{\partial t_0 \partial p_0} = (1 + s)a(1 - p_1 t) \left[\frac{1}{(1 - p_0 t_0 - i)^2} + \frac{p_0 t_0}{(1 - p_0 t_0 - i)^3} \right]$$

(5) $\quad \dfrac{\partial^2 TW}{\partial t_0 \partial p_0} = \dfrac{(1 + s)a(1 - p_1 t) \ (1 - i)}{(1 - p_0 t_0 - i)^3} > 0$

$$\frac{\partial^2 TW}{\partial t_1 \partial p_1} = \frac{(-1) \ (1 + s)a}{(1 - p_0 t_0 - 1)} < 0.$$

Multiperiod relationships

(1'') $\quad TW = Is_1 \ (1 + p_1 t_1) \ (1 + q)^{n-1} + Is_2 \ (1 + p_2 t_2) \ (1 + q)^{n-2}$

$$+ \ Is_3 (1 + p_3 t_3) \ (1 + q)^{n-3} + \cdots Is_j \ (1 + p_j t_j)$$
$$(1 + q)^{n-j}$$

$$TW = \frac{a}{1 - p_0 t_0 - i} \sum_{j=1}^{n} s_j \ (1 - p_j t_j) \ (1 + q)^{n-j}$$

$$\frac{\partial TW}{\partial p_0} = \frac{at_0}{(1 - p_0 t_0 - i)^2} \sum_{j=1}^{n} s_j \ (1 - p_j t_j) \ (1 + q)^{n-j} > 0$$

$$\frac{\partial TW}{\partial p_j} = \frac{a}{1 - p_0 t_0 - 1} s_j \ (-t_j) \ (1 + q)^{n-j} < 0$$

$$\frac{\partial TW}{\partial t_0} = \frac{ap_0}{(1 - p_0 t_0 - i)^2} \sum_{j=1}^{n} s_j (1 - p_j t_j) \ (1 + q)^{n-j} > 0$$

$$\frac{\partial TW}{\partial t_j} = \frac{a}{1 - p_0 t_0 - i} s_j (-p_j) (1 + q)^{n-j} < 0$$

$$\frac{\partial^2 TW}{\partial t_0 \partial p_0} = a \sum_{j=1}^{n} s_j (1 - p_j t_j) (1+q)^{n-j} \left[\frac{1}{(1 - p_0 t_0 - i)^2} + \frac{2 p_0 t_0}{(1 - p_0 t_0 - i)^3} \right]$$

$$= \frac{a}{(1 - p_0 t_0 - i)^3} \sum_{j=1}^{n} s_j (1 - p_j t_j) (1+q)^{n-j}(1 - p_0 t_0 - i + 2 p_0 t_0)$$

$$= \frac{a(1 + p_0 t_0 - i)}{(1 - p_0 t_0 - i)} \sum_{j=1}^{n} s_j (1 - p_j t_j) (1+q)^{n-j} > 0$$

$$\frac{\partial^2 TW}{\partial p_j \partial t_j} = \frac{a}{1 - p_0 t_0 - i} s_j (-1) (1 + q)^{n-j} < 0.$$

Let $t_0 = t_1 = t \; \forall \; j$

$$TW = \frac{a}{1 - p_0 t_0 - i} \sum_{j=1}^{n} s_j (1 - p_j t) (1 + q)^{n-j}$$

$$\frac{\partial TW}{\partial t_0} = \frac{a p_0}{(1 - p_0 t - i)^2} \sum_{j=1}^{n} s_j (1 - p_j t) (1 + q)^{n-j}$$

$$+ \frac{a}{1 - p_0 t - i} \sum_{j=1}^{n} s_j (-p_j) (1 + q)^{n-j}$$

$$= \frac{a}{1 - p_0 t - i} \sum_{j=1}^{n} s_j (1+q)^{n-j} [p_0(1 - p_j t) - p_j(1 - p_0 t - i)]$$

$$= \frac{a}{(1 - p_0 t - i)^2} \sum_{j=1}^{n} s_j (1+q)^{n-j} [p_0 - p_j(1 - i)]$$

$$> 0 \text{ if } p_0 > p_j \; \forall \; j$$

$$< 0 \text{ if } p_j > p_0 \; \forall \; j \text{ and } i = 0.$$

USE OF INPUT–OUTPUT ANALYSIS IN TAX RESEARCH

Charles W. Swenson and Michael L. Moore

ABSTRACT

In tax research involving policy implications, economic consequences resulting from potential tax law changes are frequently analyzed. Most studies have only examined economic impact in a partial equilibrium setting, however. This paper offers a methodology that can be used to determine the general equilibrium or full economic impacts of tax laws. The methodology, input–output analysis, is illustrated with examples using state and federal tax policy analyses. The examples are based on general equilibrium analysis and illustrate that tax policy intended to increase government tax collections (in one case indirectly so by encouraging economic growth) may have resulted in reduced economic welfare and tax revenues.

Advances in Taxation, Volume 1, pages 49–83.
Copyright © 1987 JAI Press Inc.
All rights of reproduction in any form reserved.
ISBN: 0–89232–782–0

INTRODUCTION

Previous studies have empirically estimated only the first-order effects of taxes. Economic effects beyond the level of entities directly dealing with the tax-influenced firms were not considered. An obvious extension of these studies would be to assess higher-order impacts, namely the multiplier effects of the tax on the economy and ultimately on tax revenues. As pointed out by Ghali and Renaud (1976) such "ripple through" economic effects can be assessed with econometric models and with input–output analysis. Input–output analysis (I–O) is generally recognized as preferable in regional or state studies given the shortcomings of regional or state econometric models. These shortcomings include the poor quality of data bases, the problem of appropriately defining regional boundaries, and "the vague notions of continuing uses of the models once they are built" (Ghali and Renaud 1976, p. 4). The objectives of this study are to acquaint the reader with I–O and to illustrate its use in tax research using two examples. In the first example we measure the effects of the unitary method of corporate income tax accounting on California's economy. In the second example we examine the national economic impact of two methods of accounting for inflation for Federal corporate income tax purposes.

THE ESSENCE OF INPUT–OUTPUT ANALYSIS

The economic method illustrated in this study is the Leonteif input–output model. Leontief developed the first empirical general interindustry model for the United States in 1936. Leontief's work has been continued by the U.S. Department of Commerce, which published input–output tables for the years 1947, 1958, 1963, and 1967. The Bureau of Economic Analysis has constructed national tables for 1972 and 1977. Regional input–output tables for California and other regions have been developed by other researchers.[1]

The input–output model represents an economy (national, regional, state, or local) as a network of flows or linkages between economic activities specified as distinct sectors. In the I–O model the economy is in, or tends toward, general equilibrium. That is, supply equals demand for all goods and services in all sectors of the economy. When an exogenous "shock" occurs in the economy, such as an increase in demand for an industry's products, an initial disequilibrium is caused. To satisfy the demand increase, the industry must purchase additional goods and services from its suppliers. These suppliers, in turn, must purchase goods and services from other supplying firms, and the other supplying firms must purchase goods and services from their suppliers, and so forth. This multiplier effect continues until the new supply equals the new demand for the economy, and general equilibrium is restored. The multiplier effect is determined by the following three-step procedure:

1. model the economy as a transactions table (a table showing the flow of goods and services, in dollars, between all sectors of the economy);
2. derive multipliers from the transaction table; and
3. multiply the exogenous shock by the multipliers.

In the following pages we present a stylized explanation of the Leontief I–O model. For an expanded discussion of the I–O model we refer the reader to O'Connor and Henry (1975).

The Transaction Table for an Economy

Whether the economy under consideration is a state, a region, or a country, the initial step in input–output analysis is to construct a transactions table for that economy. Data for construction of the transactions table is often collected from a variety of sources (see O'Connor and Henry 1975). The transactions table depicts the economy as a series of interrelated transactions between sectors for any given year. The amounts are usually in millions or billions of dollars. Figure 1 depicts a conceptual view of the transactions table, dividing the economy into four quadrants.

Quadrant I describes consumption, identifying consumption of industrial goods and services by households and other uses of goods by private investors and governments. Part of quadrant I is exports, which represents sales to other industries and final consumers outside the economy under consideration. Since these goods infrequently reappear in the economy under investigation in the same form, these sales are regarded as final. Under conventional economic theory, final demand is the motivating force in an economy, and thus quadrant I would typically contain activity-generating forces that result in changes in the economy. Quadrant II depicts production relationships in the economy, showing the ways that raw materials and intermediate goods are combined to produce outputs for sale to other industries and to final consumers. Quadrant II is the basis for the I–O model. For most state, regional, and national models it includes from 30 to 39 industries.

Quadrant III shows incomes accruing to businesses and households, depreciation, and taxes paid. These incomes are also called value-added. Since these incomes are often difficult to identify individually, they are frequently recorded as one value-added row. Quadrant III also includes payments to industries outside the economy for materials and intermediate goods which are imported into the state. Quadrant IV shows primarily

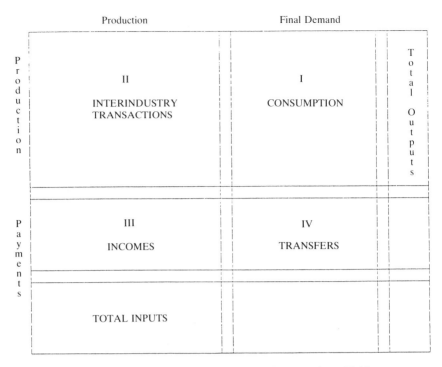

Figure 1. Conceptual View of the Transactions Table.

nonmarket transfers between sectors of the economy, and is referred to as a social transfers quadrant. The quadrant shows gifts, savings and taxes of households, government surplus or deficits, and government payments to households and other governments. The quadrant also includes purchases by final demand sectors from industries outside the state.

A Simplified Example

In this section we illustrate the use of I–O with a hypothetical two-industry economy. The hypothetical transactions table for this economy is shown in Figure 2.

In the hypothetical transactions table we see that Industry 1 purchases \$8 in goods or services from Industry 2; we have labeled this transaction total as x_{21}. We also see that Industry 1 purchases \$5 of goods or services from itself (firms within that sector purchase from other firms in that sector). We label this transaction total as X_{11}. Similarly Industry 2 purchases \$10 of goods or services from Industry 1 (x_{12}), and \$4 from itself (x_{22}). Final demand for Industry 1's products is \$25 (Y_1) and final demand for Industry 2's products is \$33 (y_2). Total output for Industry 1 (X_1) is the sum of

	Purchasing 1	Industry 2	Final Demand	Total Output
Selling 1	$5(x_{11})$	$10(x_{12})$	$25(Y_1)$	$40(X_1)$
Industry 2	$8(x_{21})$	$4(x_{22})$	$35(Y_2)$	$45(X_2)$
Value Added	$20(V_1)$	$25(V_2)$	$5(Vd)$	50
Imports	$7(M_1)$	$6(M_2)$	$-13(-m)$	0
Total Inputs	$40(x_1)$	$45(x_2)$	$50(Y)$	135

Figure 2. Hypothetical Transactions Table.

interindustry and final demand sales, or $5 + $10 + $25 = $40. Similarily, total output for Industry 2 is $45.

We see that Industry 1's value added (V_1) and imports (M_1) are $20 and $7, respectively. Note that value-added is a measure of income since it is equal to the difference between output (sales) and factor costs. When value added and imports are added to the $13 in goods and services purchases by Industry 1, the sum (total inputs or X_1) is $40. This input equals output of $40 for Industry 1. Using the same formula we can show that input and output for Industry 2 is $45. Imports and exports in this example are equal at $13, and total output for the economy is $135.

Suppose that some exogenous shock, such as an increase in demand for Industry 1's products, were to occur. When the effects of the shock have rippled through the economy, what will the new general equilibrium be? To determine the new general equilibrium we first derive "multipliers" from the transactions table, then multiply the exogenous shock times the appropriate multipliers.

To determine the multipliers we first express the transactions table as series of mathematical relationships. Using the symbols of Figure 2 we write the following equations:

$$x_{11} + x_{12} + Y_1 = X_1 \tag{1}$$

$$x_{21} + x_{22} + Y_2 = X_2 \tag{2}$$

Suppose we know the increase in total demand for Industry 1's goods and services (ΔY_1) and we wish to know what the multiplied effect on the economy will be as Industry 1 purchases additional goods and services from Industry 2 and from itself, and as this in turn causes additional goods and services to be purchased by the two industries to satisfy ΔY_1, which results in further rounds of sales and purchases, ad infinitum. We have two equations and eight variables, of which only one $(\Delta Y_1$, and thus $Y_1)$ has an assigned value. Since we have an underidentification problem (the number of equations is less than the number of unknowns) we cannot solve the system without reducing the number of unknown variables.

To do this, we introduce a set of technical conditions which assume that the situational relationships in the economy are stable. We define a set of technical coefficients as follows:

$$a_{ij} = \frac{x_{ij}}{X_j}. \tag{3}$$

In our simple economy a_{11} is equal to 0.125(5/40), a_{12} is 0.22(10/45), a_{21} is 0.20(8/40), and a_{22} is 0.089(4/45). Note that we may define x_{ij}, the sales by industry i to industry j, as $x_{ij} = a_{ij} \cdot x_j$. If the production coefficients of the economy are stable, then $x_{ij} = a_{ij} \cdot x'_j$, where x' is future production after the exogenous change in demand. Note that we assume general equilibrium (supply equals demand) both before and after the exogenous change, or $X_i = X_j$ in algebraic terms. Since we assume stability of production coefficients, we can rewrite Eqs. (1) and (2) to apply to a later period (for example, after a shock) by substituting Y'_i for Y_i, X'_i for x_i; and $X'_{ij} = a_{ij} \cdot X'_{ij}$ for X_{ij} in both of our equations as follows:

$$a_{11} \cdot X'_1 + a_{12} \cdot X'_2 + Y'_1 = X'_1 \tag{4}$$

$$a_{21} \cdot X'_2 + a_{22} \cdot X_2 + Y'_2 = X'_2. \tag{5}$$

The advantage of using the technical coefficients is now clear; the number of unknowns is now two (X'_1 and X'_2). Since the system can be solved for outputs of both industries after the change in demand, to solve for X' (either X'_1 or X'_2), we write

$$X = a \cdot X + Y \tag{6}$$

subtracting $a \cdot X$ from both sides,

$$X - a \cdot X = Y \tag{7}$$

factoring X from the left-hand side yields

$$X(1-a) = Y \tag{8}$$

dividing both sides by $(1-a)$ results in

$$X = Y/(1-a) \tag{9}$$

or the solution for X in terms of Y. If we visualize $\mathbf{X}$ as a column vector for total sales, $\mathbf{Y}$ as a column vector of final demand and $\mathbf{a}$ as the 2×2 matrix of a_{ij}s as computed above, an analogous solution to our system of equations is:

$$\mathbf{X} = (\mathbf{I} - \mathbf{a})^{-1} \cdot \mathbf{Y}, \tag{10}$$

where $\mathbf{I}$ is an identity matrix, and the -1 exponent indicates inversion (O'Connor and Henry 1975). The $(\mathbf{I}-\mathbf{a})^{-1}$ is referred to as the Leontief inverse. In our case, the Leontief inverse is a 2×2 matrix, with each element referred to as b_{ij}. When we sum each column of b_{ij}s we get an output multiplier, Q_i, for each industry j:

$$Q_j = \sum_i b_{ij} . \tag{11}$$

Following this procedure we get output multipliers of 1.48 and 1.46, respectively, for Industries 1 and 2. The significance of these multipliers is as follows: if, for example, Industry 1 experiences a $10 increase in final demand, total output for the economy (from both direct demand for Industry 1's goods and services plus indirect demand for Industry 1 and 2 goods and services) increases by $14.80. Similarly, if Industry 2's demand increases by $10, total output of the economy would increase by $14.60.

The Expanded Model

In the foregoing model we characterized the household sector as part of the final demand sector. Frequently, households are included as an industry sector in I–O. Households sell labor, managerial skills, and privately-owned resources, and they receive in payment wages and salaries, dividends, rents, and proprietor's incomes. To produce these resources they buy food, clothing, automobiles, housing, services, and other consumer goods. When we include the household sector as an industry, we capture the direct, indirect, and induced effects on an economy (using I–O) when there is an exogenous change to the economy. Multipliers including the household sector are commonly called type II multipliers; type I multipliers do not include the household sector. To derive the type II multipliers we add both the household column (previously in the final demand sector) and the household income row (previously in the value-added or income row) to the producing sector of the transactions table. We then follow the previously illustrated procedure for estimating multipliers, and we designate the type II Leontief matrix elements as b'_{ij}. Because of the reinjection effect of households, the b'_{ij} elements (and consequently type II output multipliers, which are the sum of, the b'_{ij} elements by industry) are higher than their type I counterparts.

In addition to type I and II output multipliers, researchers are often interested in effects on income or value-added (gross state products or GSP in the case of a state) and on employment as a result of an exogenous impact. Income multipliers are computed by multiplying each element of the Leontief matrix by the ratio of value added to total output for each industry, i, or:

$$v_i = \sum_i b_{ij} \frac{v_i}{X_i} \tag{12}$$

Equation (12) shows the type I income multiplier. A type II income multiplier is similarly derived by substituting b'_{ij} for b_{ij}, and v'_i for v_i, where v'_i is value-added (income) accruing to the business and household sector. The income multiplier indicates how much the economy's income will increase from a change in final demand. Thus, if the type II income multiplier for industry i is \$2, a \$1 increase in final demand for industry i's products will increase the economy's value-added income by \$2.

Employment multipliers are derived from output multipliers simply by converting from an output to an employment base. The type I employment multiplier for industry i is

$$L_i = \sum_i b_{ij} \frac{W_i}{X_i} , \qquad (13)$$

where W_i is the employment in industry i. A type II employment multiplier is derived by substituting b'_{ij} for b_{ij}. The employment multiplier tells the researcher how employment (usually expressed in person-years) will change from an exogenous change to any industry. Thus, if there is a \$1 million increase in firm demand for industry i's goods and services, and the type II employment multiplier for industry i is one person-year for each \$100,000 of final demand for industry i, then employment in the economy should increase by roughly ten full-time employees. Note that employment by industry is not an actual part of an economy's transactions table, as are employment and income by industry.

The More Complex Case: Tax Policy Analysis

The foregoing example served as a simple pedagogical device. Although the important elements of this simple model [Eqs. (3), (10)–(13)] are the same equations used to develop multipliers from a larger "real world" transactions table, real-world I–O applications are characterized by a number of complexities. One complexity is size; a typical transactions table has 30 to 39 industries and sectors composed of numerous subsectors, that is, final demand composed of exports, households, and various government final demand sectors. Calculation of the Leontief inverse from the transactions table is usually cumbersome. A second complexity is the construction of the transactions table. Ideally, a table will already exist; if one is not available, the data gathering process for table construction is extremely time-consuming. A final I–O complexity is specification of the sources of the exogenous impacts. In our simple example, the exogenous impact was additional final demand in one industry; in reality, there are often simultaneous exogenous shocks on several industries. Thus, total effect of the exogenous impacts is the sum of each industry's exogenous impact times that industry's multiplier. Also, the exogenous impact may not initially occur as a change in final demand. However, if the economy seeks equilibrium and remains structurally stable, any exogenous shock will have a multiplier effect which can be measured using I–O. Thus, an increase or decrease in tax rates will change investment and other expenditure magnitudes due to availability or nonavailability of funds, which then ripples through the economy.

In the next two sections we illustrate two applications of I–O to tax research. Both cases involve the effects of methods of income tax accounting. In the first example we measure the multiplied effects on California's economy due to that state's unitary method of accounting for corporate income taxes. In the second example we examine the impact of two methods of accounting for inflation for Federal corporate income tax purposes.

ILLUSTRATION OF THE USE OF I–O IN TAX POLICY RESEARCH: THE CASE OF FOREIGN INVESTMENT LOST BECAUSE OF THE CALIFORNIA UNITARY TAX

Most prior empirical studies have found little influence of taxes on investments in individual states. A seminal study of this nature was performed by Due (1961). Such findings are surprising, given the number of attitudinal studies indicating that taxes are an important factor in business decisions. For example, in a survey of U.S. executives performed by Belknap Data Solutions Limited for *Fortune Magazine* (1977), 20 percent of the respondents selected state and/or local attitude toward taxes on business and industry as one of the three to five most important factors in choosing a location. A survey by Tong and Walter (1980) indicated that executives of foreign firms located in the United States ranked state tax rates and local tax rates 15th and 16th, respectively, in importance out of 32 important factors for their location, and a study of Japanese executives (Nihon Keizai Shimbun 1981) reported that business taxes (and particularly the unitary tax) were important locational factors.

One particular way of determining income subjects to state corporate income taxes is through the unitary tax. Briefly, a unitary tax is a method of applying the state corporate income tax to businesses that do business partly within and partly outside the state. Under the unitary method, income subject to tax is usually apportioned to the state based on the ratios of the corporation's in-state sales, payroll, and property to the total sales, payroll, and property that are part of the same unitary business. The interdependency of corporations or parts of a corporation is a typical test for unity of business. Thus, the unitary tax is the opposite of the separate accounting used by multinationals for federal income tax purposes.

During the period 1977–1981, eleven states, including California, used the worldwide unitary method, apportioning income from worldwide operations. The impact of this simple difference in accounting—unitary apportionment versus separate accounting—can be substantial. For corporations with low in-state taxable incomes (such as those which are newly founded), apportionment of income from more profitable affiliates can greatly increase taxes. Thus, an obvious factor for conglomerates to consider is the high tax incidence on a new subsidiary in a fully unitary state (vis-à-vis a nonunitary or partially unitary state).

In this example we use I–O to estimate the impact of investments forgone in California due to the unitary tax. A survey was used to directly elicit unpublished information. The questionnaire was sent to the 56 largest Japanese manufacturers doing business in California. This targeted group represented those affected most by the California unitary tax (California Assembly 1980, 1981) and comprised the bulk of California foreign investment. Foreign services, nearly all of which were financial, comprised the remainder of Japanese investments and were excluded from the analysis for two reasons. First, they were relatively insubstantial, and second, their function was frequently to service foreign manufacturers. Consequently, decisions to locate in California were generally an endogenous function of manufacturers' locational choices.

The survey instrument (see Appendix I) elicited two types of information. The first type included attitudinal responses on the unitary tax, and overall information on fixed assets, supplies, and payroll investments in California. This latter information included the extent of actual operations in California during the previous five years, forgone operations during the previous five years due solely to the unitary tax, and projected forgone California investments in the next five years solely because of the unitary tax. These last two items were investments forgone to California and reinvested in nonunitary states. This served to limit the responses to unitary tax reactions but not to other factors such as international preference.

The second type of information sought in the questionnaire was the detailing of the above California operations for capital and supplies in 30 industrial sectors. These expenditures were to be used as data to the following hypotheses using input–output analysis.

The Hypotheses

From the preceding discussion it is clear that the California unitary tax may result in additional tax incidence on the factor inputs of a new business. It is also clear that if we accept the hypothesis of fairly high factor-demand elasticity of foreign firms (with further attitudinal evidence provided by Tong and Walter (1980) and Nihon Keizai Shimbun (1981)), then foreign firms are particularly reactive to unitary tax consequences on new state investments.

Thus, the following should hold:

H₁: The California unitary tax is an important factor in foreign firms' decisions on investment in California.

Further, if the California unitary tax is an important variable, then a significant amount of foreign investments may be made in locales other than California. It can be hypothesized that the effects of the three-factor California unitary apportionment should have resulted in potentially higher taxes on labor and capital inputs. A tax-elastic reaction, given arbitrage possibilities in nonunitary states,[2] should have resulted. This leads to a possible reaction to the unitary tax, or

H₂: Foreign firms substantially curtailed their California investment in property and payroll because of the California unitary tax.

Because of interindustry linkages in the California economy, any California investments forgone by the foreign firms would have had a multiplied effect on the California economy, or:

H₃: Forgone California investments by the foreign firms resulted in a substantial loss in California social welfare in terms of output, income, and employment.

Given that any investment would have expanded the overall state tax base for all types of taxes after giving rise to the above multiplied effect, it is posited that:

H₄: Had the unitary tax been repealed for the respondents, the increase in overall California taxes in the expanded economy would have exceeded the lost (corporate franchise) unitary taxes.

The 157 sector California Regional Input–Output Model is used in this study (California Department of Water Resources 1980). As pointed out by Schaffer (1976), when assessing regional economic impacts, a regional input–output table is highly preferable to the national I–O model. This is because the national table may show different technical coefficients than those representative of the region or state, and because the national model cannot account for intrastate–versus–interstate transactions.

Purchase of goods and services by business generate direct and indirect economic impacts, which were estimated in our survey. That is, production of these goods and services requires the output of relevant supplying industries. These in turn result in indirect and induced employment, income, and production impacts over and above those directly required. To the

Table 1. Operations in U.S. Nonunitary States as a Consequence of the California Unitary Tax of the Past Five Years

	Total	*Average*
Payroll Expenditures (in millions of dollars)	92.2	30.7
Payments for Other Goods and Services (in Millions of dollars)	1,113.9	371.3
Number of Employees	935	311.7

extent that such indirect demand requirements are met by California producers, as opposed to the import of goods and services from producers, multiplier effects will be created within the California economy.

The Aggregated California Input–Output Transactions Table

To make the questionnaire comparable, the 157-sector California transaction table was reduced to 30 industrial sectors. The primary criterion for valid aggregation is the homogeneity (or substitutability) of products between the sectors to be combined. For a discussion of this consideration as well as a general discussion of the subject, the interested reader is referred to Fisher (1958). The aggregation criteria used was essentially that used by the California Department of Water Resources (1980) to aggregate the California table into a 40-sector table.

Results—Hypotheses One and Two

Surveys were mailed to the 56 largest Japanese firms doing business in California. Japanese investment comprises the bulk of foreign California investment, so it was believed that the sample results would be large enough to generate a substantial multiplier impact on the California economy.

Of the 56 surveys mailed, 23 responses were received. Seventy-five percent of the respondents indicated that they consider the California Unitary Tax in their investment decisions. Responses on the perceived importance of the unitary tax indicated that 39 percent considered it very important (the top score of 5), 28 percent gave it a score of 4, and 28 percent gave it a score of 3.

The survey also indicated that $1.129 billion and $5.655 billion had been spent on payroll and on other goods and services in California, respectively, by the respondents, and 13,500 people had been employed. However, only 14 percent of the respondents (three firms) indicated that they had actually reduced, relocated, or not expanded because of the California unitary tax. Table 1 shows the magnitude of investments not made in nonunitary states rather than in California.

The respondents' estimated expenditures for payroll and for other products and services, and the average number of employees that would be associated with operations in other, nonunitary states rather than in California because of the unitary tax are summarized in Table 2.

Thus, Tables 2 and 3 indicate that for a small percentage of respondents the California unitary tax had a significant impact on investments, and that nearly half of the respondents planned to make a significant investment change in the immediate future as a result of the unitary tax.

The conclusion relating to H_1 is supported by the fact that although only three of the respondents actually reduced, relocated, or failed to expand their operations in the last five years because of the unitary tax, this negative reaction was substantial in economic terms. The estimated payroll lost by California was $92.7 million, or 8.2 percent of the total payroll for the respondents in California over the past five years. Payments for other goods and services lost by California was $1.12 billion, or 19.7 percent of all respondents' expenditures over the past five years. Jobs lost to California totaled 935, or 6.9 percent of all respondents' California employment.

The conclusion relating to H_2 is supported by Table 3, with ten of the twenty-three respondents indicating planned reductions in California operations. These respondents indicated that $687.4 million in payroll would be lost from California over the next five years as a result of the unitary tax, or 60.9 percent of past California payroll. Similarly, $2.79 billion in total expenditures would be lost in California, or 49.4 percent of all respondents' actual previous expenditures. A total of 6,515 California jobs will be forgone, representing 46.8 percent of all the respondents' California jobs during the past five years.

These results imply that the economic responses by the respondents are becoming increasingly large. We will now analyze total impact through multiplier analysis.

The Loss in Economic Social Welfare: Hypothesis Three

To assess the California economic impact of the respondents' answers, a

Table 2. Planned Operations in U.S. Nonunitary States as a Consequence of the California Unitary Tax Over the Next Five Years

	Total	Average
Payroll Expenditures (in Millions of dollars)	687.4	68.7
Payments for Other Goods and Services (in Millions of dollars)	2,793.2	279.3
Number of Employees	6,515	651.5

three-step process was followed. The first step was to aggregate the 157-sector input–output transactions table (California Department of Water Resources 1980) into a 30-sector table to make the table comparable to the 30-sector questionnaire. The second step was to develop output, income, and employment multipliers from this contracted table. The final multiplier appears in Appendix II.

By multiplying the changes in final demand (implied by the survey results) by the multipliers in Appendix II, the economic impact of the unitary tax on California output, employment, and income can be assessed for the survey respondents. Since the questionnaire did not provide for information on the respondents' sales by industry, demand had to be estimated. Ideally, an econometric model or some other estimation technique would be used to determine exogenous final demand (Pleeter 1980). However, since even past sales by industry were unavailable for the respondents, an ad hoc method of determining final demand was employed.

The estimate assumed that sales to final buyers by the Japanese firms exactly equalled costs. This was not unrealistic for the first few years of new plant operation. Total costs, as reported on the questionnaires, were expenditures for capital, goods and services, and payroll costs. Since profit margins of the respondents were unknown, this break-even assumption was required throughout the analysis. Total sales by the Japanese firms were assumed to fill only final demand. This is based on the assumption that the Japanese firms would export their products to the rest of the United States or the world, and that California would be the respondents' choice of a manufacturing site for a much wider area of distribution. Additional final demand (wholly Californian) would be generated by payroll expenditures.

This final demand was assumed to come from various sectors under two assumptions. The first method allocated final demand to all industry sectors based on the sectors' relative final demand proportions in the California I–O table. The second method assumed that sales by industry were in proportion to factor inputs in the industry; the factor inputs were based on the capital and the goods and services expenditure reported on the questionnaires. Final demand resulting from the respondents' payroll expenditures was allocated pro rata, according to general consumption patterns in the California I–O table.

Table 3 reports the estimated economic impact resulting from the respondents' reduction of California operations over the past five years because of the unitary tax. Estimates using each of the two multipliers under both final demand mixture assumptions are shown.

Table 4 reports comparable figures for planned foregone California investments by Japanese firms because of the unitary tax over the next five years.

Thus, the total rippled-through ten-year economic impact from lost Japanese business is substantial (approximately two percent of the total 1977

Table 3. Total Economic Impact of Forgone California Investment by Respondents—Prior Five Years (Total)

	Loss to California		
	In Total Output	*In Income (GSP)*	*In Employment (thousands of dollars)*
	(millions of dollars)		
Assuming First Sales Mixture			
Using Type I Multipliers	2,260.1	1,552.1	26.4
Using Type II Multipliers	3,960.9	1,937.9	30.2
Assuming Second Sales Mixture			
Using Type I Multipliers	2,421.1	1,492.4	24.92
Using Type II Multipliers	4,004.6	1,760.2	26.9

Table 4. Total Economic Impact of Planned Forgone California Investments by Respondents—Next Five Years (Total)

	Loss to California		
	In Total Output	*In Income (GSP)*	*In Employment (thousands of dollars)*
	(millions of dollars)		
Assuming First Sales Mixture			
Using Type I Multipliers	6,412.2	4,403.4	74.9
Using Type II Multipliers	11,237.6	5,497.9	85.9
Assuming Second Sales Mixture			
Using Type I Multipliers	6,868.8	4,234.2	70.7
Using Type II Multipliers	11,361.3	4,993.7	76.3

California economy).[3] This loss in social welfare could be significant because of the resulting loss in total California tax revenues. However, the loss in revenue from dropping the unitary tax could be offset by tax increase due to increases in investments in California. A test of this appears next.

Resulting Change in the Overall State Tax Base (Hypothesis Four)

It would be interesting to know whether loss in California Franchise Tax (from dropping the unitary tax and instead using separate accounting) would be offset by the gain in the overall state and local tax base from new investment attracted by the tax change. Table 5 below shows the estimated gain or loss in California state and local taxes resulting from the respondents' hypothetical California investments over the past five years, assuming no unitary tax. This overall tax-base gain is reduced by the estimated loss in franchise tax assuming that only the respondents were exempted from the unitary tax. The estimation procedures for these tax collections are reported in Appendix III.

Table 5 demonstrates that had the unitary tax been dropped for the respondents, there could have been a substantial increase in total California tax collections. From the I–O model perspective, this implies that the preceding multiplied effects are conservative estimates, since net gain to the public sector would also ripple through the economy. Whether a repeal of the unitary tax for all corporations would have resulted in a similar tax-base increase is beyond the scope of this study.

A SECOND ILLUSTRATION OF THE USE OF I–O: THE CASE OF ACRS VERSUS A GPL INDEXING TAXING SYSTEM DURING TIMES OF INFLATION

Although the United States is in a state of low inflation, historical evidence

Table 5. Gain or Loss in State and Local Taxes from Dropping the Unitary Tax and Attracting Respondents' Additional Investments (in millions of dollars—In Total)

	Prior Five Years				Future Five Years			
	Gain in Personal Income Taxes	Gain in Business Taxes	Loss in Franchise Taxes	Net Gain or Loss in Taxes	Gain in Personal Income Taxes	Gain in Business Taxes	Loss in Franchise Taxes	Net Gain or Loss in Taxes
Assuming First Sales Mixture:								
Using Type I Multipliers	34.2	138.4	(4.3)	168.3	96.9	392.5	(5.7)	483.7
Using Type II Multipliers	43.7	165.3	(4.3)	204.7	124.1	468.9	(5.7)	587.3
Assuming Second Sales Mixture:								
Using Type I Multipliers	32.1	137.9	(4.3)	165.7	91.2	391.3	(5.7)	476.8
Using Type II Multipliers	38.3	159.7	(4.3)	232.0	108.8	453.0	(5.7)	556.1

would indicate that this may be a temporary condition. Numerous undesirable income tax effects result from inflation. Effects on corporations include the understatements of depreciation and cost of goods sold, and the omission of monetary gains and losses. If firms alter their production, investment, and financing decisions to mitigate these effects, the tax law is nonneutral during times of inflation. This may result in economic inefficiency. Further, to the extent that the aforementioned inflationary misstatements are disproportionate across industries, horizontal inequity occurs. Neutrality requires that the tax law by itself does not bias taxpayers' decisions. Horizontal equity implies that taxpayers with identical economic situations will be taxed equivalently.

Previous studies have indicated that the bulk of corporate inflationary tax misstatements are the result of underdepreciation [see Tideman and Tucker (1976)].[4] Thus, a major goal of an inflation-mitigating tax system should be to attack inflationary misstatements of historically costed assets. The Accelerated Cost Recovery System (ACRS) under post-1980 law, with its shortening of useful lives, may provide such mitigation of under-depreciation. However, this mitigation of inflationary effects on taxation might fall on certain capital intensive industries. Gravelle (1982) and Swenson (1987) found that depreciation under ACRS should result in lopsided effects on different industries. The purpose of this study is to estimate the total economic impact of this effect using input-output analysis of the data reported in Swenson (1987).

The Impacts of Inflation on Corporate Taxation, including:

Three direct effects on corporate taxation result from times of inflation. The first effect, underdepreciation, occurs since firms must depreciate their fixed assets based on historical cost when this cost often understates their assets' inflated replacement values. Such underdepreciation decreases corporations' depreciation deductions, increases their taxable incomes, and increases their taxes. Even during periods of low inflation, this misstatement is large since it reflects years of cumulative price increases.

A second effect is the understatement of inventory values. Firms state their inventories on a historical basis, causing the cost of goods sold to be less than the inventory's replacement value. This understatement means a lowered deduction for the cost of goods sold and an increase in the corporation's taxable income, thus raising its income tax.

A final inflationary difficulty with regard to U.S. corporate taxation involves the omission of monetary gains and losses. Just like historically costed fixed assets and inventories, liabilities can be misstated during inflationary times. Historical valuation of liabilities does not account for the erosion of the principal portion of liabilities due to inflation. In anticipation of this erosion, lenders are thought to increase their interest rates, thus converting what would have been increased principal into interest.

Several serious economic consequences may occur because of the three aformentioned direct effects of inflation on corporate taxation, including:

1. erosion of real financial capital;
2. changed asset structures;
3. changed factor input mixes;
4. altered capital projects because of return requirements; and
5. increased incentives for merger.

Mitigation of Inflationary Effects

The Accelerated Cost Recovery System was shown by Feldstein (1981) and Hasbrouck (1983) to be able to mitigate against underdepreciation at certain moderately high rates of inflation. Unfortunately, as shown by Gravelle (1982) and Swenson (1987), ACRS also results in a disproportionate shift in capital among industries during inflationary periods. This induced horizontal inequity is thought to lead to decreased economic inefficiency and a loss of deadweight to the economy.[5] One way in which such disproportionate industry capital shifts could lead to a deadweight loss is through a multiplier effect on the economy.

The Inflationary Misstatements

In this section we explain the procedures used by Swenson (1987) to estimate total taxes that would be paid under ERTA (using ACRS) rules and under GPL accounting. These taxes will become inputs in the subsequent I–O analysis. Swenson's study used a Monte Carlo simulation[6] to estimate the variance of both pre-1981 and post-1980 law (which used ACRS) from general price level (GPL) accounting.[7] The data was from industry financial data in the U.S. Treasury's publication on corporate income statistics (U.S. Treasury 1982). All industries were included in the study.[8]

While much of the data needed on these industries were contained in the Treasury publication, some were missing. Accordingly, Swenson (1987) made the following assumptions:

1. FIFO, LIFO, and moving-average industry averages for inventories (Accounting Trends and Techniques, AICPA 1981) would continue in the future;
2. each industry's growth rate would follow the five-year trend calculated by U.S. Industrial Outlook (Bureau of Industrial Economics 1983);

3. inventories were turned over based on the 1980 ratio of the cost of goods sold to average inventory;
4. the tax-accounting lives of industries' fixed assets were calculated from 1980 balance sheets by dividing 1980 fixed assets by total 1980 depreciation expense (including that in the cost of sales) and by assuming pre-1981 equipment and structures to be depreciated on average by the 150-percent-declining-balance methods.

This last assumption was based upon pre-ERTA Section 167 rules (personal property was eligible for double-declining balance (DDB), 150 percent declining balance (DB) if used, and straight line (SL) if a useful life of 3 years; real property was generally eligible for 150 percent DB if new, SL if used). Real versus personal property ratios were obtained from the *Survey of Manufacturers' Data* (U.S. Department of Commerce 1980) for manufacturers, and from *Survey of Current Business* for nonmanufacturers (U.S. Department of Commerce 1981). Real growth rates of income statement and balance sheet accounts changed proportionately based on the aforementioned sales forecasts. Real fixed asset replacement was assumed to be based on capital recovery assuming straight-line depreciation.[9]

Individual industry costs of capital and effective tax rates were used in the simulation. The individual tax rates were necessary due to pronounced industry differences, that is, services (with many small companies) pay 23 percent tax rates on average, while mines and petroleum (with add-on preference taxes) pay 52 percent rates on average. Effective tax rates were calculated as gross taxes, less investment credit, plus preference taxes, divided by domestic taxable income. Weighted after-tax costs of debt and equity capital were calculated directly from 1980 industry data.[10]

The inflationary assumption for the simulation was that inflation would follow a pattern as forecasted by Box–Jenkins time series analysis. Implicit price GNP deflator was forecast built on a time series of 1930–1980 implicit price GNP deflation rates using the following model:

$$(1 - B^1) (1 - \phi_1 B^1) (1 - \phi_2 B^2) Z_t = a_t , \qquad (14)$$

where ϕ_i are autoregressive parameters, B is a backshift operator, Z_t is implicit price GNP deflator for year t, and a_t is white noise. Model parameters with standard errors in parentheses are $\phi_1 = 1.041$ (0.0418) and $\phi_2 = -0.5408$ (0.0269). Diagnostic checks indicated white noise residuals and model stationarity. Thus the model is an AR(2), indicating that price levels are a function of the previous year's price levels, and to a lesser extent, of price levels two years prior.

Table 6.   ERTA Tax Versus GPL Tax Means (in Thousands of 1980 Dollars)

ERTA Tax	GPL Tax
17,252	19,549

Note:
Data were subjected to Box–Cox power transformations roughly equivalent to a square root. Beginning fixed assets under GPL system were not indexed to allow fair comparison of depreciation on new assets (for which ACRS can be used).

Results of the Simulation

Table 6, as calculated by Swenson (1987) reports taxes under post-1980 law (using ACRS) and under GPL accounting. The figures shown are the means (over 400 replications for 20 years) of total tax for all industries (in thousands of 1980 dollars) after being subjected in a Box-Cox power transformation to correct for heteroscedasticity.[11] Parametric tests of means using Bonferroni, Tukey's HSD, and Duncan's multiple comparison procedures indicated that the two means were not equal. ACRS tax was lower than GPL tax since ACRS depreciation exceeded GPL depreciation and because current law (under ERTA) did not include monetary gains in income, as did GPL accounting. Sensitivity analyses reported in Swenson (1987) indicated that ACRS and GPL depreciation were only equivalent at inflation rates between 9 and 13 percent. Since projected (and historical) inflation rates were below these rates, it is clear why current law, using ACRS, would result in lower taxes than GPL accounting.

Swenson (1987) also estimated the 20-year variance from inflation neutrality of post-1980 law by industry, as shown in Table 7. The table indicates the post-1980 law's uneven variance from inflation neutrality by industry, which is driven largely by ACRS depreciation.

These uneven industry effects could result in more serious economic consequences when one considers that current law effectively provides more capital to some industries (through tax savings) than to others. To the extent that this capital is reinvested or distributed as dividends, the multiplied effect of such lopsided benefits might be quite large. Because of interindustry linkages in the economy, this lopsided shift in capital (and thus expenditures) could result in lower output, income, and employment than if a more even distribution of tax-related capital had occurred.[12]

The General Equilibrium Impact

To test this hypothesis, we used Swenson's data and compared the difference in tax between current U.S. law (with ACRS) and pre-1981 law to

Table 7.   Difference Between ERTA Tax and GPL Tax
Over 20 Years (in Thousands of 1980 Dollars)

Industry	Total* (1)	Percent** (2)
Metal Mining	19,144.75	0.1277
Coal Mining	25,342.91	0.4063
Oil, Gas Extr.	22,701.36	0.0557
Nonmet. Min.	19,564.74	1.4373
Construction	117,688.03	0.6550
Food Prdcts.	103,987.60	0.1508
Tobacco	12,466.86	0.1310
Textiles	40,328.87	0.3451
Apparel	8,324.11	0.0733
Lumber, Wood	57,943.42	3.2264
Furn., Fixt.	5,482.07	0.0958
Paper Prod.	63,491.03	0.3679
Printing, Pub.	22,402.85	0.0906
Chemicals	28,393.69	0.0326
Petrol. Prod.	269,210.57	0.1343
Rubber, Plast.	6,379.08	0.0473
Leather Prod.	1,824.91	0.0732
Stone, etc.	63,260.98	1.3035
Primary Mtls.	78,196.76	0.3117
Fabr. Mtls.	68,693.02	0.2150
Machinery	125,453.25	0.1673
Elect. Equip.	22,324.80	0.0125
Trans. Equip.	66,456.20	0.1653
Instruments	27,992.50	0.1535
Misc. Manuf.	5,665.90	0.0567
Transportation	−29,955.00	−0.0962
Communication	−223,383.50	−0.0669
Utilities	191,433.20	1.1897
Wholesalers	98,522.50	0.0687
Retailers	68,929.60	0.0082
Banking	−314,745.00	−0.4359
Cr. Agencies	−29,619.80	−0.1586
Sec., Omd. Brkrs.	1,250.30	0.0063
Insurance	96,737.30	0.2802
Ins. Agents	5,417.70	0.1176
Real Estate	−148,320.80	−0.6330
Holding Co.s	44,561.70	0.6261
Services	3,891.00	0.1015

Notes:
*Positive variance indicates GPL tax > ERTA tax: negative variance indicates opposite relationship.
**Column 1 divided by GPL tax.

the difference between U.S. law with GPL inflationary adjustments and pre-1981 law. Since the total amounts of taxes under each system were unequal, each industry's tax savings (over pre-1981 U.S. law) are scaled as a percent of total, economy-wide corporate tax savings. The scaled industry tax savings are then assumed to be either reinvested by the industry or partially distributed as dividends. While many studies have examined the corporation-shareholder tradeoff in benefit when taxes are increased, virtually no studies have investigated the tradeoff when taxes are reduced. Because of this uncertainty in tax savings sharing retention, two scenarios are investigated: 100 percent corporate retention, and retention in accordance with 1979–1980 dividend payout ratios in the *Statistics of Income* publication (U.S. Treasury 1982).

With regard to the firm's reinvestment of retained tax savings, Canto, Joines, and Laffer (1978) and Laffer (1980) demonstrate that increased returns to capital (which would be the primary result of ACRS's or GPL accounting's mitigation of underdepreciation) result in an increased supply of both capital and labor factor inputs. They demonstrated this analytically and empirically through an examination of 50-year trends in both factors of production. Thus, to the extent that this effect occurs and induced economic effects of higher demand result in larger supply by industry, it would seem reasonable to posit that increased spending by industries of retained tax savings would be proportionate to existing purchase patterns. Spending of tax savings by each industry was therefore assumed to be in proportion to existing national input–output table ratios for that industry.

The economic impact of the tax savings under the two tax systems was assessed using input–output analysis. Industries in the 80-sector 1977 national transaction table (Bureau of Economic Analysis 1984) were aggregated into a 38-sector economy to conform to the 38-industry scheme in the Monte Carlo simulation. Output, income, and employment multipliers were developed from the reduced transactions table and are shown in Appendix IV. Autonomous final demand changes were assumed to be generated by industry spending of the savings and by individual consumption. Industry spending was assumed to be in the same proportions as in the 1977 national transactions table. Individual consumption, resulting from dividends, was assumed to be spent proportionately in the economy (in accordance with the national transactions table ratios). Since the national table included consumption in the financial sector, the need to assume a marginal propensity to save was obviated.

The direct, indirect, and induced (type II multiplier) effects on national output, income, and employment resulting from tax savings under the two tax systems, under both corporate tax savings retention assumptions, are reported in Table 8. The estimates suggest that GPL accounting, had it been adopted, might have resulted in higher output, income, and employment than post-1980 law using ACRS.

Table 8. Output, Income, and Employment Effects
of Shift in Tax Incidence: Post-1981 Law vs. U.S. Law With GPL
Adjustments (Twenty-year Total in Billions of 1980 Dollars)

Assumption/Tax System	*Total Output*	*Household Income*	*Employment Millions*
Assuming 100 percent Retention of Tax Savings:			
Post-1980 U.S. Tax	8111.8	4105.2	1.646
U.S. Tax With GPL Adj.	8239.6	4178.0	1.660
Assuming Tax Savings Retention Based on Historical Dividends Ratio:			
Post-1980 U.S. Tax	7812.7	4164.3	1.638
U.S. Tax With GPL Adj.	7815.1	4250.0	1.638

Thus, the economic inefficiency induced by an uneven distribution of taxes among industries (under the current tax law) during times of inflation is highlighted when put to the test of a full equilibrium economic model. Ironically, ACRS was installed to promote economic growth, but the I–O model analysis indicates that economic performance might have been higher under relatively incentive-neutral GPL accounting.

CONCLUSIONS

This paper illustrates the use of input–output analysis for tax research. Two examples were presented. The first case illustrated the hypothetical effects on a state economy because of foregone investment in manufacturing facilities and the operation of these facilities because of state tax policies. The second example showed that economic inefficiency induced by horizontally inequitable distribution of taxes among industries may have diminished or offset productivity gains of ACRS.

The I–O model is characterized by strengths and shortcomings. One shortcoming is the model's static nature. If factors in the economy change substantially, then the transactions table must be updated, or any results may be of questionable value. Similarly, any large structural changes which are induced by the economic shock under investigation will invalidate the results. Thus, if a massive tax change is expected to result in drastic changes in corporate and personal investment/consumption decisions, use of the I–O model to investigate the multiplied effect of the tax law change would be inappropriate.

A second shortcoming of I–O is a lack of existing transactions tables. While national tables and some state tables have been published (we have cited some of them), tables do not exist for many states. The use of I–O is thus effectively precluded for such states, since construction of a transactions table is a time-consuming process that may be beyond the scope of many accounting researchers. A final difficulty with I–O is the measurement of the exogenous changes (by industry) which drive the results. Our two applications of I–O illustrate that such measurements can be difficult; our small sample in the California unitary tax case and our assumption-laden simulated input in the inflationary accounting case were useful but not ideal.

The major strength of I–O in tax policy research is that it is a general equilibrium model. To the extent that researchers are interested in how tax laws affect both business and individual welfare, a partial equilibrium model may be inadequate. A second strength is that I–O is often a more accurate and simple general equilibrium model than are econometric models. The shortcomings of regional and state econometric models were discussed in the first section. National econometric models involve scores of simultaneous equations and may be beyond the scope of many accounting tax researchers. A final strength of I–O is its potential simplicity. Once a researcher has obtained multipliers, it is a relatively simple mathematical procedure to multiply exogenous impacts for each industry by related industry output, income, and employment multipliers. We hope that this paper has illustrated the use of I–O, and that this knowledge will encourage its use in tax research.

NOTES

1. The most relevant state tables have been by the California Department of Water Resources (1967) for California, for Georgia as reported in Schaffer (1976), for Washington by Tiebout (1969), and for Utah by Bradley (1967). See also the references in Schaffer (1976).

2. For example, a firm otherwise indifferent about whether to choose Arizona or California could locate in Arizona to avoid higher taxes because of the California unitary tax.

3. Of course, a complete analysis would also consider extra social costs of the new firm's locations in California. These costs would include new schools, and so forth. Since a satisfactory regional economic model for estimating this cost is not available, this step was not included.

4. Previous studies have shown that except for a sudden jump in inflation (when monetary gains dominate the depreciation effect for that year only) underdepreciation dominates both monetary gains or losses and undercosting of cost-of-goods-sold effects. See, for example, Tideman and Tucker (1976).

5. For a discussion of welfare loss and economic inefficiency the reader is referred to McClure and Thurske (1975).

6. Since the objective of Swenson's 1987 study was to determine the complex interrelationships between inflation rates and taxation with minimal confounding, the use of actual data from prior years (which would have been subject to macroeconomic fluctuations, etc.) would have been inappropriate. Further, an analytic study could have proven intractable due to the complex, nonlinear relationships of the variables involved, nor would it have allowed for realistic macroeconomic tax policy implications, e.g., actual interindustry shifts in taxable

incomes due to ACRS. The use of the 20-year period was to assure that "steady state" inflationary depreciation occurs. Note that the "steady state" inflation rate was already achieved at the start of the experiment due to prespecified truncation of the inflationary distributions.

7.   See Casler and Hall (1985) who demonstrate that price level accounting is a reasonable surrogate for replacement costs with aggregate data. General price level accounting was determined by the method provided for in Financial Accounting Standards Board (FASB) Option No. 33. Under FASB Opinion No. 82 (effective 12/15/84) the GPL reporting requirements of Opinion 33 were suspended, and only current cost data need be disclosed. The FASB eliminated the GPL requirement because it felt that reporting two different types of price-level adjusted accounting detracted from the usefulness of the information.

8.   The agriculture, forestry, and fishing industry was excluded from the analysis since industry statistics vary so widely (e.g., inventory turnovers for catfish farms versus forest-growing firms) that reliable industry-average statistics were not obtainable. Since this industry only accounts for one percent of total corporate tax revenues, its omission should not affect any of our conclusions. The motor vehicle transportation manufacturing industry has such cumulative large tax loss carryovers, and such a small projected growth (as of 1980), that it is unlikely to pay any taxes in the next 20 years. Since, by paying no taxes, this industry would not (in the sense defined in this study) vary from inflation neutrality, it was excluded so as not to bias the results.

9.   Thus, for example, if industry A's straight-line depreciation for the year was $100,000, then $100,000 (in current dollars) of additional fixed assets would be acquired as replacements to maintain a fixed stock of productive capital. This replacement was also multiplied by the industry's projected growth rate, if any. The straight-line recovery assumed that calculated useful lives were accurate. Useful lives are derived directly from Statistics of Income balance sheets. These balance sheets generally conform to GAAP (generally accepted accounting principles) balance sheets and hence GAAP useful lives.

10.   Costs of debt were calculated by dividing after-tax interest expense (interest expense times one minus the calculated effective tax rate) by total debt. Cost of equity was after-tax taxable income divided by owner's equity. Weighted returns were obtained by adding 1) after-tax return on debt times the ratio of debt to debt plus equity, plus 2) after-tax return on equity times the ratio of equity to debt plus equity.

11.   The simulation was based on a sample size of 400. Each sample had identical starting values and seed; thus the results were not autocorrelated. The sample size selected was based on a two-step multiple comparison procedure by Dudewicz, Ramberg, and Chen reported in Kleijnen (1975). The method assumed that the variances of variables to be compared (in this case, deflated and discounted tax payments) were unknown and possibly unequal. The sample size was designed to result in detecting a five percent or less difference in true (population) means. The heteroscedasticity assumption resulted in sample sizes larger than necessary to satisfy pairwise tests with more restrictive distribution assumptions (e.g., Bonferroni tests). To insure that the simulation's results were not invalid, certain validation procedures (Van Horne, 1971) were performed. Inflation rate forecasts to 1983 were correct within two standard errors, as were industry sales forecasts. Corroborative results were obtained when the inflation rate followed a random pattern using actual inflation rates from 1930–1980. Sensitivity analyses and construct validity tests (e.g., using undiscounted dollars) did not significantly change the simulation's results. See Swenson (1987) for a thorough discussion of the simulation.

12.   There are several reasons why this might occur. Since value added is usually highest in manufacturing, ACRS, which favors utilities, real estate, and communications (see Swenson 1987) could result in lower income than GPL accounting. Also, to the extent that ACRS benefits non-labor-intensive industries, employment (and hence household income) might be lower under ACRS than under GPL. Other factors, such as dividend payout ratios and interdependence on other sectors of the economy (as opposed to heavy exportation or importation) are also important. The issue is so complex that it reduces to an empirical question.

REFERENCES

American Institute of Certified Public Accountants, *Accounting Trends and Techniques* (AICPA, 1981).

Box, George E. P., and Gwilym M. Jenkins, *Time Series Analysis: Forecasting and Control* (Holden-Day, 1976).

Bradley, I. E., "Utah Interindustry Study: An Input-Output Analysis," *Utah Business and Economic Review* (July-August 1967), pp. 1–13.

Bureau of Economic Analysis, "Input–Output Structure of the U.S. Economy—1977," *Survey of Current Business* (May 1984).

Bureau of Industrial Economics, *U.S. Industrial Outlook* (B.I.A., 1983).

California Assembly, "Unitary Apportionment." Hearings before Assembly Revenue and Taxation Committee, State Publication Nos. 750, 767, 810, 886 (1980).

California Assembly, "Unitary Method of Apportionment: New Developments." Hearing before California Assembly Revenue and Taxation Committee (Dec. 16, 1981).

California Department of Water Resources, "California Statewide Input–Output Model Base Year 1967" (State of California, 1980).

California Franchise Tax Board (1981) *Annual Report* (State of California, 1982).

Canto, V. A., D. H. Joines, and A. B. Laffer, "Taxation, GNP, and Potential GNP," presentation before American Statistical Association (August 1978).

Casler, T. W., and D. J. Hall, "Firm-Specific Asset Valuation Accuracy Using a Composite Index," *Journal of Accounting Research* (January 1985), pp. 110–122.

Due, J., "Studies of Local Tax Influences on Location of Industry," *National Tax Journal* (1961), pp. 163–173.

Feldstein, M., "Adjusting Depreciation in An Inflationary Economy: Indexing Versus Acceleration," *National Tax Journal* (January 1981), pp. 29–43.

Financial Accounting Standards Board, *Statement 33* (FASB, 1977).

Financial Accounting Standards Board, *Statement 82* (FASB, 1984).

Fisher, W. D., "Criteria for Aggregation in I–O Analysis," *Review of Econometrics and Statistics* (Vol. 40, No. 3, 1958), pp. 250–260.

Fortune, Facility Location Decisions, Fortune Magazine (Fortune, 1977).

Ghali, M., and B. Renaud, *The Structure and Dynamic Properties of a Regional Economy* (Lexington Books, 1976).

Gravelle, J. G., "The Effects of the 1981 Depreciation Revisions of Income From Business Capital," *National Tax Journal* (January 1982), pp. 1–20.

Hasbrouck, J., "The Impact of Inflation upon Corporate Taxation," *National Tax Journal* (March 1983), pp. 65–81.

Kleijnen, J. P. C., *Statistical Techniques in Simulation* (Marcel Dekker, Inc., 1975).

Laffer, A. B., *The Ellipse: The Expectation of the Laffer Curve in a Two Factor Model*, (H. C. Wainwright, 1980).

Louis Harris and Associates, "Attitudes of the Nation's Corporate Leaders Toward California as a Business Location," unpublished paper for Commission of Economic Development (State of California, February 1978).

McClure, C. E., and W. R. Thurske, "A Simplified Version of the Harberger Model I: Tax Incidence," *National Tax Journal* (March 1975), pp. 1–28.

Nihon Keizai Shimbun, "Foreign Countries Show Rising Zeal to Invite Japanese Enterprises," *The Japan Economic Journal* (December 29, 1981), pp. 14–15.

O'Connor, R. and E. W. Henry, *Input–Output Analysis and Its Applications* (Mafner Press, 1975).

Pleeter, S., *Economic impact analysis: Methodology and applications* (Martinus Nijhoff, 1980).

Schaffer, W., ed., *On the Use of Input–Output Models for Regional Planning* (Martinus-Nischoff, 1976).

Standard and Poor's, Inc., *Industry Outlook* (Standard and Poor's, Inc., 1980).

Swenson, C. W., "An Analysis of ACRS During Inflationary Periods." *The Accounting Review* (January 1987), pp. 117–136.

Tideman, T. N., and D. P. Tucker, "The Tax Treatment of Business Profits Under Inflationary Conditions," in M. S. Aaron, ed., *Inflation and the Income Tax* (The Brookings Institution, 1976).

Tiebout, C. M., "An Empirical Regional Input–Output Projection Model: The State of Washington, 1980," *Revue of Economics and Statistics,* (LI, 1969), pp. 334–40.

Tong, H. and C. K. Walter, "An Empirical Study of Plant Location Decisions of Foreign Manufacturing Investment in the United States," *Columbia Journal of World Business,* (Spring 1980), pp. 66–73.

U. S. Department of Commerce, Bureau of Economic Analysis (1950), "New Structures and Equipment by Using Industries, 1972," in Peter E. Roughlin and Bea Staff, *Survey of Current Business* (July 1980), pp. 45–54.

U. S. Department of Commerce, Bureau of the Census (1981), *Expenditures for Plant and Equipment, Book Value of Fixed Assets, Rental Payments for Building and Equipment, Depreciation and Retirement* (U. S. Government Printing Office, 1981).

U. S. Treasury (Internal Revenue Service), *Statistics of Income: Corporation Income Tax Returns* (U. S. Government Printing Office, 1982).

Van Horne, R. L., "Validation of Simulation Results," *Management Science* (January 1971), pp. 247–258.

Wheaton, W., "Interstate Differences in the Levels of Business Taxation," *National Tax Journal* (Vol. 36, 1983), pp. 83–94.

APPENDIX I: CALIFORNIA UNITARY TAX INPUT/OUTPUT QUESTIONNAIRE

Company Name _____

Address _____

_____

Optional _____

Name of person
completing questionnaire _____

Telephone Number _____

I. In your investment decisions, do you consider the California Unitary Tax?

_____ Yes   _____ No

If you answered YES to Question I:

How important is the California Unitary Tax in your decision process?

Very Important   Unimportant

5   4   3   2   1

II. In the past five years what was the approximate total of expenditures for payroll and expenditures for other products and services (capital type expenditures, goods for resale and other expenses for products and services) and average number of employees in your California operations?

    A. Payroll $ _____
    B. Other goods and services $ _____
    C. Number of employees $ _____

III. In the past five years did you ever reduce, relocate, or not expand California operations in orde to reduce your California Unitary Tax?
             _____ Yes   _____ No

If you answered YES to Question 3, what was the appropriate total of expenditures for other goods and services and the number of employees as a consequence of the operations in "nonunitary" U.S. states during the past five years?

    A. Payroll $ _____
    B. Other goods and services $ _____

IV. In the next five years, what do you estimate will be the approximate expenditure for payroll and expenditures for other products and services and average number of employees which will be associated with operations in other "non-unitary" states rather than in California because of the unitary tax?

    A. Payroll $ _____
    B. Other goods and services $ _____
    C. Number of employees $ _____

Instruction for Question 5

Compiling the information in Question 5 is not as difficult as it appears. In most cases information will not be required in more than half of the categories and can be obtained from accounting records of purchases of materials used in your manufacturing operations or for resale, operating expenses, and purchases of operating assets.

For example, Design Systems, Inc., manufactures office furniture. The financial information is traced to the input–output question as follows:

Input–Output Category
(i.e., expenditures made to firms
which provide the following goods
or services)

Operations . . .
Purchases

Lumber	8	Lumber and wood products
Hardware	16	Fabricated metals and products
Upholstery materials	7	Textile products
Metal parts, nails, screws, etc.	16	Fabricated metals and products

Expenses . . .

Insurance	26	Finance, insurance and real estate services
Utilities	24	Utilities
Legal and Accounting	27	Services
Postage	30	Government enterprise
Advertising	27	Services
Transportation	22	Transportation and warehousing. See Questions 2A, 3A, and 4A
Truck expenses	22	Transportation and warehousing
Repair and maintenance	27	Services

In addition, Design Systems purchased followed fixed assets during the previous five-year period.

Manufacturing machinery	18	Industrial machinery
Copy machine	19	Light duty equipment
Truck	20	Motor vehicles and transportation equipment

V. What was the approximate amount of your expenditures (both for capital type expenditures, goods for resale and other expenses for products and services) made to firms which provide the following primary products or services? The first column should provide the detail of the amount indicated in Question 2B, and the second column should provide the detail of the amount indicated in Question 3B. What do you estimate will be the approximate amount you plan to spend on operations during the next five years which will not be located in California because of the Unitary Tax? Column 3 should provide the detail of the amount indicated in Question 4B.

Total other goods and
services from Question 2B $ _____
Total other goods and
services from Question 3B $ _____
Total other goods and
services from Question 4B $ _____

	Detail of the above amount	Detail of the above amount	Detail of the above amount
1. Agriculture, forestry and fishery products	$ _____	$ _____	$ _____
2. Mining, petroleum and natural gas production	$ _____	$ _____	$ _____
3. New construction	$ _____	$ _____	$ _____
4. Repair construction	$ _____	$ _____	$ _____
5. Ordinance (artillery, ammunition, tanks, guided missles, etc.)	$ _____	$ _____	$ _____
6. Food processing (meat, dairy, canned and frozen foods, grain mill products, bakery products, beverages, etc.)	$ _____	$ _____	$ _____
7. Textile products	$ _____	$ _____	$ _____
8. Lumber and wood products	$ _____	$ _____	$ _____
9. Furniture and fixtures	$ _____	$ _____	$ _____
10. Paper products (pulp, paper, paperboard, etc.)	$ _____	$ _____	$ _____
11. Printing and publishing	$ _____	$ _____	$ _____
12. Chemicals, drugs, plastics, paints and allied products	$ _____	$ _____	$ _____
13. Petroleum refining and related products	$ _____	$ _____	$ _____
14. Glass, stone and clay products	$ _____	$ _____	$ _____
15. Primary metals processing (steel works, castings, etc.)	$ _____	$ _____	$ _____
16. Fabricated metals and products (metal containers, fabricated structural steel, machine products, etc.)	$ _____	$ _____	$ _____
17. Farm, construction and mining equipment (farm machinery, steam engines, turbines, etc.)	$ _____	$ _____	$ _____

18. Industrial machinery (metal working machinery, machine shop products, other industrial machinery, etc.) $ ____ $ ____ $ ____

19. Light-duty equipment (computers, office equipment service industry machines, radio and TV receiving sets, communication equipment, etc.) $ ____ $ ____ $ ____

20. Motor vehicles and transportation equipment (trucks, aircraft, ships and boat building and repairing, bicycles, railroad equipment, etc.) $ ____ $ ____ $ ____

21. Scientific equipment (computers, office equipment, clocks, photographic and optical goods, jewelry, musical instruments, toys, sporting goods, etc.) $ ____ $ ____ $ ____

22. Transportation and warehousing (truck, water, air, pipeline, railroad, etc.) $ ____ $ ____ $ ____

23. Communications (telephone, telegraph, radio or TV broadcasting, etc.) $ ____ $ ____ $ ____

24. Utilities (electricity, gas, water, disposal of wastes, etc.) $ ____ $ ____ $ ____

25. Wholesale and retail trade (selling of merchandise to commercial and personal consumers) $ ____ $ ____ $ ____

26. Finance, insurance, and real estate services (insurance or real estate operators, etc.) $ ____ $ ____ $ ____

27. Services (hotels, personnel, repair services, accounting, advertising, legal, engineering, etc.) $ ____ $ ____ $ ____

28. Amusements (production and distribution of motion pictures, theatrical productions, sportings events, etc.) $ ____ $ ____ $ ____

29. Medical, educational and non-
profit organizations (doctors,
hospitals, educational services,
etc.) $ _____ $ _____ $ _____
30. Government enterprise (postal
services, government-provided
goods and services, etc.) $ _____ $ _____ $ _____

APPENDIX II: MULTIPLIERS—CALIFORNIA I–O MODEL

Sector	Gross Output Type I	Gross Output Type II	Income (GSP) Type I	Income (GSP) Type II	Employment* Per Million-dollar Demand Type I	Employment* Per Million-dollar Demand Type II
1	2.33	3.28	1.35	1.45	1.21	1.26
2	2.08	3.14	1.44	1.62	1.04	1.05
3	2.27	3.82	1.33	1.53	1.10	1.15
4	1.80	3.37	1.31	1.66	1.07	1.15
5	2.29	3.92	1.33	1.54	1.06	1.10
6	2.84	4.10	1.24	1.30	1.06	1.08
7	2.76	4.41	1.29	1.41	1.07	1.32
8	2.61	3.90	1.30	1.40	1.13	1.23
9	2.51	4.12	1.31	1.48	1.10	1.27
10	2.55	3.99	1.31	1.43	1.13	1.30
11	2.12	3.70	1.36	1.61	1.09	1.27
12	2.64	4.08	1.29	1.41	1.12	1.16
13	2.65	3.83	1.26	1.33	1.02	1.09
14	2.11	3.62	1.35	1.58	1.12	1.20
15	2.73	4.26	1.26	1.36	1.08	1.10
16	2.59	4.16	1.29	1.43	1.14	1.21
17	2.56	4.16	1.30	1.44	1.10	1.14
18	2.32	3.93	1.33	1.54	1.12	1.19
19	2.18	3.82	1.34	1.57	1.13	1.21
20	2.63	4.32	1.30	1.44	1.10	1.15
21	2.31	3.94	1.33	1.54	1.17	1.27
22	1.94	3.46	1.34	1.63	1.15	1.22
23	1.37	2.55	1.22	1.61	1.04	1.13
24	2.14	3.24	1.32	1.47	1.05	1.06
25	1.42	2.74	1.25	1.69	1.13	1.44
26	1.52	2.22	1.29	1.47	1.07	1.10
27	1.89	3.37	1.58	2.06	1.17	1.36

(continued)

Appendix II (*continued*)

Sector	Gross Output		Income (GSP)		Employment* Per Million-dollar Demand	
	Type I	Type II	Type I	Type II	Type I	Type II
28	2.28	3.77	1.35	1.53	1.12	1.22
29	1.63	3.32	1.32	1.79	1.05	1.47
30	1.37	3.48	1.19	1.93	1.05	1.62

Note:
* In Person-years

APPENDIX III: PROCEDURES FOR ESTIMATING TAX REVENUE IMPACTS FOR TABLES 5 AND 6

State Personal Income Tax

Personal income tax was assumed to increase by the change in payroll times the average California income tax rate. The change in payroll was calculated as the payroll to employment ratio rate (by sector from the I–O table) times the calculated change in employment. The average tax rate (3.5 percent) is total taxes over total adjusted gross income (Franchise Tax Board 1981) for all Californians, and assumed the homogeneity of California taxpayers. The 3.5 percent rate remained fairly constant from 1978–1982, and was thus used throughout the study.

State-Local Business Taxes

Per Wheaton (1983), the business tax rate of California is 10.2 percent. This rate is computed by dividing total business taxes (state and local property, payroll, corporate income, utility, stock and document transfer, and severance) by "business income" (value added less payroll).

Thus, the business tax increases were assessed by multiplying increased state GSP (less payroll) times 10.2 percent. In addition, anticipated sales increases (computed as a percent of GSP based on 1977 data) increased the overall business tax rate to 24.01 percent.

California Frachise Tax

Loss in franchise taxes assuming that only the respondent corporations were exempted from the unitary tax was calculated as follows:

	Loss in Franchise Taxes by Exempting Respondents From Unitary Tax for:	
	Past Five Years (Total in Millions of Dollars)	Future Five Years (Total in Millions of Dollars)
Total Expenditures per Survey	7,989.2	10,263.7
Less Assumed Capital Expenditures (7.3 percent per California I–O table ratio)	583.2	749.3
Total Operating Expenditures	7,406.0	9,514.4
Time Net Income Percent (average for all corporations per Franchise Tax Board *Annual Report* 1981)	× 4.67%	× 4.67%
State Net Income	345.9	444.3
Times Tax Rate (9.3 was average rate for 1978–1982)	× 9.3 %	× 9.6 %
	32.2	42.7
Times Portion of Tax Attributable to Unitary Apportionment (see explanation below)	× 13.3 %	× 13.3 %
Total Unitary Tax for Respondents	4.28	5.68

Their expenditures included actual expenditures of the prior five years (assumed to remain constant in the future five years) plus forgone expenditures in the past five years (for past only) or plus forgone expenditures in the next five years (for future only). The 13.3 percent unitary tax is determined as follows:

	Income Apportionment Assuming:		
Ratio (Total to California)	Unitary	Separate Allocating	Difference
	%		
Sales	80	NA	—
Payroll	100	NA	—
Property Average	100	NA	
(= Income Apportionment Ratio)	93.3	80%	13.3%

The above estimation procedure is conservative (i.e., it would tend to overstate the respondents' unitary tax impact) in that payroll and property expenditures actually in California (as listed by the respondents) are assumed to be allocated as such. The 80 percent sales figure is the within-state final demand (exclusive of exports) to total demand ratio from the California I–O table, and is assumed to apply to the respondents. The analysis implicitly assumed that the calculated net incomes are equivalent to allocated income (assuming the respondents' worldwide incomes were aggregated and allocated). This was a necessary assumption since the respondents' worldwide incomes were unknown and allocation was thus not possible.

APPENDIX IV: TYPE II MULTIPLIERS (ROUNDED) FOR 34-SECTOR ECONOMY–U.S. ECONOMY

Sector	Output	Household Income	Employment Per ** Million-dollar Demand
1	2.73	1.22	1.00023
2	2.66	1.11	1.00014
3	2.38	1.18	1.00010
4	1.74	1.24	1.00003
5	2.38	1.21	1.00012
6	2.89	1.07	1.00013
7	3.14	1.10	1.00008
8	2.58	1.14	1.00004
9	3.38	1.22	1.00023
10	3.25	1.31	1.00025
11	2.95	1.22	1.00016
12	2.98	1.33	1.00025
13	3.00	1.23	1.00012
14	2.71	1.33	1.00020
15	2.96	1.18	1.00008
16	2.81	1.12	1.00001
17	3.13	1.34	1.00088
18	2.69	1.29	1.00006
19	3.12	1.27	1.00006
20	2.92	1.03	1.00012
21	2.79	1.32	1.00011
22	2.79	1.36	1.00022
23	3.35	1.21	1.00015
24	2.96	1.41	1.00019
25	2.57	1.30	1.00029
26	2.69	1.31	1.00018
27	2.49	1.37	1.00003
28	1.90	1.22	1.00026
29	2.47	1.08	1.00008
30	2.07	1.32	1.00001
31	2.33	1.38	1.00116
32	1.51	1.00	1.00003
33	2.40	1.35	1.00001
34	2.10	1.89	1.00058

Notes:
*The 38-sector economy in the Monte Carlo simulation was further contracted to 34 sectors to make it comparable to the aggregation scheme in the national transactions table.
**In Person Years.

LOCAL REVENUE POLICY IN LESS DEVELOPED COUNTRIES:

THE CASE FOR ENERGY CONSUMPTION TAXATION

Charles R. Enis, William T. Stuart,

and John J. Hourihan

ABSTRACT

Land taxes are a common source of revenue at the local level in less developed countries (LDCs). In the Philippines such taxation has reached its limits as an effective tax, usually as the result of resistance fostered by local patron-clientage. This paper specifically analyzes the adverse effect of this form of social structure on land taxation. To mitigate this problem, an energy consumption tax (ECT) is proposed. Such a tax is demonstrated to stabilize declining local revenues since it is better tailored to the needs of local polity; moreover it encourages efficient energy deployment in concert with national economic development goals.

INTRODUCTION

In the field of social and economic development, it is now generally ac-

Advances in Taxation, Volume 1, pages 85–107.
Copyright © 1987 JAI Press Inc.
All rights of reproduction in any form reserved.
ISBN: 0–89232–782–0

cepted that the major focus of development efforts should be directed toward directly improving the quality of life of individuals rather than relying on the secondary benefits from national sector economic growth (Cochrane 1979).[1] Local development programming, especially in rural areas, typically involves three activities:

1. identifying priority poverty categories;
2. working directly with representatives of these categories to design and implement programs for improving their quality of life, individually and collectively; and
3. strengthening the capacity of local government units to serve as revenue generators and administrators.

The first two of these activities represent attempts to ensure that it will be the disadvantaged groups which will be the direct, primary beneficiaries of development programs. The significance of the third activity is to remedy the shortage of locally generated funds. This is particularly true in cases where direct subsidies from national or even international agencies are no longer adequate to finance and administer local projects (Sommers 1978, p. 11).

The focus of this paper is on the strengthening of local government units, especially their capacity as generators of local revenues. We show that land taxation, traditionally relied on as a local source of revenue, is incapable of an expansion adequate to meet contemporary local development needs. Moreover, we show that efforts to collect land taxes more efficiently stand to be sabotaged by patron-client systems, powerful political-economic forces commonly encountered in LDCs.[2] There is, then, a real need for alternative sources of reliable revenues which are both cost-effectively collectable and relatively unthreatening to pervasive patron-clientage. For purposes of amplification and explication, we will discuss at some length the case of the Republic of the Philippines, which typifies the conflict between the land tax and the system of patron-clientage.

We will first discuss the problems of funding local development programs in less developed countries with special emphasis on the Philippine case, and demonstrate the inadequacies of land taxation. We identify the system of patron-clientage typical of LDCs as the major cause of the unreliability and inadequacy of land taxation, and then examine energy consumption taxation as a supplement to land tax systems that have reached their limits as revenue generators. This alternative form of levy is administratively feasible at local levels and is distinctly more congenial to those forms of political decision making that are influenced by patron-clientage. We conclude with an argument for the compatibility of energy consumption taxation with local and national development goals.

LAND TAXATION IN LDCs: THE PHILIPPINES

In many LDCs land is a traditionally exploited tax base because it is visible and cannot be removed from a local jurisdiction. Furthermore, land ownership is a proxy for ability to pay, and can be seized and sold to satisfy tax deficiencies. Thus, at the local level, land tax systems are relatively equitable, certain, and convenient. Nevertheless, in spite of the availability and advantages of land taxation, problems in administration and compliance persist. Many LDCs lack the administrative machinery for adequate tax enforcement; in most the population lacks the willingness or the capacity for compliance.

In the Philippines, local governments would seem to have numerous advantages in fiscal management: their personnel are drawn largely from permanent residents who know the people and the technical and financial resources of the area; moreover, they are generally more accountable to local populations than are central line agencies. In many ways local governments are indeed the natural unit for taking the lead in identifying local needs, assuming the role of people's advocate in the development process, and facilitating responsive, coordinated action by a variety of local and external agencies which are responsible for development activities in their respective communities.

For the past decade, fiscal decentralization has been an important goal of the social and economic development policy of the Philippine national government. Such decentralization would feature a reduction in grants-in-aid by the national government, a decline in direct central government expenditures in local jurisdictions, and a growth in locally generated revenues which would allow local governments to be financially self-reliant (as evidenced in Presidential Decree 464, the Local Autonomy Act, and the Decentralization Act). However, as noted in a recent evaluation of the Real Property Tax Administration Program in the Philippines:[3]

> While Philippine local government expenditure has increased in absolute amount over the 1970–1979 period . . . local government is a declining share of total (central and local) government expenditure over the (same) period. The ratio of local government expenditure to central government expenditure declines from .23 in 1970 to .11 in 1979. During the same period, central government grants to local government decreased from 51 to 39 percent of local expenditures. Thus, while grants as a share of local government expenditures are shrinking, local government expenditure growth lags behind central government expenditure growth. (Holland, Wasylenko, and Bahl 1980)

The figures illustrating these trends are presented in Table 1, where it can be seen that while the absolute amount of funds generated and spent by local government units has increased in the past decade, the proportion of this amount to continued direct government expenditures has declined. In

Table 1.   Trends in Philippine Local Government Finances: 1969–1979

Year	(1) Total Central Government Expenditures (in million pesos)	(2) Total Local Government Expenditures (in million pesos)	(3) Local Government Expenditure— Central Government Grants (in million pesos)
1969	3,611	817	327
1970	4,053	931	454
1971	4,429	1,033	475
1972	5,588	1,314	590
1973	7,041	1,465	765
1974	13,025	1,698	971
1975	20,168	2,202	1,339
1976	21,300	2,388	1,453
1977	22,600	2,914	1,905
1978	27,110	3,237	2,189
1979	34,380[a]	3,781[a]	2,307

Year	(4) Local Government Grants (in million pesos)	(5) Local to Central Expenditures Ratio (2)/(1)	(6) Excess local[b] to Central Expenditures (3)/(1)	(7) Grants as a Percent of Local Government Expenditure (2) − (3) / (2)
1969	490	0.23	0.09	60
1970	477	0.23	0.11	51
1971	588	0.23	0.11	54
1972	725	0.23	0.11	55
1973	700	0.18	0.09	48
1974	727	0.13	0.07	43
1975	863	0.11	0.07	39
1976	953	0.11	0.07	39
1977	1,009	0.13	0.08	35
1978	1,048	0.12	0.08	32
1979	1,474	0.11	0.07	39

Notes:
[a]Estimates
[b]Local expenditures in excess of central government grants, see column (3).
Sources: Budget of the National Government for Fiscal years 1957–1975;
President's Budget Message (Calendar Years 1976–1979);
Commission on Audit Reports on Local Government (1969–1971);
Ministry of Finance (1972–1979); in Holland, Wasylenko, and Bahl 1980, p. 16.

other words, the policy of fiscal decentralization has failed to achieve the objective of local fiscal self-reliance. In fact, as shown in Table 2, the major sources of noncentral government revenues have remained virtually unchanged over the past decade.[4]

Table 2. Changing Importance of Local Government Finance
(Excluding Grants), 1969–1979

	As Percentage of Revenues			
(1)	*(2)*	*(3)*	*(4)*	*(5)*
	Property	*Business*		*Other Locally*
Year	*Tax*	*Tax*	*Charges*[a]	*Raised Revenue*[b]
1969	31	29	34	5
1970	35	20	25	20
1971	31	22	27	20
1972	30	27	27	15
1973	30	31	26	13
1974	26	33	29	11
1975	26	32	31	11
1976	26	31	31	12
1977	30	25	33	12
1978	30	27	31	11
1979	32	29	29	10

Notes:
[a] Charges include registration fees (for items such as carts or cattle) marriage fees, secretary's fees, and fishery rentals; they exclude fees and charges on the operation of economic enterprises.
[b] This consists of the fees and charges in the operation of economic enterprises, namely the operation of public utilities, markets and slaughterhouses, toll roads and bridges, and cemeteries.
Sources:
Commission on Audit Reports on Local Governments (1969 to 1971 data); Ministry of Finance (1972 to 1979 data); in Holland, Wasylenko, and Bahl 1980, p. 20.

Column 2 of Table 2 has special relevance because the national government has consistently considered the land tax as the major source of potential revenue for financing local development. In fact, under the Real Property Tax Code, all revenues generated by this tax are to be retained locally and used for financing public service-oriented programs at the local government level (Sommers 1978).

Moreover, as indicated by a survey conducted in 1976, the projected sums to be generated by an improved real property tax mapping and collection system were to be substantial, with an average projected increase of 96.3 percent in the assessed value of property (see Table 3), and an increased collection efficiency projection of 75 percent (Holland, Wasylenko, and Bahl 1980). Because of the importance placed on the land tax, the Philippine government and the United States Agency for International Development have spent millions of pesos during the past decade in an effort to improve the tax mapping of local jurisdictions and the efficiency of real property tax assessments and collections. Although there has been some absolute increase in real property tax collections, the percentage of collections to total revenues has remained virtually unchanged, as was shown in Table 2.

Thus, although tax mapping efforts have nearly doubled the land tax base

Table 3.   The Assessed Value of Property Before/After Tax Mapping

	Taxable Assessed Value (in million pesos)		Increase	
	Before Tax Mapping	After Tax Mapping	Net Pesos	Percentage
Total for all Municipalities	160,361.1	314,782.4	154,421.3	96.3
Total Adjusted Sample[a]	127,749.6	233,545.4	105,795.5	82.8
Average Municipality, Adjusted	21,291.6	38,924.2	17,632.6	82.8

[a] Low and High Extremes Deleted
Source: Sommers 1978, p. 12.

for Philippine municipalities (see Table 3), the amount collected has not increased in proportion. This observation is surprising because the Philippines "administrative machinery" in terms of personnel and hardware is superior to that in most LDCs. Compliance rather than administration, therefore, appears to be the weak link in local revenue management.

There appear to be many reasons for the failure of tax compliance. Chief among them is patron-clientage, a social, economic, and political phenomenon especially common in LDCs. There are two analytically separable aspects to patron–client systems: the patrons' vested-interest protectionism of their felt needs, and their very real obligations to ensure substantial benefits for their clients.

Patron-client systems are structurally precarious, intersticial systems; they mediate the demands and resources from the higher-level or national sector and those at the lower-level, local domain (Stuart 1972). And as Wolf (1966) has remarked, although the exchanges flowing to the patron from the client may not be as immediately tangible as those going the opposite direction, they are by no means inconsequential. In addition to esteem, the patron receives critical information about the functioning of local activities under the immediate aegis of his derived power and about the state of his rivals' power blocs. As a clear sign of his right to the title of patron, he must recruit additional personnel to swell the ranks of his own bloc; in this way, the patron must maintain and increase the ramifying set of mutual patron-client responsibilities to guarantee his continued success.

Thus it is that patron-clientage indeed requires that the patron—the effective local-level policy maker and legislator cum executive—act in ways which are typically contrary to rational management. This is the result of the need to please those at the national level while at the same time "feathering his nest" as well as that of his clients.[5] Let us examine this phenomenon of patron-clientage in the Philippines which is typical of many and perhaps most LDCs in this respect.

Patron-Clientage and Land Taxation: The Philippines

In the Philippines, local government personnel might seem to have considerable advantages in efficiently performing expanded roles in the generation and management of resources which are necessary for an increased role in community economic development. There are, however, barriers to efficiency: the ambiguities inherent in the need for officials to act both as rational administrators of locally generated revenues and as responsible superiors in the pervasive patron–client relationships.[6]

From Spanish colonial times onward, the patron-client system has been inextricably linked to extensive social ties, including those based on biological or fictive kinship. As Vreeland et al. (1976) have noted, patron-clientage

> was basic to the social, economic, and political life of the Filipinos. The landlord [traditionally the major example of patron], although customarily taking about half of the harvest, provided his tenants with various forms of security—cash loans, rations to tide the family over the preharvest shortage, assistance in family crisis, financing the education of a promising child, or assuming the important social role of godparent; in exchange the tenant offered a variety of personal services . . . [such as] . . . labor on demand and social deference (Vreeland et al. 1976, pp. 55, 285).

In recent times, particularly since universal suffrage was introduced in 1937, other ties have come to bind the patron and client together. According to Vreeland et al (1976), "the landlord depended on the political loyalty of his tenants at election time and in return served as a powerful intermediary on their behalf in dealing with state authority and as adjudicator and mediator in local disputes." Moreover, beginning even during the Spanish era and accelerating after the Second World War, the more traditional patron–client relationships (landlord–tenant) were significantly modified in both their content and structural arrangement. This was due primarily to the emigration of the rural elites (landowners) to the major urban centers, particularly Manila.[7] This resulted in a loss of both leadership and resources to the local level. This emigration, coupled with the government-sponsored land-reform programs of the 1970s (which broke up many of the remaining large estates), left the peasantry without their former sources of security, resources, and leadership—the patrons. However, even as the traditional elites consolidated themselves in the urban sector, the rural power vacuum was being filled by a vote-driven form of patron-clientage, which in many ways resembled "ward-heeling," once common in the United States. The result was that the

> functions of patron–client exchange were almost entirely transferred to the institutions of government—the administration and the political parties—that came to operate an elaborate patronage system of nationwide scope. (Vreeland et al. 1976, p. 67)

In reality, the changes in the patron–client system in the Philippines have not been as clear-cut as the passage from Vreeland et al. would indicate. While it is true that many of the large landholdings have been broken up in some geographical areas, particularly in Luzon and parts of Mindanao, they have remained intact in others, especially in the Visayas and the Bicol regions. In some areas such as central and northern Palawan, large land-holdings never existed and neither did the traditional basis of a landlord-tenant or patron-client relationship. The point is that regardless of whether the politically influential local leaders are "traditional" or "nouveaux," they continue to be embedded in pervasive sets of kinship and pseudo-kinship ties and obligations called patron-clientage. The new patron elites normally originate from the lower-middle economic class that is shop owners, teachers, boat captains, and so forth. Although "homegrown," they are, if anything, even more ethnically and familially linked to their local clients, the owners of "minifundia" (tiny parcels of land), than was true in the past when patrons themselves owned large parcels ("latifundia"). As their part of the bargain, patrons are expected to protect client landholdings from increased (or even efficiently collected) taxation. Thus there has arisen a relatively new group of patrons—called "lideres"—who are in effect political brokers. They perform a middleman role, gathering blocs of votes and mobilizing political supporters of party candidates in exchange for distributing valued resources, including cash and access to jobs, but always involving the attempt to protect their followers (or clients) from expropriation through land taxes. Such patronage-clientage remains strongly personalistic in character; it remains a strong force which works counter to the ideal of rational compliance and management.[8] Whether at the most local "barangay" level or at the relatively high level of the province, the clients both expect and receive some form of payment for their loyal support of their local patron–cum–political leader.

Patron-Clientage: A Summation

We have noted that the technical and administrative skills required for efficient land taxing exist in the Philippines, especially since modern tax mapping was introduced in 1976. Despite this increase in tax base, only about half of the potential has been, in fact, collected (for example, see Table 2 and Table 3). Why has this been the case? Perhaps to some degree it is the result of bureaucratic inefficiency in the implementation of good tax-monitoring and collecting procedures. To some degree, perhaps, it is the result of a relatively low level of commitment on the part of local-level, often appointed, civil servant collectors. We believe, however, that the major cause of the revenue shortfall based on land taxation has to do with the ways in which patron-clientage undermines the efficiency and increase of land tax collection. The question is one of compliance rather than administration.[9]

First of all, to the degree that land taxes can be collected, (especially in increased amounts and in a rational manner) it would be at the expense of the independent operation (and, therefore, the political-economic machinations) of the patron. Specifically, the implementation of a rationally controlled system would act to interdict the patron's financial resource base. This would be likely to undermine the effective control over clients exercised by the patron when he has discretionary power over patronage resources. To the degree that the local patron is a land-owner, any increased taxation on land would affect him as well. Thus the patron will be disinclined to comply with increased or more efficiently collected land taxation.

Second, and perhaps more important than the role of patron in sabotaging land tax compliance in order to benefit himself, is the significance of the mutual system of obligations between the patron and his clients. As noted above, one of the very important services the patron must supply to his clients (who are likely to be "minifundia" owners) is to protect them from efficient or increased land taxation. Indeed, for the patron to fail to buffer his clients from taxation is to risk the loss of their support.

Consequently, to the degree that they act primarily as key figures in a system of patron-clientage, local-level, politically influential leaders—whether formally recognized bureaucrats, informal political entrepreneurs, or elected officials—may be expected to thwart compliance with land taxation. To act otherwise would be to risk the loss of patronage, the basis for their influence, and as a result to risk being voted out.

We have shown that patron-clientage, a common if not universal feature of LDCs, subverts and indeed is antithetical to compliance with land taxation. What such countries need to facilitate the effective decentralization of local community and economic development programs is some form of revenue generation and management that is not as threatening to local interest or as easily sabotaged. Clearly, some form of taxation is required, but it must be one that is less likely to provoke the patron's hostility either on his own behalf or that of his clients. In what follows, we propose just one such local revenue tax source, namely, an energy consumption tax. Such a form of levy will be shown to neither threaten the patron nor to alarm the source of his political clout, his clientele. Moreover, the energy consumption tax (ECT) is feasible, because it requires less, not more direct enforcement cost than land taxes.

ENERGY CONSUMPTION TAXATION

Consumption and Taxation in LDCs

Consumption taxation provides an additional tax base at the local level, and encourages economic growth at the national level. Because LDCs consume much of their gross national product (GNP), analysts have proposed various forms of consumption taxation to divert funds from consumption to government investment (Musgrave and Musgrave 1980, pp. 798–808). Moreover, consumption taxes promote economic growth because they encourage savings and investment without forcing a choice between present and future consumption (Musgrave and Musgrave 1980, pp. 234, 299). The poor, of course, would pay a disproportionate share of a consumption tax because they spend greater portions of their income than the rich. One can mitigate such an adverse impact on vertical equity by imposing higher rates on luxury goods and lower rates on necessities (Kaldor 1967). Although luxury goods are prevalent in LDCs (for example, cars, televisions, and stereos in the Philippines), a personal consumption tax would be difficult to impose because of the strong penchant for and ease of evading taxes. Compliance with consumption taxes is weak where the retail sector consists of many small, unstable enterprises which conduct a significant volume of transactions off the books (for example, sari-sari stores and street foods in the Philippines) and where commerce is channeled through a large informal sector, and involves local kinship networks (Clarke 1973–1974).

Local governments would benefit from a "tax handle" that could serve as a practical surrogate for consumer goods. Energy is one such surrogate. All products share energy as an input, and many economists consider it one of the major factors of production.[10] Indeed, some authorities believe that energy input represents a truer value of production than prime cost (Odum 1971). Moreover, while fossil fuel energy is the basis of all modern economic activity, it is scarce and expensive in non–oil–producing LDCs.

Some Consequences of Energy Consumption

Relative to developed countries, LDCs spend a greater portion of their GNP on energy resources. The Philippines, like many other LDCs, has gone deeply in debt to finance energy imports. This has placed a serious drain on foreign exchange, which has discouraged development programs. In addition, LDCs need foreign exchange to acquire capital goods that are unavailable domestically.

High energy cost translates into higher production cost which results, ceteris paribus, in higher prices for export goods. To make their export goods more competitive, LDCs (including the Philippines) devalue their currency. Unfortunately devaluation means that it takes more units of local currency to pay for imported oil (Lehner 1982). For instance, from 1973 to 1981 the portion of export earnings applied to oil imports in the Philippines rose from 11 to 36 percent. The balance of payment problems suffered by oil-importing LDCs as a result of this vicious cycle could be ameliorated if OPEC nations were more willing to invest in the economies of LDCs or even to hold the currencies of these nations (Powelson 1977, pp. 24–25). But OPEC nations, for the most part, invest their financial resources in the less risky economies of developed nations. As a result, LDCs suffer disproportionately from rising energy prices. Declining petroleum prices resulting from the recent oversupply of oil are likely to be of little help to some LDCs, including the Philippines, because they are subject to long-term contracts that were negotiated during periods of high prices. Energy conservation and management is still essential for those LDCs striving for economic growth. The case of the Philippines is again instructive. Imports for oil as a percentage of exports has continued to rise in recent years, from 11.0 percent in 1973, to 30.2 percent in 1979, to 42.5 percent in 1982. Even with the recession, the 1983 figure was still 34.5 percent.[11]

To achieve economic growth, LDCs should divert energy from consumption to investment activities.[12] A consumption tax on energy should create disincentives for the use of energy in other than productivity-enhancing activities (Cordes 1980). An energy consumption tax (ECT) should favor those basic domestic industries (like textiles, rubber products, and pharmaceuticals in the Philippines) that play an economic development role (Powelson 1977). Rather than to decrease total energy consumption per se, the primary goal of an ECT should be to channel it efficiently into economically desirable productivity. Indeed, one of the factors which retards economic development is the insufficient use of energy in economic growth activities (Odum 1971).

Energy Intensive Products

All products require energy as an input; however, some products require more energy than others. Hereafter, we refer to them as energy-intensive products (EIPs). We use the term "product" in its broad or "product concept" meaning, which includes consumer influences such as status, image, and atmospheric and shopping amenities, like lighting, temperature, and convenience (Nickels 1976).[13] In general, EIPs are the luxury goods consumed by upper- and middle-class households rather than necessities consumed by the poor. When a country squanders expensive imported energy in the production and consumption of EIPs, unfavorable economic consequences can disproportionately affect the poor. Indeed, such energy deployment results in the inhibition of the production of export goods from which foreign exchange can be earned to pay for imported oil; cost-push inflation; and the diversion of energy from basic industries, which in turn retards growth and solidifies unemployment. Shortages, inflation, and unemployment thus become social costs of EIPs that are borne by the poor. These social costs are not necessarily reflected in the market prices paid by the rich.

Mismatching various energy sources and applications can also create social costs that are not embodied in market prices. Because energy from one source may not be easily substituted for energy from another, physical measures such as BTUs, kilowatt-hours, and entrophy become important considerations in the deployment of scarce energy resources. Entropy is the theoretical measure of the energy that cannot be transformed into mechanical work in a thermodynamic system.[14] Low-entropy energy has the capacity to perform the mechanical work required by the production process (Burness et al. 1980). Its cost is absorbed in product prices as direct variable overhead in that the BTUs needed for production vary directly with the units produced.[15] As the final output is a tangible product which may satisfy a domestic need or may be exported to attract foreign currency, the consumption of low-entropy stock in such activities could be considered a social good.

Countries need low-entropy energy consumption to develop basic, modern industries (Burness et al. 1980). Because it has little potential for mechanical work, high-entropy energy should be used to heat and cool space and in other ways which permit its cost to be absorbed in product prices as indirect fixed overhead. Whereby the BTUs consumed are unrelated to the number of tangible units produced (Burness et al. 1980). When goods are produced though the consumption of low-entropy stocks in high-entropy applications (for example, apparel sold in air conditioned malls in the Philippines), such goods can be considered "demerit goods" in a social sense since they involve the diversion of scarce, low-entropy energy from basic industries (Loehr 1976).

If imported, such sources of low-entropy energy as oil, coal, and natural gas are especially costly for LDCs. When these sources are employed in a high-entropy application (like using natural gas to air condition a home), social costs similar to those associated with EIPs result (Buchanan and Stubblebine 1962). To free low-entropy energy for industrial production, high-entropy energy sources such as solar power, wind, geothermal power, biomass, and small-scale hydro-electricity could be developed for lighting, heating and cooling where it is cost effective (Lovins 1977). The Philippines, for instance, has made some progress in exploiting such high-entropy energy sources as geothermal (underground steam) and biomass (the burning of *ipil–ipil* trees). By 1983 the Philippines government had recognized the problems posed by a high dependence on imported fossil fuels and instituted a program for the development of indigenous energy resources. In addition, the government started a companion program for "effective energy demand management in the modern sector" (U.S. Agency for International Development 1983). The ECT proposed here would be an economically appropriate and technically feasible component of the companion program.

Incidence and Rate Structure

The distributions of the tax burden and the statutory incidence differ for many forms of consumption taxes. For the ECT, the "point of taxation" is the time of energy purchase which is usually simultaneous with its utilization. When this tax is imposed in the factor market, the buyer will attempt to shift the tax in the direction of the final consumer.[16] The ability to shift the ECT depends upon the ratio of the elasticity of demand to the elasticity of supply between buyers and sellers throughout the distribution channels. A tax is shifted to the extent that demand is inelastic and supply is elastic (Browning and Browning 1979). The statutory tax incidence falls on the energy purchaser (factories and stores, for example) while the ultimate burden can either be shifted forward to the consumer or shifted backward to the energy producer. The forward shifting of the tax burden discourages the purchase and, eventually, the production of EIPs. In short, the ECT is an indirect tax targeted at the EIP consumer.

In addition to influencing the incidence of an ECT, elasticities on the demand side govern the relative progressiveness of an ECT—that is, the degree to which the tax burden is associated with the ability to pay. The ECT disregards ability to pay, in the sense that the tax is impounded in the cost of goods and services rather than imposed as a direct function of income. Anyone can avoid the tax, however, by curtailing discretionary expenditures on EIPs. Thus the incidence of an ECT is progressive if consumption is limited to the rich. Although EIPs tend to be luxury items that feature more heavily in the outlays of affluent households, the distribution of consumption patterns with respect to income is an empirical question. Energy consumption can be used as a proxy for income in most LDCs because the poor have few energy-consuming appliances. For example, in the Philippines less than 40 percent of households have electricity. However, energy consumption has been shown to be a weak proxy for income in more developed countries (see Burgess and Paglin 1981, p. 45).

The effective rate structure of an ECT is a function of income elasticity, E_y, and price elasticity, E_p of demand for EIPs (Buchanan 1964). If E_y is high (>1), the tax burden will increase with income. On the other hand, if E_p is high (>1), the increase in the tax burden will be mitigated. In other words, the effective ECT rate structure will be progressive, regressive, or proportional depending on whether E_y is greater than, less than or equal to E_p. Consider the following equations:

$$E_Y = \frac{\dfrac{\Delta Q}{Q}}{\dfrac{\Delta Y}{Y}} \tag{1}$$

$$E_P = \frac{\dfrac{\Delta Q}{Q}}{\dfrac{\Delta P}{P}} \qquad (2)$$

$$\frac{E_Y}{E_P} = \frac{\dfrac{\Delta P}{P}}{\dfrac{\Delta Y}{Y}} = E_R \qquad (3)$$

where ΔQ = the increase in quantity (Q) consumed, ΔP = the increase in price (P), ΔY = the increase in income (Y), and E_R = the elasticity ratio.

If $E_R > 1$, the effective structure is progressive.
If $E_R = 1$, the effective structure is proportional.
If $E_R < 1$, the effective structure is regressive.

According to Eq. (3), an ECT would be progressive in circumstances where individuals would be willing to pay a percentage increase in price for EIPs that was greater than a percentage increase in their incomes (Due 1970). Such a situation may be typical of LDCs with an emerging middle class. As income for members of this class increases, and as they accumulate a consumer surplus, they tend to shift their consumption patterns from subsistence to luxury items, consistent with their rising status. Since these items are likelier to be EIPs, the incidence of the ECT would fall differentially on this category of consumers. This new burden would discourage such consumption patterns, thereby channeling income into savings and investment and channeling energy resources into development activities.

One can use the ECT, therefore, to discriminate in favor of economic activity that provides momentum for growth and development through the ECT rate structure. When one wants favorable tax treatment, the rate should be a flat charge per BTU so that the unit production cost, including tax, equals the price the energy user pays. Furthermore, a negative tax rate to subsidize and thus encourage the use of energy in highly desirable development applications cannot be ruled out. However, one should reserve the tactic of implementing marginal-cost pricing for circumstances in which the maximum possible social benefit results from the deployment of energy stocks (Musgrave and Musgrave 1980). On the other hand, for energy use scenarios associated with demerit goods or those with a high social cost, one should employ a tax rate such that the marginal cost (including tax) equals the marginal revenue (Baumol and Bradford 1970). This policy of implementing profit-maximizing pricing will reduce energy consumption and increase tax revenues.

Table 4. A General Model for Energy Consumption Tax Rates

$$\text{ECT}_{jit} = \sum_{i=1}^{N} Q_{jit} \, r_{jit},$$

where ECT_{jit} = the statutory ECT imposed upon energy user j for application i during period t; Q_{jit} = a physical measure of energy units consumed (for example; BTUs) by user j for application i during period t; and r_{jit} = the unit price to user j for application i during period t.

$$r_{jit} = B + \sum_{k=1}^{m} (\pm X_k); \; P_1 < P_E < P_2;$$

where P_1 = the price per energy unit based upon the point where average revenue equals marginal cost (including the ECT); P_2 = the price per energy unit based on the point where marginal revenue equals marginal cost (including the ECT); P_E = price per energy unit after the imposition of the ECT; B = a base rate per BTU consumed; and $X_k \ldots X_m$ = weighted energy consumption attributes; attributes that have positive coefficients are associated with externalities and hence will increase the unit tax rate. Attributes that have negative coefficients are associated with economic development and will decrease the unit tax rate.

The following is a list of some possible X_k attributes that should have the $(+)$ or $(-)$ coefficients as designated:

	+	−
X_1	high-entropy application	low-entropy application
X_2	household usage	industrial usage
X_3	retail sector	manufacturing sector
X_4	peak-period usage	slack-period usage
Energy applied to the manufacture of:		
X_5	domestic goods	export goods
X_6	luxury items	necessities

A general model for developing a schedule of ECT rates to discriminate for or against various energy deployments appears in Table 4.[17] The final price the energy purchaser pays per BTU is influenced by the ECT rate, which is a function of the X_k coefficients in Table 4. A preponderance of positive coefficients will drive the tax rate in the direction of profit-maximizing pricing, while negative coefficients will drive the rates toward marginal-cost pricing. The quantity, magnitude, and precise functional relationship of the X_k factors presented in this general model will, of course, vary considerably across LDCs and across local jurisdictions within a nation: a separate analysis of these factors extends beyond the scope of this discussion. Nevertheless, any quantitative model employed in the formulation of an ECT or other energy policy should blend energy and economic measures of efficiency (Milon 1981).

High imported energy costs have already triggered successful conservation efforts in the Philippines and other LDCs. If oil prices should fall as a result of recent or future oil gluts, one could use the ECT to support and continue the conservation ethic. Although the world may occasionally find itself oversupplied with energy stocks, the specter of fossil fuel depletion remains.

An ECT should be integrated into the overall tax structure of an economy; it should not be evaluated in a vacuum but rather in concert with cultural and political constraints and with social and economic goals. Because an ECT is designed to augment rather than replace existing tax revenue sources, the adopting LDC should maintain a proper balance between the ECT and other taxation forms (for example, income, land, excise, and import taxes). If an ECT is too harsh and the cost of luxury consumption becomes prohibitive, creative and productive citizens may emigrate to other countries that afford them a higher standard of living, thus siphoning off essential human resources. A nation must also coordinate its ECT with taxes in the import-export sectors, otherwise the physical components of EIPs will have to be imported, and high taxes on the energy used to produce export products may render them noncompetitive in world markets.

The case for an ECT can be made for many countries (the Philippines is but one example) whose development is limited by a combination of factors which include the precariousness of an international trade imbalance, especially a reliance on expensive, imported fossil fuels; a system of local taxation easily subverted by patron-clientage; and other revenue inefficiencies at the local level.

LOCAL COMPLIANCE AND ADMINISTRATION

Like land taxes, the ECT is suited to local administration. As the previous discussions suggest, an LDC must consider many variables if it is to rely on an ECT as a successful fiscal tool: the energy needs of its basic industries; the sources and cost of available fuels, including high-entropy alternatives; its distribution of income; the preferences, attitudes and life-styles of consumers; and the number and classes of energy users. Such factors are best monitored at the local level.

Local policies can influence the attitudinal and institutional effects on energy conservation that may alter the relevant elasticities which determine tax incidence (Bruner 1980). Furthermore, only local administration can provide the flexibility needed to implement a rate structure that distinguishes between certain user classes. For example, peak and slack periods of energy utilization vary across jurisdictions; thus, local monitoring would facilitate the application of higher rates during peak demand periods to encourage more uniform consumption patterns and save energy.

Land taxes are also suited to local administration since they depend on a visible tax base and require relatively little administrative or compliance effort. When dominated, however, by the local political structure (for example, patron-clientage), land taxes become an inadequate revenue generator. While the ECT appears to present a substantially more complex and unwieldy administrative burden for a local LDC government, on the whole it can be rather convenient. To begin with, the ECT "point of taxation" is the point at which energy flows from the producer or utility to the user. Whether private or state-owned, the utility collects the tax directly from users in the same manner that a retailer collects sales taxes from consumers. Since there are fewer energy suppliers than land owners, the local government has fewer contacts in the collection process. Moreover, energy is not visible and cannot be owned in the same sense as land; its taxation is thus less likely to be viewed by the taxpayer as an expropriation of property.

Energy flows are more easily monitored than income or other consumption flows, since mechanical apparatuses can be used. In fact, the technology to classify, measure, and record energy flows exists wherever modern energy stocks exist. The intervention of mechanical devices such as technologically sophisticated meters helps assure the production of reliable data needed for decentralized fiscal management (Arens and Loebbecke 1980).[18] An income tax is easy to evade because it is a "self-imposed" tax: the taxpayer supplies the data and voluntarily reports taxable income, thereby controlling to an important degree the information flow that supports the tax base. The taxpayer is thus in a position to underreport income. By contrast, because it can easily monitor energy consumption the taxing authority controls the information flow and the taxpayer cannot underreport the tax base.[19] Because the taxing authority also controls the energy flow, and since failure to comply with the tax could result in the interruption of service, the ECT should have a high compliance rate.

There is of course an important similarity between the ECT and land taxes, namely that significant administrative costs in both cases are invested in structuring and setup efforts. A fundamental question regarding land taxes is whether the base should be the value of the land, the actual income it produces, or the income it could potentially produce (Musgrave and Musgrave 1980, p. 805). Once this issue is resolved, the next stage involves measuring each taxpayer's land holdings, usually through assessment. The appropriate rates are then applied to the assessed values to arrive at the amount of tax to be collected from each landowner. The structuring and setup of the ECT similarly involves the delicate and difficult task of determining which energy applications are advantageous and which are detrimental to economic development. The formulation of specific rate schedules for different energy markets is not easy; there is often the danger that the efficient operation of various markets may be disrupted. The sophistication needed to structure a workable, equitable ECT may be beyond the design capabilities of local governments, but once in place, an ECT is relatively easy to administer. There are many international development agencies that can assist in such a project, offering economic and technical consulting services such as energy balance studies (Loehr 1976, pp. 132–147). Additionally, in areas where there are multinational corporations there are usually large international public accounting firms which perform services such as financial and energy audits, and fiscal management consulting (Simich and Strauss 1978, pp. 52–59). Such services would be valuable in organizing an ECT that would blend in with local economic planning and fiscal administration (Cy Cip 1967, pp. 41–45).

A local government can thus raise additional revenues by imposing an ECT rather than raising land taxes. Moreover, the distribution of the tax burden will itself change: as property ownership and EIP consumption both serve as proxies for ability to pay, the redistribution of the tax burden should occur among the upper- and middle-income classes. By encouraging conservation, the ECT should also help lower fuel imports and thus stymie the drain on foreign currency. These benefits would encourage wealth retention within the national economy.

CONCLUSION

Most LDCs are still largely agrarian in the predominant mode of production, and have traditionally exploited land as a primary tax base. Land taxes are becoming less sufficient to underwrite the costs of local economic development. This has become even more the case where the LDCs are tied to the purse strings of the developed nations, especially the United States, which requires not only that projects it aids benefit the local populace but that the local beneficiaries demonstrate some capacity to generate their own resources for development. Land taxation is typically not up to further exploitation, primarily because the local-level patron–client systems frustrate the increased exploitation of that resource.

It is necessary, therefore, for many and perhaps most LDCs to seek alternative local revenue sources which ideally are less regressive than the traditional land taxation and less easily challenged by pervasive patron-clientage. Moreover, it is desirable that this alternative form of levy be feasible and less costly to implement, and that it redirect local consumption from the purchase of import luxury goods to savings and investment—at least in effect if not purposely so on the part of consumers.

We have identified consumption taxes as the sort which may be expected to answer the needs for local development funding. Specifically, we have suggested that energy consumption taxes which may be a cost-effective surrogate for poorly enforceable excise taxes on luxury goods, and which may be the best alternative to (or at least the best complement of) land taxes.

We have seen that whereas compliance with increased, rationally scheduled land taxes is likely to be effectively subverted by the endemic patron-clientage typical of LDCs, the ECT stands to be significantly less vulnerable to such challenges. In particular, ECTs, by virtue of their exploitation of essentially nonindigenous and unowned resources, seem to alarm neither patrons nor their clients to the degree that land taxation does.

In sum, given the very real local crises in revenue generation and management confronting LDCs, especially those obligated to demonstrate local-level fiscal self-reliance of a sort that does not victimize the poor, the ECT offers a feasible and relatively equitable revenue source. Finally, such taxation is supportive not only of local development goals and self-determination but also of national goals of reducing foreign imports.

Of course the ECT is no panacea. We offer it only as a feasible, cost effective way of funding local development in LDCs.

NOTES

1. Despite the dynamic philosophy of public policy since 1980, Cochrane in a personal interview attests to the current relevance of his earlier work. Hourihan, who has revisited the Philippines on numerous occasions, confirms the earlier conclusions of Cochrane (1979) which are especially relevant given the recession years of the 1980s.

2. Patron-client systems (or simply patron-clientage) are systems of informal interpersonal contracts which benefit both the client and patron and are frequently encountered in LDCs. Such systems are typical where the central government is weakly represented at the local level, and where the patron acts as an unofficial "broker" between clients and the urban-based political and economic policies and personnel. From the perspective of the central authorities, such phenomena represent frustrating economic "irrationality" as well as inefficiency (Stuart 1972).

3. For the description of specific revenue data presented here, we have relied heavily on the work of Orr (1978), Sommers (1978), and Holland, Wasylenko, and Bahl (1980). But while we owe a considerable debt to them in this respect, the anthropological analyses of the materials is of our own design. We should note also that the inspiration to undertake the present analyses came from Cochrane's (1980) cross-national project.

4. Although the data included in Tables 1 and 2 date from the late 1970s, we feel that the data still hold and that the conclusions based on them still follow. Our thanks to E. Hullender (personal communication), of the USAID, for confirming this point. An important factor which complicates the systematic updating of tax system data is that "neither the World Bank or the IMF releases detailed information on the structures of their member countries tax systems" concerning deductions, credits, special incentives, and so on (Rabushka and Bartlett 1985, p. 73).

Note however, that data on the Philippine National Government Cash Budget, 1980–1984, document a dramatic increase in overall surplus/deficit, from a modest −0.3 billion pesos in 1979 to very substantial −12.2 in 1981 and −14.4 in 1982. As percentages of GNP these figures represent 0.1 in 1979 to 4.0 in 1981 and 4.2 in 1982. (Annex I, *The Philippine Economy: Recent*

Events, unpublished document, USAID, April 3, 1984, Table 18.) The implications of such central government revenue figures for local government financing include the need for local governments to become more self-reliant, especially through developing efficient, feasible revenue sources. See also U.S. General Accounting Office (1986).

5.   We have kept the term patron-clientage sex-neutral in this sentence. It is worth noting, however, that such systems are typically dominated by males in LDCs. In Latin America, for instance, such systems are common, but even where females are the key operatives, they are referred to as "patrones," and not "matrones" as one would expect in good grammatical usage. Such a male bias in patron-clientage politics is thus the rule, and is in keeping with male domination of the political and economic arenas in most of the Third World.

6.   See for example, Hollnsteiner (1963, 1979), Gagelonia (1974), Vreeland et al. (1976), and Mangahas, Miralao, and Delos Reys (1976).

7.   Actually, even in the colonial period the large landowners frequently maintained second homes in Manila, Cebu, and other large cities, in addition to their rural estates. The phenomenon discussed here emphasizes an essentially permanent move to the urban areas and a reinvestment of capital in the industrial and/or commercial sectors by the erstwhile traditional elites.

8.   A caveat is in order. While it might well be the case that these distinctive kinship properties of Filipino patron-clientage are a result of nonlineage kin-group structure of social relationships at the local level, Goody (1976, pp. 115–120) has shown how corporate lineage organizations will produce different forms of superordinate political structuring. One of the anthropological consequences is that social scientists have perhaps been too willing to impose a model of European patron-clientage (for example, feudalism or Latin patron-clientage) where a distinctive, non-European model would be preferable, especially in the analyses of the implementation of local-level development schemes. At the present, we can but acknowledge this as a possible limitation of our argument.

9.   Although the impact of patron-clientage on undermining efficiency specifically in tax collection has not to our knowledge been addressed elsewhere in the literature, the argument is strongly implicit in Wolf (1966).

10.   According to Boulding (1978), the three classical factors of production—land, labor, and capital—should be restated as knowledge, energy, and materials; accordingly, commodities are produced by the application of a knowledge structure that directs energy toward the selection and conversion of materials into finished goods. As Boulding (1978, pp. 173–178) states, "land, labor and capital, the conventional trinity, are each highly heterogenous aggregates of the three real factors, knowledge, energy and materials."

11.   Annex II, "Lines of Inquiry," *The Philippine Energy Sector and AID Assistance Strategy*, unpublished USAID document, February 1984, p. 7.

12.   For a discussion of the use of taxation to channel resources into developmental activities, see Due and Friedlaender (1981).

13.   For example, 'A' and 'B' purchase identical shirts—the "physical product." 'A' purchases his shirt from a fashionable boutique in an air-conditioned shopping mall while 'B' purchases his shirt from a vendor in an open-air market. According to the product concept 'A' and 'B,' in an important sense, have purchased different products. 'A' has received the benefits of air-conditioned comfort and status, 'B' has not. Because indoor lighting and air conditioning require the consumption of energy, 'A' has purchased an EIP. Shopping malls such as Makati in the Philippines are increasingly common in urban areas of LDCs.

14.   In physics and ecology, entropy represents the relative tendency toward disorder—that is, the breakdown of matter and the production of heat. Thus, high-entropy fuels are those which break down (or burn) quickly, producing little heat (or work) for the amount consumed; by contrast, low-entropy fuels are those which burn slowly, producing great amounts of heat (energy) in relation to the amount consumed. The irony for development is that the entropically "better' fuels, such as fossil fuels, are costly for oil-importing LDCs. By contrast, the

entropically higher energy sources (wood, charcoal, and so on) are indigenous and relatively inexpensive.

15. A BTU tax was proposed in the Energy and Development Act of 1973. For a discussion of this tax see Hudson and Jorgenson (1974, pp. 501–508).

16. Energy costs incurred within a given relevant range of activity may be either variable (such as the cost of power to operate factory machinery) and constant on a per unit basis with respect to production volume, or fixed (like the cost of lighting a building) and inversely variable on a per unit basis with respect to production or sales volume. Those buyers of energy who are manufacturers incur both types of energy costs, while merchandisers incur only the latter. Regardless of type, all costs (including the ECT) throughout the distribution channel must ultimately be absorbed by the price paid by the final consumer if the availability of a given finished product is to continue.

17. The attributes listed in Table 4 were drawn from previous discussions.

18. Our argument in the present paper is not that the Philippines government is better than other LDCs at undertaking and monitoring taxation. Philippine local officials are probably typical of central government control at local levels. Given relatively weak central control in rural and town areas, it is important to lessen the temptation for local government agents–cum–patrons to undermine the tax collection to the benefit of themselves and their clients. This, we suggest, is best accomplished by having the taxed item (low-entropy fuels) publically visible through prominent hard-to-sabotage instruments or meters which measure the amount of use. By contrast, effective monitoring and taxation of high-entropy, locally produced energy resources (such as wood) would be highly unlikely.

19. No system of controls can completely prevent tax evasion. A sophisticated tax evader can tamper with a meter so that it will underreport energy consumption. This act may or may not be discovered by the auditors. However, the intervention of mechanical devices at least discourages the nonprofessional tax evaders which are numerous in LDCs. Such devices do not eliminate the need for auditors but do increase the productivity of such skilled individuals who are in short supply in LDCs.

REFERENCES

Arens, A. A., and J. K. Loebbecke, *Auditing, An Integrated Approach*, 2d ed. (Prentice-Hall, 1980).

Baumol, W. J., and D. F. Bradford, "Optimal Departures from Marginal Cost Pricing," *American Economic Review* (June 1970), pp. 265–283.

Boulding, K. E., *Ecodynamics: A New Theory of Societal Evolution* (Sage Publications, 1978).

Browning, E. K., and J. M. Browning, *Public Finance and the Price System* (Macmillan, 1979).

Bruner, R. D., "Decentralized Energy Policies," *Public Policy* (Winter, 1980), pp. 71–91.

Buchanan, J., "Fiscal Institutions and Collective Outlay," *American Economic Review* (May 1964), pp. 227–235.

Buchanan, J., and W. C. Stubblebine, "Externality," *Economica* (November 1962), pp. 371–384.

Burgess, G., and M. Paglin, "Lifeline Electricity Rates as an Income Transfer Device," *Land Economics* (February 1981), pp. 41–47.

Burness, S., et al., "Thermodynamic and Economic Concepts as Related to Resource-Use Policies," *Land Economics* (February 1980), pp. 1–9.

Clarke, D. G., "The Urban Informal Sector and National Accounting," *Development and Change* (No. 1, 1973–1974), pp. 54–57.

Cochrane, G., *The Cultural Appraisal of Development Projects* (Praeger, 1979).

_____, *Local Revenue Administration Project: An Outline* (Maxwell School of Citizenship and Public Affairs, Syracuse University, 1980).

Cordes, J. J., "The Relative Efficiency of Taxes and Standards," *Public Finance* (No. 3, 1980), pp. 339–343.

Cy Cip, W., "Professional Practice in Developing Countries," *The Journal of Accountancy* (January 1967), pp. 41—45.

Due, J., *Indirect Taxation in Developing Countries* (Johns Hopkins, 1970).

Due, J. F., and A. F. Friedlaender, *Governmental Finance: Economics of the Public Sector,* 7th ed. (Irwin, 1981).

Gagelonia, P. A., *Philippine History* (Navotas Press, 1974).

Goody, J., *Production and Reproduction* (Cambridge University Press, 1976).

Holland, D., M. Wasylenko, and R. Bahl, *An Evaluation of the Real Property Tax Administration Project* (Local Revenue Administration Project, Maxwell School of Citizenship and Public Affairs, Syracuse University, 1980).

Hollnsteiner, M. R., *The Dynamics of Power in a Philippine Municipality* (Community Development Research Council, University of the Philippines, 1963).

_____, *Society, Culture and the Filipino* (The Institute of Philippine Culture, Ateneo de Manila University, 1979).

Hudson, E. A., and D. W. Jorgenson, "U.S. Energy Policy and Economic Growth, 1975–2000," *The Bell Journal of Economics and Management Science* (Autumn, 1974), pp. 461–514.

Kaldor, N., "The Expenditure Tax in a System of Personal Taxation," in R. M. Bird and O. Oldman, eds., *Readings on Taxation in Developing Countries,* 2d ed. (Harvard Law School, International Tax Program, 1967).

Lehner, U. C., "Cheaper Petroleum is a Long Time Coming to the Philippines," *Wall Street Journal* (April 7, 1982), p. 1;1.

Loehr, W., "Public Policy and Energy Balance," *The Journal of Energy and Development* (Autumn 1976), pp. 132–147.

Lovins, A. B., *Soft Energy Paths: Toward A Durable Peace* (Ballinger Press, 1977).

Mangahas, M., V. A. Miralao, and R. P. DeLos Reys, *Tenants, Lessees, Owners: Welfare Implications of Tenure Change* (The Institute of Philippine Culture, Ateneo de Manila University Press, 1976).

Milon, J. W., "An Economic and Energetic Framework for Evaluating Dispersed Energy Technologies," *Land Economics* (February 1981), pp. 63–76.

Musgrave, R. A., and P. B. Musgrave, *Public Finance in Theory and Practice,* 3d ed. (McGraw-Hill, Inc., 1980).

Nickels, W. G., *Marketing Communications and Promotion* (Grid, 1976).

Odum, H. T., *Environment, Power and Society* (Wiley, 1971).

Orr, K., "Social Soundness Analysis—Edited Field Notes," Annex XIV, in W. A. Sommers, ed., *Philippines—Real Property Tax Administration* (USAID, Department of State, 1978).

Powelson, J. P., "The Oil Price Increase: Impacts on Industrialized and Less Developed Countries," *The Journal of Energy and Development* (Autumn 1977), pp. 10–25.

Rabushka, A., and B. Bartlett, *Tax Policy and Economic Growth in Developing Nations* (Agency for International Development, 1985).

Simich, S., and R. Strauss, "The Energy Audit," *The Journal of Accountancy* (November 1978), pp. 52–59.

Sommers, W. A., *Philippines–Real Property Tax Administration* (USAID, Department of State, 1978).

Stuart, W. T., "The Explanation of Patron-Client Systems: Some Structural and Ecological Perspectives," in A. Strickon and S. M. Greenfield, eds., *Structure and Process in Latin America* (The University of New Mexico Press, 1972), pp. 19–42.

U. S. Agency for International Development, *Technology Transfer for Energy Management*, PID document (U. S. Agency for International Development, 1983).

U. S. Agency for International Development, *The Philippines Economy: Recent Events*, unpublished document (U. S. Agency for International Development, 1984).

U. S. General Accounting Office, *The Philippines: Accountability and Control of U. S. Economic Assistance*, Briefing Report to Senator Edward M. Kennedy (U. S. General Accounting Office, May 1986).

Vreeland, N., G. Hurwitz, P. Just, P. Moeller, and R. Shinn, *Area Handbook for the Philippines* (U. S. Government Printing Office, 1976).

Wolf, E. R., "Kinship, Friendship, and Patron-Client Relations in Complex Societies," in M. Banton, ed., *The Social Anthropology of Complex Societies*, ASA Monograph 4 (Tavistock Publications, 1966).

FEDERAL TAX REFORM:

ANALYSIS OF TWO CONSUMPTION TAXES

Herbert G. Hunt, III

ABSTRACT

Tax reform is needed now more than ever before in the United States. Previous attempts at tax reform have failed to accomplish the type of changes needed to eliminate the inequities, inefficiencies, and complexities that have led to widespread dissatisfaction with the current income tax system. Consumption taxes have received renewed attention recently and two of these, the value-added tax and the expenditure (or consumed income) tax, have been suggested as possibilities for significant federal tax reform. Successful tax reform will be accomplished only after a thorough analysis of the short- and long-term economic, social and behavioral effects of the alternatives. This paper provides a discussion of the pros and cons of these two consumption taxes by examining factors likely to be differentially affected by them. These factors include the tax base, equity, economic neutrality, productivity, convenience, prices and inflation, immunity to evasion, transition problems, and political considerations.

Advances in Taxation, Volume 1, pages 109–130.
Copyright © 1987 JAI Press Inc.
All rights of reproduction in any form reserved.
ISBN: 0–89232–782–0

INTRODUCTION

For a number of years, economists have advocated significant tax reform to alleviate the inefficiencies and inequities inherent in our current tax system. In the past, politicians have been unwilling or unable to grapple with the substantive issues of tax reform. Recently, however, huge federal budget deficits combined with increased awareness of the deficiencies of the current tax system have created a political environment conducive to significant federal tax reform. As Break maintains, "never has the time been riper for embarking on that crusade so dear to our hearts—federal tax reform" (1984, p. 1). Break suggests that the time is ripe not because reform can be more easily accomplished now than at any other times, but because the need for reform of the United States tax system has reached a critical level. Indeed, this need can no longer be ignored.

The tax reform process is normally characterized by a set of competing and often mutually exclusive tax policy objectives that create difficult choices for policymakers. For example, equity may be achieved only at the expense of greater administrative complexity and may also affect neutrality (Musgrave and Musgrave 1976, p. 211). Furthermore, many substantive issues affecting the desirability of alternative tax systems may be either inadvertently overlooked or unclear. The main objective of this paper is to examine on an a priori basis some of the more important issues regarding two consumption taxes which have received recent attention by economists and politicians. Awareness of these issues should be helpful to policymakers in designing new and better tax systems and should provide an impetus for researchers to examine the issues in greater detail.

The scope of this examination is limited to consumption taxes for two reasons. First, as pointed out in the following sections, significant and lasting tax reform will be most easily achieved by starting with a clean slate and building from the ground up (the "bottom-up" approach). Such an approach would be required with a federal consumption tax since such a tax does not currently exist. Second, the two consumption taxes most often mentioned as reform possibilities, the value-added tax (VAT) and the personal expenditure tax (ET), possess quite different qualities with respect to a number of factors which could seriously affect their respective desirability. The differential qualities of the two taxes raise a number of issues that must be addressed prior to the legislative process.

The paper is arranged as follows. The next section discusses the issue of true tax reform versus the tinkering approach that Congress has followed in recent years. The third section briefly examines the reform options currently available and suggests that a consumption tax may be the best vehicle for true tax reform in this country. A discussion of the issues raised by the consideration of a VAT and an ET is presented in the fourth section. The final section includes a summary and conclusions.

TAX REFORM VERSUS AD HOC TINKERING

Webster's New Collegiate Dictionary (1977) defines reform as an action "to amend or improve by change of form or removal of faults or abuses . . . to put or change into an improved form or condition . . . ." Although significant tax legislation has been signed into law four times in the past six years,[1] the efforts fall short of fulfilling the spirit of truly meaningful tax reform.[2] Indeed, despite its title, the Tax Reform Act of 1984 (TRA) is a gargantuan legislative product that rivals only the Internal Revenue Code of 1954 in its scope, significance, and complexity. At best, the excruciating detail of the legislation and its excessive use of cross-referencing drastically impairs the professional tax advisor's ability to advise clients, and will definitely not facilitate the job of IRS auditing agents (Eustice 1984).

The concerns alluded to by Eustice are symptomatic of at least three basic problems evident in recent tax legislation. First is the apparent inertia on the part of most members of Congress to do anything but tinker with the present income tax system in their attempts at reform (Break 1981; Eustice 1984). "Tinkering" is used here to describe incremental technical changes made to the existing tax base as opposed to significantly expanding the tax base itself. Given the complexity in the system to begin with, tinkering may yield slightly more equity but does so at the expense of simplicity. This problem is particularly evident with TRA (Eustice 1984). Second, the speed with which recent tax laws have moved through the committees and houses of Congress prompts one to question the amount of serious study received by these important pieces of legislation.[3] For example, the fact that several of the liberal provisions contained in the Economic Recovery Tax Act of 1981 (ERTA) were either rescinded or postponed by later acts sheds doubt on the adequacy of the initial analyses. This seesaw activity with respect to tax legislation not only inefficiently consumes the resources of government, lobbyists, and the public, but increases the perceived instability of tax laws. This perceived instability and the associated uncertainty regarding the future causes further inefficiencies by affecting the level and time horizon of business decisions (Halperin 1983). A third problem is the extent to which special interest groups affect the form and content of tax legislation. Regardless of policymakers' best intentions, the realities of the political process and the pressure exerted by special interests have exacerbated many of the problems discussed above. In particular, the tinkering approach that Congress has taken in the past is likely due to strong pressure from lobbyists to retain existing tax breaks.

Given the deficiencies in the tax legislative process, one is left wondering whether significant tax reform is possible, and if so, how it can be best accomplished. The answer to the first question depends heavily on the answer to the second. That is, the degree to which policymakers are successful in their attempts at true tax reform (as opposed to mere tinkering) will be determined by the approach they take to the reform process and the diligence with which the process is carried out. Break suggests that the best policy alternative at this point would be a commitment by the government "to a serious and systematic study of tax reform, combined with widespread public discussion of all its aspects. . . . The basic emphasis . . . would be as much on the process by which tax reform should be planned, discussed and achieved as it is on the specific reform proposals to be considered" (1984, p. 7). Thus, successful tax reform legislation would be preceded by a planning process involving input from many sectors of society.

> The goal would be to collect, organize, and integrate the results of existing research studies of the economic effects of taxation; to simulate the short- and long-run effects of alternative tax reform packages; to determine the areas of agreement among fiscal experts and to identify the nature of, and the reasons for, their disagreements; and, most important of all, to develop the widest attainable understanding of the present federal tax system together with the most general consensus possible concerning its reform (Break 1984, p. 7).

The only item that must be added to the above agenda is a thorough analysis of the behavioral implications of the various tax reform possibilities. Policymakers (and others) often fail to consider the effect of tax changes on basic behavioral patterns (Crumbley 1973). Consequently, economic models are often misspecified and the intended fiscal effect is not achieved.

Based on the above discussion, a number of points can be made. First, historically high budget deficits, and public and private dissatisfaction with the current income tax system should combine to provide both motivation and opportunity for basic tax reform. Second, the experiences with recent tax law changes clearly illustrate the necessity for a more bottom-up approach to tax reform (as described above). Specifically, the tax reform process should be characterized by careful and thorough analyses of all the factors which affect, or are affected by, tax law changes. Input into this process should be solicited from many sources and the analyses should be completed prior to the legislative process. Indeed, it is a waste of resources to enact major tax legislation in one year, only to rescind the law the following year. Last, the problems introduced by special interest groups and lobbyists are likely to remain as long as the current political reward system remains intact. However, with respect to the type of tax reform process under examination here, political gamesmanship and preferential treatment for favored taxpayer groups could be minimized through the appointment of a bipartisan Presidential commission. In this manner, the policy options could hopefully be articulated and presented to Congress as objectively as possible.

TAX REFORM ALTERNATIVES

Although there are any number of possible forms that a tax system could take, political and practical considerations narrow the realistic alternatives considerably. The Treasury Department has studied four different tax systems as reform possibilities. These are a simple flat-rate tax (FT), a modified flat-rate tax (MFT), an ET and a VAT (United States Treasury Department 1984).[4] Similar to the present system, the first two alternatives would calculate tax liability on the basis of some measure of income. However, the FT alternative would broaden the tax base considerably by disallowing most deductions, exclusions, and credits currently allowed, and would impose a single flat rate on taxable income. The MFT would also broaden the tax base somewhat, but would retain some of the "politically untouchable" deductions currently allowed, such as the mortgage interest deduction and the charitable contribution deduction (Birnbaum and Blustein 1984). The rate structure for the MFT would likely include three or four moderately progressive tax rates.

The ET and VAT are both consumption-based systems under which taxes would be levied on the basis of consumption (however defined) instead of income.[5] An ET is levied directly on persons rather than transactions and would involve many features of the current income tax system including individual tax returns, periodic withholding by employers, and estimated tax payments. All borrowing and dissaving would be included in the tax base of an ET, but a deduction would be allowed for all saving and investment. Thus, the main difference between an ET and a comprehensive income tax is the treatment of saving and borrowing (Carlson and McLure 1984). The ET could be designed using one flat rate or could incorporate graduated rates to make the tax more progressive. The VAT is a transaction-based tax similar to a national sales tax, but instead of being collected only at the point of retail sale, is imposed and collected at each stage of production (that is, as "value" is added).[6] Thus, individual taxpayer reporting would not be required under a VAT. The VAT could be imposed at a single rate or incorporate different rates for different categories of goods and services.[7]

Although not currently under study, another reform alternative is a comprehensive income tax (CIT). Such a system would be based on a broad definition of economic income with few or no exclusions, deductions, or credits (Robinson 1984). For example, the definitions of income provided by the early tax theorists Robert M. Haig and Henry C. Simons provide a starting point for the type of tax base envisioned by a comprehensive income tax. Haig defined income simply as "the money value of the net accretion to one's economic power between two points of time" (1921, p. 7). Similarly, Simons (1921) defined income as "the algebraic sum of (1) the market value of rights exercised in consumption and (2) the change in the value of the store of property rights between the beginning and end of the period in question"(1921, p. 50).[8] These two definitions have been combined into the so-called Haig-Simons income concept which is widely accepted in U.S. tax policy debate. Haig-Simons income is defined as consumption plus change in net worth (Bradford 1982). Note that a comprehensive income tax base would differ from the tax base proposed for the FT in that the former would include all accretions in wealth plus consumption, while the latter would omit many items not currently considered taxable, such as gifts, bequests, and unrealized gains. Due to the broadening of the tax base, the rate structure under a CIT would be significantly lower than the current one (Robinson 1984).

A complete examination of the above alternatives is beyond the scope of this paper. However, to support the contention that consumption taxes may play a part in future tax reform, the following observations are made.

A true FT would likely mitigate many of the problems inherent in our present system such as the built-in incentives to shelter income (often inefficiently) at higher income levels. In addition, a FT would greatly simplify tax planning and compliance by unraveling the complex web of deductions, exemptions, and credits that comprise the Internal Revenue Code. However, the tenacity with which most individuals cling to their favorite deductions and tax breaks has led many to conclude that the most that can be hoped for in terms of income tax reform is an MFT [for example, see *Newsweek* (1984)].

An MFT also has the potential to simplify the tax code and to alleviate some of the inequities and inefficiencies prevalent in the current system. For example, several proposals that have come before Congress in recent years would greatly simplify the tax rate structure and eliminate many deductions allowed under the present system. For example, the Bradley-Gephardt Fair Tax Act (H.R. 800 and S. 409) and the Tax Reform Bill of 1986 (H.R. 3838). However, the battle lines over which deductions and exemptions should be allowed under an MFT are already tightly drawn and the extent to which Congress will be willing (or able) to accomplish significant income tax reform is unclear. In addition to the problems Congress is likely to face in its attempt to legislate an MFT, policy makers will also be under pressure in future years to modify the system in order to achieve various social and economic objectives (Friedman 1986). This, in turn, would likely result in a complex system with many of the same problems and abuses as the current one. Indeed, what started out in 1913 as a low-rate, simple income tax has developed into the complex system that we have today.

A CIT may be appealing theoretically because it would possess a number of qualities considered important for a tax system. For example, the tax could have distinct advantages with respect to simplicity, horizontal equity, and efficiency (Goode 1980; Robinson 1984). However, a CIT would also involve significant measurement and implementation problems (Bradford 1980; Robinson 1984). In addition, requiring taxpayers to include things such as the fair market rental value of owner-occupied housing in income may be politically costly for some legislators. Without a complete analysis of these and other issues related to a CIT, no conclusions can be reached on its acceptability. Such an analysis is left for future research.

Consumption taxes offer realistic alternatives to the present system. Since a consumption tax would be "written on a clean slate," it could be structured so as to accomplish tax reform objectives as efficiently as possible and alleviate many of the problems associated with income tax.[9] Indeed, a consumption tax has at least the theoretical potential to provide a superior tax base with respect to both equity and efficiency (United States Treasury Department 1977; Institute for Fiscal Studies 1978; Bradford 1980) and would eliminate the tax burden on savings (Bradford 1982; Galper and Steuerle 1984). Recent calls for a consumption tax (for example, Lee 1983; Ornstein 1983; Thurow 1983; Brannon 1984), the results of a recent government survey,[10] and the recent introduction of a consumption tax bill in Congress[11] seem to indicate that the public may be favorably disposed to a consumption tax.[12] Thus, at some point policymakers are likely to face the question of the type of consumption tax that should be instituted in the United States. The answer has important implications for the success of tax reform in solving the problems of the current U.S. tax system.

In summary, although flat-tax proposals seem to be both popular and ubiquitous, and may potentially offer some advantages over the present tax system, policymakers may at some point wish to consider some type of consumption-based tax in order to achieve significant and lasting tax reform. A VAT and an ET, or slight variations thereof, appear to be likely candidates. Legislation aimed at these taxes should be preceded by careful and thorough analyses of the variables which will affect their success (Break 1984). The remainder of this paper raises several issues that should be examined. The scope of the discussion is limited to factors likely to be differentially affected by an ET and a VAT.

ISSUES AFFECTING THE CHOICE OF A CONSUMPTION TAX

A number of factors are likely to affect policymakers' choices of tax systems. Most of these factors are highly interrelated, and these interrelationships often necessitate the trade-off of one policy objective against another (United States Treasury Department 1984, pp. 18-19). This section is structured to facilitate a discussion of the issues surrounding the choice of a consumption-based tax and should not be construed as indicating the relative importance or separability of the issues. Table 1 provides a brief summary of the points discussed below.

Consumption Tax Base

Theoretically, both the VAT and the ET could be based on similar broad definitions of consumption. However, due to several practical and political considerations, and to administrative differences that would likely arise between the two taxes (for example, with respect to reporting and collection procedures), the actual tax base would probably differ between the VAT and the ET (McLure 1973; Graetz 1980). This would appear to be an important issue, especially given the widespread concern with the erosion of the current income tax base (United States Treasury Department 1984). A number of issues that have implications for the tax base under each of the two consumption taxes are discussed below.

With respect to the ET, a clear distinction between business and personal expenses is important, since the former would be deductible from the consumption tax base while the latter would not (United States Treasury Department 1984). However, as experience with the U.S. income tax system has shown, this distinction is not always easy to make, and a thorough reexamination of business versus personal expenses would be required under the ET (Graetz 1980). Another major issue is the treatment of housing and other consumer durables under the ET. The basic question is whether the purchase of houses and other durable assets constitutes consumption or saving at the time of purchase. If the purchase is considered saving, then the difficult problem of imputing annual rental values arises. As a practical matter, this issue would probably be resolved by using a cash basis approach whereby the amount considered consumed each year would be equal to the cash payments (that is, interest and principal) made on the purchase (Due and Friedlaender 1981; United States Treasury Department 1984). A third major issue which would arise under an ET is the appropriate treatment of gifts and bequests.[13] The question here is whether gifts and bequests should be included only in the tax base of the recipient, or whether they also represent consumption to the donor (United States Treasury Department 1984). While taxing both donor and donee would result in double taxation of the item in question, taxing only the donee allows gifts among relatives to lessen tax liability (Due and Fiedlaender 1981), and would have enormous distributional implications (United States Treasury

Table 1. Summary of Relative Strengths and Weaknesses of a Value-Added Tax (VAT) and an Expenditure (Consumed Income) Tax (ET)

FACTOR	VAT	ET
1. Comprehensiveness of Tax Base	Pressure to exclude several items including housing, banking and insurance services, foreign consumption, urban transit service, food for home consumption and popular itemized deductions. Vulnerable to specific exemptions and deductions.	Problems distinguishing between business and personal expenditures, and handling housing, durable goods purchases, and gifts and bequests. Pressure to allow popular itemized deductions. Flexibility for adjusting progressivity without specific exemptions and deductions.
2. Equity	Susceptible to loss of horizontal equity; relatively costly to achieve vertical equity.	Both horizontal and vertical equity could be easily maintained.
3. Economic Neutrality	Susceptible to specific exemptions and deductions which could favor some types of consumption over others.	Somewhat less susceptible than the VAT due to the flexibility of a progressive rate structure.
4. Productivity	Significant levels of revenue with relatively low tax rates. Monitoring and enforcement costs minimized by fewer taxpayers and self-enforcement features.	Enforcement costs likely to be very high due to number of taxpayers and voluntary reporting requirements.
5. Convenience	Costly for business due to start-up, compliance and financing costs. No reporting by individual taxpayers.	Costs to employers similar to income tax, very costly to individual taxpayers due to unfamiliarity and complicated reporting procedures.
6. Prices and Inflation	Prices likely to increase somewhat, possibly leading to inflation pressures.	Little or no direct effect.
7. Immunity to Evasion	Low level of motivation by businesses to evade, taxes underground economy, "collected at the source."	Problems of evasion similar, or greater than, those under the current income tax. Underground economy could continue to operate.

(continued)

Table 1 (continued)

FACTOR	VAT	ET
8. Transition and Implementation Problems	Creates incentive to consume before the tax takes effect. How to treat previously taxed income would be minor consideration.	Questions of how to treat previously taxed income and old debt create significant transition problems. Tax could easily be made retroactive to avoid early consumption.
9. Political Issues	Significant opposition from state and local governments. Many fear growth of government due to ease of raising revenues with the tax.	No specific drawbacks.

Department 1984).[14] Finally, several questions arise with respect to the various itemized deductions that are currently allowed under the income tax. The deductibility of these items under an ET depends on whether they are considered consumption. Graetz (1980) suggests that itemized deductions would most likely be allowed for state and local sales and income taxes, charitable contributions, extraordinary medical expenses, and some interest.

The 1984 Treasury Study (United States Treasury Department 1984, pp. 222–223) identifies several items that would likely be excluded from the consumption tax base under a VAT. First, owner-occupied housing would likely be excluded due to the difficulty of valuing the housing consumed by owner occupants. Furthermore, it would be unfair and distortionary to tax tenant-occupied residential housing if owner-occupied housing were exempt. The Treasury study suggests that one alternative would be to tax the value of all newly constructed housing but exclude the rental value of both tenant and owner-occupied housing. Alternatively, the cost of materials for construction, repairs, and alterations could be taxed as it is now under many state retail sales taxes. Second, medical care, educational expenses, and religious and welfare expenses would probably be excluded from the tax base for social and distributional reasons. Third, certain banking and insurance services would probably escape taxation due to the problem of defining value added for them. Fourth, the consumption expenditures of Americans traveling abroad could not be collected easily and would, therefore, escape taxation. However, a VAT could be charged on some items that foreigners purchase in the United States. Last, there would be pressure to exclude urban transit service since it is heavily subsidized.

The Treasury study estimates that the proposed treatment of housing and the exclusions mentioned above would result in a consumption tax base equal to approximately 77 percent of total personal consumption expenditures in 1988. Some tax theorists (for example, McLure 1973) have suggested that food for home consumption would likely also be excluded from the tax base since it constitutes such a large portion of the budget of low-income families.[15] The effect of this exclusion would be reduction of the tax base from 77 percent of total personal consumption to approximately 65 percent (United States Treasury Department 1984).

In summary, both the ET and the VAT tax bases would be vulnerable to erosion based on practical, political, administrative, or equity considerations. While the relative extent of this erosion is difficult to assess on an a priori basis, the issue is important to study since the rate or rates at which any new tax would be imposed will be inextricably tied to the comprehensiveness of the base. In general, it would appear that a comprehensive tax base could be more easily maintained with an ET than with a VAT. Since the ET would be applied at the individual taxpayer level and would likely be characterized by a multiple rate structure, tremendous flexibility would exist for adjusting the progressiveness of the tax without eroding the tax base (Carlson and McLure 1984). Alternatively, the multiple-rate structures and numerous exemptions that would likely be introduced under a VAT to decrease its regressiveness have created significant administrative and compliance problems in the European countries that currently have a VAT (Aaron 1981).

Equity

Since Adam Smith first proposed equity as a necessary criterion for a "good" tax in his 1776 classic,[16] other tax theorists (for example, Mill 1909; Pigou 1952) have established equity as one of the most important concepts for any tax system. Equity is usually measured along two different dimensions. The most commonly discussed form of equity, referred to as horizontal equity, exists when there is equal treatment of similarly situated taxpayers. Unfortunately, the concept of similarly situated taxpayers is somewhat ambiguous since there are several alternative bases on which to determine a taxpayer's situation (income, wealth, amount consumed, and so forth). However, in political discussions and in the literature, the term tax equity is used to imply that the intended measure is implicit in the tax base (Sommerfeld, Anderson, and Brock 1984). For example, under a consumption tax, equity is measured with respect to the amount consumed, while under an income tax, equity is measured with respect to income. Thus, two similarly situated taxpayers within a consumption-tax environment would each consume equal amounts of income but would not necessarily have equal income or wealth. In pure form (with no exemptions or deductions), the ET and the VAT would perform equally well with respect to horizontal equity. However, once exemptions or deductions were introduced into either system, there would be a loss of horizontal equity since the amount of tax paid would no longer depend solely on total consumption but would also be affected by the form of consumption. For example, if medical expenses were deductible from the consumption tax base, two taxpayers with equal total consumption would pay different amounts of tax if their relative level of medical services differed. Of the two systems, the VAT is probably more susceptible to a loss of horizontal equity because as is evident with sales taxes in many states, it is relatively easy to make specific exceptions to the comprehensive tax base with this type of tax. While specific exceptions could be made under an ET as well, as suggested in the previous section, many adjustments under an ET would be more efficiently accomplished by adjusting the rate structure.

The second concept of equity, generally referred to as vertical equity, is related to the taxpayer's "ability to pay." This concept of equity "suggests that unequally situated taxpayers should be treated differently. Specifically, it suggests that those who have a greater tax-paying ability should pay a larger part of the total taxes so that, in the aggregate, the tax collections are 'equitably' distributed among all taxpayers" (Sommerfeld, Anderson, and Brock 1984, p. 28). The application of the vertical equity criterion is made somewhat difficult by the fact that there is no simple measure of ability to pay, and there is no agreement on how unequally situated taxpayers should be treated (Sommerfeld, Anderson and Brock 1984, p. 29). Under the current income tax system, a progressive tax-rate structure is used in an attempt to achieve vertical equity. A similar notion of vertical equity could be applied in the case of a consumption tax. Indeed, the form of the ET most often mentioned as a reform possibility contains a progressive rate structure similar to the present system (United States Treasury Department 1977; Graetz 1980; United States Treasury Department 1984). Thus, it appears that vertical equity, as operationalized in the current system, could be achieved with an ET.

Critics of the VAT argue that it would unfairly burden the poor and allow the rich to accumulate wealth tax-free since the marginal propensity to consume is inversely related to income. However, there are ways that the regressivity of a VAT could be reduced and its vertical equity increased. For example, since lower-income taxpayers spend a greater proportion of their resources for basic necessities, one option would be to exempt certain necessities of life (food, housing, clothing, and so forth) from tax. Similarly, necessities could be taxed at a low rate and luxury goods at a higher rate. Indeed, both of these methods are currently used in many of the European countries that have a VAT. The increase in vertical equity achieved by these methods would not come without costs, however. As pointed out above, the introduction of exemptions and multiple rates would cause some loss of horizontal equity. In addition, efficiency would be negatively affected in a number of ways as the European experience has shown (Aaron 1981). In fact, most of the participants in a recent conference on the VAT agreed that it would be preferable for the United States to use other taxes and transfer payments to alleviate the distributional consequences of a VAT rather than introduce multiple rates and exemptions (Aaron 1981, p. 16). However, the costs and benefits of these options should be carefully weighed against the ease with which both horizontal and vertical equity could be maintained with an ET.

Economic Neutrality

The 1984 Treasury Study on Tax Reform identifies economic neutrality as an important criterion for an ideal tax system.[17] Economic neutrality requires that the tax system interfere with private decisions as little as possible. For example, the tax system should not unnecessarily distort choices about how income is earned and spent, or cause businesses to modify their production techniques and financing decisions (United States Treasury Department 1984). In pure form, both a comprehensive ET and a comprehensive VAT would be relatively neutral with respect to the choice of consumer goods and the choice of present or future consumption. However, the neutraility of either tax would be compromised by introducing exemptions or deductions since consumption decisions would then be distorted by the availability of tax-favored goods. Both the VAT and the ET would be subject to special interest exceptions. However, legislators may be more reluctant to introduce exemptions or deductions under an ET since this would increase the record-keeping requirements for individuals and would be relatively costly from a compliance point of view. Furthermore, as pointed out earlier, certain objectives can be most easily accomplished under an ET by manipulating the rate structure rather than introducing distortionary exemptions and deductions. Overall, it is difficult to predict which of the two consumption taxes would be least likely to distort economic decisions since this depends on the comprehensiveness of the tax base chosen. However, the ease with which deductions and exemptions can be introduced under a VAT and the extent to which this has occurred in Europe should not be overlooked by policy makers.

Productivity

Productivity has recently become an important consideration in the design of tax systems (Sommerfeld, Anderson and Brock 1984). The productivity of a tax measures the ease of raising revenues relative to the costs involved. Although the potential administrative costs of the ET and VAT are unknown at the present time, at least two qualities of the VAT favor it with respect to productivity. First, once the collection machinery is in place, additional revenue can be easily generated with a VAT by simply increasing the tax rate. For example, the Treasury study (United States Treasury Department 1984, p. 222) estimates that each percentage point of a VAT would yield $20 to $24 billion in revenue, depending on whether food consumed in the home was included in the tax base. Furthermore, additional revenue would come at a relatively low cost since a change in the tax rate would not appreciably increase administrative costs. Second, in light of the tremendous "tax gap" (the difference between the theoretical and the actual tax base) inherent in the current tax system and the voluntary reporting requirements for individuals under an ET, the monitoring and enforcement costs of an ET are likely to be very high. The same type of costs are also likely to be significant in the case of the VAT. However, because there are far fewer business taxpayers than individual taxpayers,[18] a higher percentage of taxpayers would potentially be subject to IRS audit under a VAT.[19] Furthermore, the fact that businesses would merely collect the VAT rather than bear its full burden (United States General Accounting Office 1981)[20] and the self-enforcement features of the VAT collection and reporting process (Musgrave and Musgrave 1976; United States General Accounting Office 1981; Carlson and McLure 1984)[21]should minimize enforcement costs.[22]

Convenience

Adam Smith's third maxim of taxation stated in part that "every tax ought to be levied at the time, or in the manner, in which it is most likely to be convenient for the contributor to pay it" (1910, p. 652). Sommerfeld, Anderson, and Brock suggest that, in practice, the convenience criterion is often the controlling factor and that convenient taxes often encounter the least opposition (1984, p. 29). Depending on one's perspective, the convenience, and therefore the compliance costs, of the two consumption taxes would be expected to differ considerably. In fact, one of the most significant differences between the VAT and the ET is in the area of compliance costs. In the case of the VAT, the tax is relatively simple to understand, is withheld at the source and requires no reporting by individuals. On the other hand, most businesses would be required to collect and submit taxes, and to report periodically under such a system. The costs associated with setting up new accounting and reporting systems and the periodic compliance costs under a VAT would likely be significant for these businesses (Barker 1972; Parker 1976). Furthermore, certain aspects of the compliance costs of the VAT may indirectly affect neutrality by burdening some businesses more than others. For example, there is evidence that compliance costs of the VAT are disproportionately high for small firms (Godwin and Sanford 1983) and that some forms of the VAT would impose differential financing costs across firms (Crum 1983).

Alternatively, the bulk of the compliance costs of an ET would be incurred by individual taxpayers. As under the current system, employers would be required to withhold and periodically submit tax payments to the government and to provide certain substantiating evidence to taxpayers and the IRS. Individual taxpayers would be required to report annually to the IRS in much the same manner as they do now. However, because all cash inflows (that is, loans as well as income) and all cash outflows for investment or savings purposes would be reported under an ET in order to calculate net consumption, the reporting process could be more complicated for many taxpayers than it is currently. In addition, due to the novelty of the reporting requirements of an ET, significant relearning and start-up costs would be incurred by most taxpayers. Thus, while it is not clear what level of compliance costs would be associated with either of the two consumption taxes, it is likely that the compliance cost burden of a VAT or an ET would be differentially distributed.

Prices and Inflation

One common criticism of the VAT is that it would increase prices and could fuel additional wage and price inflation over an extended period (Due and Friedlaender 1981). However, the extent to which this would occur depends on several variables, including the ability and willingness of producers to shift the tax forward by raising their prices (Unites States General Accounting Office 1981) and the response of prices to the removal of any tax which the VAT might replace (McLure 1973). A careful consideration of these variables led McLure to conclude that, "it seems highly likely that introduction of a tax on value added will raise prices by about the amount of the tax" (1973, p. 181). While this increase in prices would have at least a minor effect on the economy, critics of the VAT offer several reasons why they believe it would lead to additional rounds of price increases with more significant effects. First, since the wage and pension contracts of many individuals provide for cost of living adjustments (COLAs) for changing prices, the price-level effect of the VAT could be expected to feed into these contracts by increasing the Consumer Price Index (CPI).[23] This initial round of price increases would then be followed by a series of similar increases as the effects spread throughout the economy. Second, there is concern that businessmen could "hide" the tax in the price of goods, thereby providing an opportunity to increase prices more than the amount of the tax (Bartlett 1984). These price increases, in turn, would feed into the COLAs as indicated above. Third, in addition to the probable increase in government spending that would accompany a jump in the CPI (due to indexed entitlements), the ease with which tax revenues could be raised with a VAT has led some to express concern that the VAT would be used as a "money machine" at the expense of controlled spending (for example, Bartlett 1984; and Heller 1984). The resulting increase in government expenditures could subsequently impact prices and worsen inflation.

An ET would not likely be subject to these same criticisms since it would not have any direct effect on prices. In light of recent experiences in this country with wage and price inflation, policymakers would be remiss not to give due consideration to the possible inflationary effects of a VAT.

Immunity to Evasion[24]

Policymakers should be concerned not only with the administrative productivity of a tax, but also with the system's ability to thwart tax evasion. While no tax system can guarantee full compliance, immunity to evasion will help ensure that everyone pays their fair share, and that the original goals of the system will be realized. There are significant differences between the VAT and the ET with respect to reporting and collection procedures that may differentially affect taxpayers' abilities and motivations to evade the taxes.

As pointed out earlier, the ET would require voluntary reporting by individuals while a VAT would require reporting by businesses. Therefore, a central issue here is the likelihood of compliance with the reporting requirements of these two groups. Two observations are in order. First, the bulk of the VAT burden would likely fall on one group (consumers) while it would be collected and reported by another group (businesses). Aside from outright confiscation of the taxes, businesses have little to gain by failing to comply with reporting requirements (other than bookkeeping costs). Second, much of the tremendous "tax gap" inherent in the current system can be traced to individuals' failure to report income. There is little reason to believe that voluntary reporting by individuals would be better under an ET.

The method by which each of the two taxes would be collected may also provide differential incentives and opportunities for evasion. Although the underground economy would continue to create a tax leakage under any system, the fact that the VAT would be collected at the point of purchase gives it a distinct advantage over an ET in taxing the underground economy. This advantage stems from the fact that, regardless of the source of consumption dollars, those used to consume in the legal economy would all be exposed to the VAT. The same is not true for the ET. Since actual collections of tax dollars under an ET would be made either by withholding and remittance by employers or by taxpayers' voluntary payments, an individual operating in the underground economy would be relatively immune from the tax.

Related to evasion is the notion of the utility of tax dollars to the tax-payer. Although the "rational man" model would predict that taxpayers consider their total tax liability in evaluating the economic impact of taxes on their financial situation, a recent IRS-commissioned study found that some tax dollars (those paid above withholding) have more utility than other tax dollars (those withheld by the employer). The report states that "people tend not to be aware of the amount of money paid through with-holding. They do not 'miss what they never have.' Far more salient to them is the amount owed after withholding. People are motivated to avoid having to pay extra tax when they file" (Westat 1980, p. 11). Since the VAT would, in effect, be totally withheld at the source and therefore not require tax-payers to pay "high utility" dollars at tax-reporting time, it would have an advantage over the ET in terms of taxpayers' tendencies to avoid paying taxes. Although there would be some type of withholding (by employers, for example) under an ET, the amounts withheld would be only a rough approximation of the total tax liability since there would be no necessary relationship between income subject to withholding and expenditures. Thus, incentives and opportunities might exist under an ET for taxpayers to underreport cash inflows and exaggerate amounts saved.

Transition and Implementation Problems

While there are several transitional considerations that would affect the VAT and the ET similarly, two of these considerations have different effects on two taxes. First, since the imposition of a VAT would increase the cost of future consumption relative to current consumption, it would create an incentive for consumers to withdraw savings and incur debt in order to purchase goods and services before the tax took effect (Bartlett 1984). This window of opportunity for tax avoidance in the short run would not exist with the imposition of the ET since this tax could be made retroactive. With the VAT, however, the time interval that would elapse between enactment of the tax and its effective date would likely be significant and would cost the Treasury some potential revenues.

The second transition problem that would differ between the two con-sumption taxes is the treatment of existing wealth under an ET (United States Treasury Department 1977; Graetz 1980; Carlson and McLure 1984; United States Treasury Department 1984). While the question of how to treat previously taxed income would arise with both the VAT and the ET, the problem would be particularly significant with respect to the ET since nonexempt income would be subject to progressive tax rates twice, first under the income tax structure when it was earned, and then under the ET when the income was used for consumption. Furthermore, a unique ques-tion arises under the ET regarding the treatment of debt incurred prior to the imposition of an ET. Normally a deduction would be allowed for repayment of debt under an ET, since all borrowing is included in the tax base. However, it would be inequitable to allow a deduction for the repayment of old debt since the original borrowing was not included in the tax base. Unfortunately, any attempt to distinguish between new debt and old debt would be fraught with compliance problems (United States Treasury Department 1984, p. 210).

Political Issues

Unfortunately, political considerations usually have the effect of compromising the ideals of tax legislation, and a consumption tax would certainly not be immune to their influence. While consumption taxes in general share a number of political shortcomings (for example, they are viewed as allowing unreasonable wealth accumulations by high-income individuals), the VAT has two characteristics that may work against it. First, due to the VAT's similarity to a sales tax and the probability that it would be collected in much the same fashion, state and local government officials fear that through imposition of the VAT, the federal government would be limiting their ability to use sales taxes as revenue sources (Heller 1984; Kleine 1984). Although there is no reason why a federal VAT cannot coexist with state and local sales taxes, the fact that tradition is on the side of the state and local governments promises to make this a hotly debated issue with significant overtones.

Second, one of the major advantages of the VAT, the ease with which it generates revenue, is also a major political liability (Bartlett 1984; Heller 1984; Kleine 1984). The fact that tremendous amounts of revenue can be raised with relatively low tax rates is likely to cause a political schism between proponents of the VAT and fiscal conservatives who worry that the VAT would be used to fund endless numbers of federal programs.[25]

SUMMARY AND CONCLUSION

Despite many changes of the tax laws in the United States in recent years, the Internal Revenue Code of 1954 continues to expand in size and complexity, and its provisions continue to create incentives for inefficient and often unproductive behavior. The widespread dissatisfaction with the current tax system caused by these problems and the inequities that result have created an environment conducive to significant federal tax reform. Any attempt at major tax reform should be preceded by a period of study in which tax reform alternatives are carefully examined to determine their respective short- and long-term economic, social, and behavioral effects.

Only by approaching the reform process in this way will policy makers avoid many of the problems that have plagued previous attempts at tax reform.

In light of the limited success in accomplishing significant tax reform by tinkering with the current income tax laws, policy makers at some point are likely to give serious consideration to a consumption tax in their search for tax reform possibilities. The VAT and the ET represent the two most likely candidates since they have been the subject of recent study by both economists and the United States Treasury. In keeping with the spirit of a careful and thorough analysis of tax reform alternatives, this paper provides a preliminary examination of a number of factors generally considered important for the success of a tax system with an emphasis on those likely to be differentially affected by the two consumption taxes. The analysis raises a number of issues that policymakers should consider and illuminates areas for further research. Hopefully, this endeavor will assist policymakers and researchers in focusing on important issues and in designing and implementing better tax systems.

NOTES

1. The Economic Recovery Act of 1981 (Public Law 97–34), the Tax Equity and Fiscal Responsibility Act of 1982 (P. L. 97–248), the Tax Reform Act of 1984 (P. L. 98–369), and the Tax Reform Act of 1986 (P. L. 99–514).

2. The Accelerated Cost Recovery System (ACRS) contained in the Economic Recovery Tax Act of 1981 is one notable exception. ACRS replaced a very complicated depreciation system which had been characterized by uncertainty and litigation.

3. For example, TRA took barely four months to go from House Ways and Means Committee release to presidential signature (Eustice 1984).

4. Slight variations on these taxes have also received recent attention. For example, a national sales tax has been offered as an alternative to a VAT. In substance, these variations do not differ much from those mentioned and are not specifically discussed.

5. However, see McLure (1973) or Carlson and McLure (1984) for a description of an income–based VAT.

6. See McLure (1983) or Carlson and McLure (1984) for discussions of the ways in which the VAT can be calculated.

7. Both single-rate and multiple-rate VATs are currently used in Europe (Aaron 1981).

8. See Sommerfeld, Anderson, and Brock (1984, pp. 91–96) for a more thorough examination of income concepts.

9. The United States Treasury Department's report to the President (1984) identified several goals of fundamental tax reform including lower tax rates, increased equity, simplicity, and fairness, and economic and revenue neutrality.

10. The survey, conducted by the Advisory Council on Intergovernmental Relations, found that 52 percent of Americans said they would prefer higher sales taxes to increases in other taxes.

11. Representative Cecil Heftel (D–Hawaii) introduced a bill in November, 1983, calling for the replacement of the corporate and individual income taxes with a comprehensive consumption tax.

12. Carlson and McLure (1984) make a similar observation: "In recent years there has been a remarkable shift of opinion from income toward consumption as the preferred means of raising federal revenues. This shift has been exemplified by increased interest in the consumed income or personal expenditure tax, by structural shifts in the income tax that move its base from income toward consumption, and by revived interest in some form of federal sales tax" (p. 147).

13. See McLure (1973), Slitor (1973), Graetz (1980), and Bradford (1982) for more detailed discussions of the treatment of gifts, bequests, and other items under a consumption tax.

14. This assumes a progressive rate structure for the ET.

15. McLure (1973) also suggests that household utilities and medical expenses would be excluded from a VAT tax base for the same reason.

16. *The Wealth of Nations* (Smith 1910).

17. As one reviewer pointed out, "many of the provisions in both the current and proposed tax packages contain investment *incentives* that reflect both Congressional and Presidential objectives." While this is certainly true, the U.S. Treasury report maintains that "any deviation from economic neutrality represents implicit endorsement of governmental intervention in the economy—an insidious form of industrial policy based on the belief that those responsible for tax policy can judge better than the marketplace what consumers want, how goods and services should be produced, and how business should be organized. It should be interesting to see whether the Treasury position on economic neutrality will influence the tendency by Congress and the President to use tax incentives to accomplish social and economic objectives" (1984, p. 13).

18. The General Accounting Office (1981) estimates the number of businesses that would be involved in collection and reporting under a VAT at between 5 and 15 million, depending on exemptions. Franklin (1985) estimates that over 103 million individual income tax returns will be filed in 1986.

19. I am grateful to an anonymous reviewer for pointing this out.

20. Theoretically, the VAT is a tax on consumption. However, it may not be possible for all businesses to shift the entire tax burden to the final consumer (United States General Accounting Office 1981, p. 23). In fact, France's experience with the VAT has shown this to be true. A recent study found that almost 28 percent of the VAT burden in France fell on businesses, government and financial institutions, rather than on consumers (Balladur and Courtiere 1981).

21. One of the main advantages claimed for the VAT is the so-called "self-policing" aspect offered by the invoice method of collecting the tax. "What this usually means is that at most stages, one taxpayer's VAT collections are another taxpayer's VAT credits; the seller's desire to minimize the tax paid to the government is offset by the buyer's desire to maximize the tax for which credit can be claimed" (United States General Accounting Office 1981, p. 32).

22. This, of course, is true only for businesses operating "above board." Businesses operating underground and barter transactions would burden enforcement more under a VAT than under an ET.

23. However, see Brannon (1984) in which the author suggests that Congress could enact a law requiring the use of a price index which did not include the VAT component in all contract negotiations subsequent to a VAT adoption.

24. See Slitor (1973, pp. 243–247) for a detailed discussion of several problematic items under an ET.

25. However, in a study of 12 countries with a VAT and 12 countries without a VAT, Stockfisch (1985) failed to find evidence that a VAT increased government spending or increased the ratio of total taxation to total economic activity.

REFERENCES

Aaron H. J., "Introduction and Summary," in H. J. Aaron ed., *The Value-Added Tax: Lessons from Europe* (The Brookings Institution, 1981), pp. 1–18.

Balladur, J., and A. Coutiere, "France," in H. J. Aaron, ed., *The Value-Added Tax: Lessons from Europe* (The Brookings Institution, 1981), pp. 19-29.

Barker, P. A., "The Value-Added Tax: The Cost to the Businessman," *The Journal of Accountancy* (September 1972), pp. 75–79.

Bartlett, B., "Revenue-Raising Redux: It's VAT Time Again," *Wall Street Journal* (August 2, 1984).

Birnbaum, J. H., and P. Blustein, "Most Forecasters Say a Tax Rise is Inevitable: The Question is How," *Wall Street Journal* (July 27, 1984).

Bradford, D. F., "The Case For a Personal Consumption Tax," in J. A. Pechman, ed., *What Should Be Taxed: Income or Expenditure?* (Washington: Brookings Institution, 1980), pp. 75–113.

Bradford, F. F., "The Possibilities for an Expenditure Tax," *National Tax Journal* (September 1982), pp. 243–251.

Brannon, G. M., "The Value-Added Tax is a Good Utility Infielder," *National Tax Journal* (September 1984), pp. 303–312.

Break, G. F., "The Reagan Tax Reform Fits an Old Scheme, but Will it Play?," *Tax Notes* (September 28, 1981), pp. 691–693.

_____, "Avenue to Tax Reform: Perils and Possibilities," *National Tax Journal* (March 1984), pp. 1–8.

Carlson, G. N., and C. E. McLure, Jr., "Pros and Cons of Alternative Approaches to Taxation of Consumption," proceedings of the Seventy-Seventh Annual Conference of the National Tax Association Tax Institute of America (November 1984), pp. 147–154.

Crum, R. P., "The Short-Run Neutrality of Selected Value-Added Tax Forms with Respect to Financing," (unpublished Ph.D. Dissertation, University of Kentucky, 1983).

Crumbley, D. L., "Behavioral Implications of Taxation," *The Accounting Review* (September 1973), pp. 759–763.

Due, J. F., and A. F. Friedlaender, *Government Finance: Economics of the Public Sector* (Richard D. Irwin, Inc., 1981) pp. 349–373.

Eustice, J. S., *The Tax Reform Act of 1984: A Selective Analysis* (Boston: Warren, Gorham and Lamont, 1984).

Franklin, C., "Projections of Returns to be Filed in Fiscal Years 1986–1993," *SOI Bulletin* (Fall 1985), pp. 61–67.

Friedman, M., "Tax Reform Lets Politicians Look for New Donors," *Wall Street Journal* (July 8, 1986).

Galper, H., and Steurle, E., "Tax Incentives for Savings," *SOI Bulletin* (Spring 1984), pp. 1–8.

Godwin, M., and Sandford, C., "Simplifying VAT for Small Traders," *Accounting and Business Research* (Autumn 1983), pp. 279–288.

Goode, R., "The Superiority of the Income Tax," in J. A. Pechman, ed., *What Should be Taxed: Income or Expenditure?* (Washington: Brookings Institution, 1980), pp. 49–73.

Graetz, M. J., "Expenditure Tax Design," in J. A. Pechman, ed., *What Should be Taxed: Income or Expenditure?* (Washington: Brookings Institution, 1980), pp. 161–276.

Haig, R. M., "The Concept of Income—Economic and Legal Aspects," *The Federal Income Tax* (Columbia University Press, 1921).

Halperin, R., "The Perceived Instability of Tax Legislation and its Effect on Consumption-Investment Decision," *Journal of Accounting and Public Policy* (Winter 1983), pp. 239–262.

Heller, W. W., "A Rocky Road to Tax Reform," *Wall Street Journal* (November 28, 1984).

Institute for Fiscal Studies, *The Structure and Reform of Direct Taxation* (London: Allen and Unwin, 1978)

Kleine, R., "National Consumption Taxes: The View from the States," *National Tax Journal* (September 1984), pp. 313–321.

Lee, S., "Consider the Saving Grace of a Consumption Tax," *Wall Street Journal* (March 8, 1983).

McLure, C. E., Jr., "Economic Effects of Taxing Value Added," in R. A. Musgrave, ed., *Broad-Based Taxes: New Options and Sources* (The John Hopkins University Press, 1973), pp. 155–204.

Mill, J. S., *Principles of Political Economy* (London: Longmans, Green, and Co., 1909).

Musgrave, R. A., and P. B. Musgrave, *Public Finance in Theory and Practice* (McGraw-Hill, 1976).

Newsweek, "Second-Term Tax Plans," (November 19, 1984), pp. 48–50.

Ornstein, N. J., "A Levy to Erase Future Deficits," *New York Times* (October 20, 1983), p. 27.

Parker, S. K., "Compliance Costs of the Value-Added Tax," *Taxes* (June 1976), pp. 369–380.

Pigou, A. C., *A Study in Public Finance* (MacMillan & Co., 1952).

Robinson, J. R., "Tax Reform: Analyzing a Comprehensive Income Tax," *Journal of Accounting and Public Policy* (Spring 1984), pp. 29–38.

Simons, H. C., *Personal Income Taxation* (University of Chicago Press, 1921).

Slitor, R. E., "Administrative Aspects of Expenditures Taxation," in R. A. Musgrave, ed., *Broad-Based Taxes: New Options and Sources* (The John Hopkins University Press, 1973), pp. 227–263.

Smith, A., *The Wealth of Nations* (New York: E. P. Dutton & Co., 1910).

Sommerfeld, R. M., H. M. Anderson, and H. R. Brock, *An Introduction To Taxation* (Harcourt Brace Jovanovich, 1984).

Stockfisch, J. A., "Value-Added Taxes and the Size of Government: Some Evidence," *National Tax Journal* (December 1985), pp. 547–552.

Thurow, L. C., "Where Credit is Not Due," *Newsweek* (November 21, 1983), p. 86.

United States General Accounting Office, "The Value-Added Tax—What Else Should We Know About It?" (U. S. General Accounting Office, 1981).

United States Treasury Department, *Blueprints for Basic Tax Reform* (U.S. Government Printing Office, 1977).

United States Treasury Department, *Tax Reform for Fairness, Simplicity and Economic Growth*, Vol. 1 (U. S. Government Printing Office, 1984).

Webster's New Collegiate Dictionary, (Springfield, Mass: G & C Merriam Company, 1977).

Westat, Inc., *Individual Income Tax Factors Study: Qualitative Research Results* (Prepared for the Internal Revenue Service, U. S. Department of the Treasury, February 1980).

THE FIRST YEAR OF SAFE HARBOR LEASING ACTIVITY:

A LOOK BACK AT OBJECTIVES AND RESULTS

Michael H. Morris, and James L. Wittenbach

ABSTRACT

This study investigates the effects of safe harbor leasing, one of the most controversial provisions of recent tax legislation. Through a survey of *Fortune* 500 firms and an analysis of congressional testimony, this study expands on results of previous research to address the questions raised by the controversy and analyzes safe harbor leasing from the standpoint of the stated objectives. The analysis raises questions about the intended equitable adjustment to ACRS (the Accelerated Cost Recovery System), suggests that the provisions were not well directed to the target population, and finds that participants believed the provisions were unimportant in reducing mergers and stimulating investment.

Advances in Taxation, Volume 1, pages 131–152.
Copyright © 1987 JAI Press Inc.
All rights of reproduction in any form reserved.
ISBN: 0–89232–782–0

INTRODUCTION

The Economic Tax Act of 1981 provided the opportunity for safe harbor leasing activity. Under the safe harbor provisions, transactions structured as a lease were treated as a lease for federal income tax purposes, even though the transaction was, in substance, a conditional sale or a financing device. As a result, companies could readily transfer the investment tax credit (ITC) and depreciation deductions with respect to property subject to the lease. Firms with tax benefits but little or no earnings could "sell" their benefits through tax leases to other companies with profits to shelter. The advantage from the transaction to the buyer or lessor was a reduction of taxes. The seller or lessee of the tax benefits received instant cash for the transfer of the ITC and/or depreciation, and effectively reduced the property's cost.

The following example illustrates the benefits to be realized from a safe harbor lease transaction:

> The ABC Corporation acquires new five-year ACRS equipment on September 1, 1981 at a cost of $2,000,000. Because the ABC Corporation already has NOL and ITC carryovers it cannot use the additional investment tax credit of $200,000 and depreciation deductions of $2,000,000. However, by entering into a safe harbor sale lease-back transaction with a profitable corporation, the tax benefits will not be lost but will be divided between the lessor and lessee through a negotiated transaction. The purchaser (lessor), for example, may agree to buy the equipment for $2,000,000 with a ten percent down payment and sign a note payable over eight years to ABC Corporation for $1,800,000. The purchaser may sell the equipment back to ABC Corporation at the end of the lease for a token amount. The rent that the purchaser charges is exactly equal to the principal and interest payment on the note so that the only cash that changes hands is the downpayment.
>
> This transaction entitles the lessor to the tax benefits, including the ITC and the tax shield provided by the recovery deductions, which at a 46 percent tax rate and 15 percent discount rate are worth $900,000 in present value terms. Of course to get these benefits, the lessor must incur a cost (the negotiated down payment and increased tax on the excess of rent revenue over interest expense throughout the lease) which is equivalent to the benefit transferred to the lessee.

The safe harbor leasing provisions were added to the 1981 tax bill because the U.S. Administration was urged to offer something to distressed industries.[1] Since unprofitable businesses could not benefit directly and immediately from the liberalization of tax credit and depreciation rules under the Accelerated Cost Recovery System (ACRS), the safe harbor leasing provisions appeared to be a natural correction to the "unlevel playing field for corporations."[2] In this way, the provisions attempted to equalize the cost of asset acquisitions for profitable and unprofitable firms. The Joint Committee on Taxation argued that by making investment incentives the same for all firms, the allocation of resources would be more efficient (Joint Committee on Taxation 1981). The U.S. Treasury was also convinced that safe harbor leasing would "significantly increase the level of investment" (Chapoton 1981). The provisions were also supported on the grounds that they would eliminate the build-up of tax credits and tax deductions that may have resulted in increased merger activity (Joint Committee on Taxation, 1981). In summary, by providing a free market for the sale of tax benefits, investment would be stimulated and merger activities reduced, resulting in a more efficient and more equitable system with less government involvement.

As attractive and innocent as the provisions first appeared, major controversies soon surrounded safe harbor leasing. The timing of the provisions was inappropriate. The budget deficit was growing significantly and these provisions were viewed as an excessive loss of revenue. To grant benefits to the corporate sector while cutting benefits to many other sectors did not rest well with many elected officials. In addition, several large, very profitable businesses significantly reduced or eliminated their tax liabilities by purchasing tax benefits. These firms, although clearly acting within the spirit and letter of the law, were perceived by many as major abusers of the provisions. As a result, questions were raised about the equitable sharing of the tax burden (Pell 1982). Others argued that these provisions resulted in a misallocation of resources. Senator Orrin G. Hatch, in hearings before the Senate Finance Committee (Hatch 1982), argued that by subsidizing unprofitable firms, resources were diverted from more efficient sectors of the economy, and inefficient or unproductive firms were able to continue doing business.

Throughout the controversy, the Treasury argued that the provisions were operating exactly as intended (Chapoton 1981). If the provisions were operating as intended, why were they so controversial and, considering the long-term nature of the provision's objectives, why were they repealed after only one year?

This study, in combination with the results of prior studies, addresses the questions raised by the controversy and analyzes safe harbor leasing from the standpoint of the stated objectives and the resulting economic effects. A survey of *Fortune* 500 firms was used to collect data on actual safe harbor lease activity and participant perceptions. The questionnaire, which is included in the Appendix, was designed to generate the information needed to determine if the provisions accomplished what was intended in terms of helping distressed industries, stimulating investment, and preventing merger activity. Because there is a buyer for every seller of tax benefits, an analysis of the nondistressed industries that benefited from safe harbor leasing is included. This study also examines whether the safe harbor leasing provisions made the tax laws more equitable across various segments of the economy or whether they resulted in a misallocation of resources. Further-more, it gives consideration to alternative provisions that may have resulted in lower transaction costs, more efficient allocation of resources, and the prevention of perceived abuses.

The study also investigates the policy-making process in this case and what can be learned from it. By examining congressional testimony sur-rounding safe harbor leasing, an attempt is made to determine whether policy makers underestimated the revenue loss or failed to anticipate the abuses. Were the provisions somehow pushed through Congress without an adequate investigation? As things developed with respect to these provi-sions, another interesting question arises with respect to Senate Finance Committee Chairman Robert Dole's promise to repeal the provisions retro-active to February 19, 1982. Did Senator Dole effectively stop the safe harbor leasing deals subsequent to that date as he intended?

Economic and policy-making issues are also investigated here for future reference. Strengths and weaknesses of the provisions are isolated to serve as input for future tax changes. More specifically, the tax depreciation system has long been used as a faucet to turn the investment flow on or off. In a similar manner, safe harbor leasing was used to stimulate investment in certain areas and reduce merger activity. What is learned about the suc-cesses or failures of this experiment can have important implications for the design of future investment incentive systems.

The second section discusses the methods used to collect the data and the time period analyzed. The next section contains the analysis which, in conjunction with two previous studies of safe harbor leasing and congressio-nal testimony surrounding the provisions, serves as the basis for the con-clusions in the final section of the study.

METHODOLOGY

A survey of *Fortune* 500 firms was used here to expand and, in certain areas, to confirm the results of previous studies of safe harbor leasing. The U.S. Department of the Treasury (U.S. Treasury 1982) summarized data from 2,000 companies that had filed information returns (Form 6793) with the Internal Revenue Service. Form 6793 (Safe Harbor Lease Information Return) allowed the Treasury to estimate total safe harbor leasing activity and the revenue effect as well as the division of benefits between the lessor and lessee. This data was only for 1981 (about one-half of the time period of safe harbor leasing) and contained no information on the effects of the provisions on company behavior.

About the same time, Arthur Andersen and Company (Arthur Andersen and Company 1982) was engaged by a group of firms to survey participants in safe harbor leasing deals. They collected information on actual transactions and on the decision-making process of a random sample of 75 firms for the same time period of the Treasury study, with which their findings agreed.

This study expands on previous research by opening up the time period analyzed to include the entire period prior to safe harbor leasing repeal. It also incorporates input from individual firms on how their behavior was affected by safe harbor leasing. In addition, since lobbyists from large corporations reporting losses were primarily responsible for pushing the safe harbor leasing provisions through Congress, this study concentrates on the activities of large corporations (Kirkland 1981). A questionnaire was mailed to the controllers of each of the *Fortune* 500 firms in July of 1982, requesting information on their actual activities and their perceptions of safe harbor leasing. Investigation was made of the amounts and timing of leasing deals as well as the methods used, the reasons for involvement or noninvolvement, and the effectiveness of the provisions. A second mailing was made two weeks after the first to maximize the response from the population of *Fortune* 500 firms. The results of this study of *Fortune* 500 firms, in comparison with previous studies, provide and indication of the extent of involvement of large firms in safe harbor lease activity.

TIME PERIOD STUDIED

One of the requirements of the safe harbor lease provisions was that the qualifying property had to be leased within three months after it was placed in service. The Economic Recovery Tax Act (ERTA) was enacted on August 13, 1981, so the deadline for property placed in service on the enactment date was November 13, 1981. This date takes on increased significance because of a special exception that allowed property placed in service between December 31, 1980 and ERTA's enactment date to be considered placed in service on the enactment date. The first deadline associated with safe harbor leasing activity, therefore, was November 13, 1981. This survey was designed to include measurement of the safe harbor leasing activity before this date.

The enactment of ERTA defined the initial period of study for this investigation and the enactment of the Tax Equity and Fiscal Responsibility Act (TEFRA) defined the closing date. Although special cutoff dates exist for certain industries and extensions were granted for deals begun before Congress repealed the law, safe harbor leasing deals faced restrictions on the use and benefit of the provisions as of July 2, 1982. This study investigates the safe harbor leasing activity during the unrestricted period from ERTA enactment to July, 1982.

ANALYSIS

Investigation of some general characteristics of the results shows that a wide distribution of industries responded to the questionnaires. In total, 114 different four-digit Standard Industrial Classification (SIC) Industries were represented by the 229 firms responding to the study. The wide distribution of industries made the sample representative of the population of *Fortune* 500 firms[3] and the high response rate of 45.8 percent indicated the relevancy of and interest in the topic. The sample, taken as a whole, was a net purchaser of safe harbor tax benefits, with 20.8 percent of the sample involved in buying benefits while 13.7 percent sold tax benefits. In total, therefore, about one-third (20.8 percent plus 13.7 percent) of the sample firms were involved in safe harbor lease transactions.

The results also revealed the general characteristics that the *Fortune* 500 companies purchased about 25 percent more tax benefits than they sold (see Table 4). Although the provisions were designed to help distressed companies (sellers), the *Fortune* 500 involvement was primarily as nondistressed benefactors (buyers) of the safe harbor leasing provisions. A natural result of allowing for the purchase of tax benefits through safe harbor leasing is that some of the largest and strongest firms (profitable *Fortune* 500 companies) were made stronger as a result of being able to purchase tax benefits from distressed industries. On the other hand, the success of the safe harbor leasing provisions was totally dependent on these eager buyers of tax benefits.

Industries Involved

The safe harbor lease provisions were designed to provide assistance to distressed industries, including what has been referred to as the "sick six" (steel, airlines, automotive, railroads, mining, and paper). Obviously the benefits of the lease provisions could not be limited to these industries because of the need for buyers of the tax benefits. In fact, all firms had the potential for being parties in a safe harbor lease transaction. Therefore, a natural question is what industries were involved, or who benefited from the safe harbor lease provisions?

Table 1 displays the industries that sold safe harbor tax benefits. The largest participating industries are listed in order by the amount of safe harbor lease property sold, with the percentages of the sample as indicated. The "sick six" are represented (with 33.8 percent of total sample property sold), although not at the top of the list in terms of property sold. For example, the nonferrous metal industry, electrical machinery, conglomerates, communication, and utility industries sold more tax benefits than the "sick six."

Table 1.   Safe Harbor Lease Property Sold by Industry

Selling Industry	Property Sold as a Percentage of Total Sample Property Sold
*Steel	9.2
Metal—nonferrous	9.2
Electrical and Electronic Machines	8.1
Conglomerates	7.8
Communication	7.6
*Automobiles	6.8
Utilities	6.2
*Railroads	6.1
*Paper	6.0
Rubber	5.4
Lumber	5.0
Financial	4.4
Oil and Gas Extraction	4.0
Cement hydraulics	3.9
*Mining	3.7
*Aircraft	2.0
Other[a]	4.6
	100.0

Notes:
[a]None of the specific industries that are grouped in the "other" classification sold more than two percent of the total safe harbor lease property of the sample.
*Members of the "sick six."

An interesting analysis centers around the other side of the tax benefit transfer. Table 2 presents the major industries from the *Fortune* 500 group that purchased safe harbor tax benefits. The food industry appears to be the major buyer of tax benefits, with many other profitable industries benefiting from the transfer of tax benefits. In analyzing one of the survey responses concerning why firms buy tax benefits, four out of five buying firms said they sought to reduce current taxes, rather than create carry-forwards or obtain refunds of prior taxes. Several of the industries, (such as oil and gas extraction and electrical machinery) appear both as buyers and sellers of tax benefits. The industrial groupings are quite broad and could easily include both profitable and unprofitable companies or subgroups that would allow an industry to appear on both sides of a tax benefit transfer. No transaction was found, however, where a company from one four-digit SIC was transferring benefits to another company from the same four-digit SIC.[4]

Not all the industries shown in Table 2 were part of the targeted beneficiaries of safe harbor leasing, but each received some of the benefits as a result of the free market mechanism that allowed for the benefits to be purchased or sold. Although it is obvious that for every seller there must be

Table 2. Safe Harbor Lease Property Purchased by Industry

Purchasing Industry	Property Purchased as a Percentage of Total Sample Property Purchased
Food	24.1
Oil and Gas Extraction	9.5
Chemicals	9.4
Fabricated Metal	8.1
Wholesale-Retail Trade	7.3
Electrical and Electronic Machinery	7.1
Communications	6.9
Petroleum Refining	6.5
Printing and Publishing	4.5
Utilities	3.7
Nonelectric Machinery	2.5
Construction	2.3
Other[a]	8.1
	100.0

Note:
[a]None of the specific industries that are grouped in the "other" classification purchased more than two percent of the total safe harbor lease property of the sample.

a buyer, the extent to which these purchasing industries participated in the benefits from safe harbor leasing worked against the objective of helping distressed industries and creating a level playing field for corporations. Recent studies (Arthur Andersen 1982; U.S. Treasury 1982) indicate that about 15 percent of the benefits accrued to the lessor. The fact that 15 percent was lost by the lessee and gained by the lessor maintained, in part at least, the uneven playing field.

Method of Transferring Tax Benefits

For those companies buying and selling tax benefits (survey results indicated that both depreciation and investment tax credits were transferred in almost all safe harbor lease transactions), the questionnaire investigated the methods employed to make the transfer. This is particularly important since it directly addresses the efficiency of safe harbor leases. The Treasury had argued that safe harbor leasing relaxed the many restrictions on tax-oriented leasing that allowed for less complicated agreements. The simplified tax-benefit packages were transacted in a competitive bidding environment that had the potential for reducing the need for and cost of brokers and lawyers (Chapoton 1981).

The results of this survey, however, suggest that a large number of the safe harbor transactions were made with the assistance of middlemen.

Table 3. Method of Transferring Tax Benefits for Buying and Selling Companies

Method	Percent of Selling Companies	Percent of Buying Companies
Direct Dealings	27.6	55.6
Use of Financial Intermediary	62.1	40.0
Both Direct and Intermediary	10.3	4.4
	100.0	100.0

Table 3 provides an indication that, on average, slightly over 50 percent of the buyers and sellers used financial intermediaries. Studies have shown that about one percent of the tax benefits was used to cover costs to third parties (U.S. Treasury 1982), which is 1 percent less for the seller for whom the provisions were designed. For the firms selling tax benefits in this study, less than one-third were able to deal directly and avoid the additional transaction cost of transferring the tax benefits.

The crucial question regarding efficiency is how much of the tax benefit actually goes to the lessee (seller of benefits). Studies by the U.S. Treasury (1982) have indicated that on average 15 percent is retained by the lessor, 1 percent is retained by intermediaries and 84 percent reverts to the lessee. That means that for every $1 of tax benefit directed to a company in a distressed industry, $1.19 ($1.00/.84) is diverted from the Treasury. These average figures become even more pronounced for weaker-loss companies. Since lessors may have to recapture the benefits on property disposed of by the lessee,[5] weaker (or riskier) lessees will have to compensate the lessors for absorbing the increased risk. As a result of their weaker negotiating position, the competitive bidding framework of safe harbor leasing causes the more distressed companies to receive a lower percentage of the benefits. This characteristic of the market-place does not appear to be consistent with the objective of helping distressed industries.

Equity and Perceptions of Equity

The ACRS was instituted to stimulate investment and simplify the tax depreciation system used by businesses. Because ACRS is beneficial only to profitable firms, they might view it as their subsidy. Safe harbor leasing was viewed as a correction to this lopsided subsidy, albeit a "back-door" method for a direct subsidy. It was meant to put unprofitable firms on an approximately equal footing with profitable firms in the sense that they could sell their unuseable tax benefits to others. Upon closer examination, however, strong arguments can be made against the equity issue.

First of all, by indirectly subsidizing distressed companies, the Treasury may have helped some firms that were inefficient or poorly managed, or that were no longer serving the needs of the nation. By creating a mechanism that subsidized unprofitable companies, the efficient allocation of resources could have become distorted.

Although the provisions may have leveled the playing field in the capital-intensive corporate arena, it did not level the playing field for taxpayers in general. The benefits are clearly biased toward the unprofitable capital-intensive firms, because unprofitable firms outside this group would have little to sell in the way of depreciation or tax credits.[6] It is difficult to find equity in provisions that cut taxes for one sector of the economy with substantial revenue losses to the Treasury, while simultaneously cutting benefits to other sectors. When one realizes that 45 percent of corporations did not pay taxes before safe harbor leasing, (House of Representatives, Subcommittee on safe harbor leasing oversight, 1982) it is surprising that enough congressional support existed to enact a measure that would increase the corporate nontaxpaying percentage.

Probably just as important as the issue of equity is the perception of equity by participants. As mentioned earlier, not only were the tax benefits not uniformly distributed to lessees because of varying degrees of negotiating strength, but certain lessors were able to completely eliminate their tax liabilities. Although it is obvious that safe harbor leasing necessitates a buyer for every seller of tax benefits, one would hope that such benefits were widely distributed. When one firm or group of firms outside the targeted distressed industry group buys tax benefits to such an extent as to eliminate their current tax liabilities and obtain refunds of prior tax payments,[7] the general public may regard such activity as an abuse or an unfair use of a legal loophole. As one senator suggested, safe harbor leasing provisions "undermine public respect and confidence in our tax laws." (Pell 1982) In a society where tax collection is dependent on self-compliance, such perceptions carry a heavy weight.

Timing of Safe Harbor Lease Transactions

The period of study for this investigation runs from the initial establishment of safe harbor leasing (with ERTA) up to the time limitations were placed on it by TEFRA. However, the time period is divided into several segments. The first deadline faced by firms interested in the safe harbor provisions was November 13, 1981. All property placed in service in 1981, including the amounts before ERTA's enactment date, was eligible under the safe harbor provisions if leased on or before November 13 of that year. To measure the amounts of tax benefit transferred before the first deadline (which, incidentally, represented a windfall to firms that purchased property without knowing of the provision), the end of the first subperiod is defined as November 13, 1981.

Approximately 72 percent of the sample firms were calendar year taxpayers. Since many firms postpone the closing of leasing deals until they are certain of their profit picture, safe harbor leasing activity had the potential to be quite high late in the year. To provide an indication of the tax benefit transfer occurring late in the year and to separate the activity in 1981 from that in the following year, the end of the second subperiod is set at December 31, 1981.

Another significant timing event before TEFRA's enactment was the announcement by Senate Finance Committee Chairman Robert Dole that safe harbor leasing should be repealed or substantially modified retroactive to February 19, 1982. His announcement received a great deal of press and created considerable uncertainty in the leasing market. As a result, buyers were reportedly avoiding purchase of tax benefits (Apcar and Herman 1982) and Congress believed that leasing deals were drastically reduced subsequent to that date.[8] To measure the extent to which Senator Dole's announcement curtailed safe harbor leasing activity, February 19, 1982 serves as the division between the third and fourth subperiods.

Results on the timing of safe harbor lease transactions are presented in Table 4. The subperiod with the largest activity was the first three months after enactment of ERTA. This suggests that many firms were taking advantage of the windfall provided by the retroactive application of the safe harbor provisions to property placed in service in early 1981. The fact that the *Fortune* 500 were net sellers in the first subperiod could possibly reflect the deadline of November 13th, subsequent to which sellers would lose the tax benefits on property placed in service before August 13th. Sellers may have been pressured to find a wider distribution of buyers (outside the *Fortune* 500 group) that were willing to purchase benefits before their tax position had been finalized. The results also suggest that the tax-benefit transfers occurring in the last four and one-half months of 1981 exceeded the transfers in the first six months of 1982. The firms' calendar year-ends and the retroactive application in 1981 explain a large portion of the activity in 1981 and the subsequent decline in 1982. By comparing the second and third subperiods, which are essentially equal in length, the effects of increased activity before the calendar year end are clear.

One of the surprising results in Table 4 is the significant amount of activity taking place in the final subperiod. In spite of the uncertainty created by Senator Dole, and the caution exercised on the part of buyers at the time, selling activity increased by a factor of about 4.5 and buying activity increased by a factor of nearly 2 (on a per diem basis) over the activity of the third subperiod. Senator Dole's announcement appeared to have little impact on safe harbor leasing activity. Perhaps one explanation

Table 4. Timing of Safe Harbor Leasing Transactions

Subperiods	Sell[a]		Percent of Total Sold	Purchase		Percent of Total Purchased
	Property Sold (Millions)			Property Purchased (Millions)		
	Total	Per Diem		Total	Per Diem	
	$			$		
through 11/13/81	2,061	22.4	51.3	1,783	19.4	35.4
11/14/81–12/31/81	891	19.0	22.2	1,250	26.6	24.8
1/1/82–2/19/82	84	1.7	2.1	350	7.0	7.0
2/20/82/–7/1/82	978	7.5	24.4	1,649	12.7	32.8
	4,014		100.0	5,032		100.0

Note:
[a] The seller of property (and the accompanying tax benefits) is the lessee in the lease transaction.

is that many leases contained complex unwind measures (clauses that revoke the agreements when the law is changed) and indemnification provisions (financial guarantee) designed to protect lessors. At any rate, activity as measured by the amount of property transacted increased rather than decreased.

One final result portrayed in Table 4 was that the *Fortune* 500 firms as a group were net purchasers of tax benefits. Although the provision was designed to help the firms in distressed industries, the large profitable firms were also significant beneficiaries as a result of the negotiated transfer of tax benefits. Because *Fortune* 500 firms are larger, more stable, and on average more profitable, one would expect them to be net purchasers of tax benefits.

Separating the data by the timing of safe harbor leasing transactions not only makes it possible to gauge the strength of warnings issued by the Chairman of the Senate Finance Committee, but also allows for estimation of the participation by *Fortune* 500 firms. The Treasury estimated the value of safe harbor leased property to be $19.3 billion in 1981 (U.S. Treasury 1982). Using the data of Table 4 for 1981, eliminating property sold by one *Fortune* 500 company to another and projecting the results to the total population of *Fortune* 500 firms[9] revealed that slightly over 50 percent of total safe harbor leasing property transferred was sold by or purchased by a *Fortune* 500 company. Converting these estimates to tax benefits revealed that *Fortune* 500 companies ended up with over 38 percent of the total 1981 tax benefits from safe harbor lease transactions.[10] Although the Treasury indicated that there were no real barriers to leasing by small companies (U.S. Treasury 1982), the country's largest 500 firms played a significant role in the market for safe harbor deals.

Safe Harbor Leasing Objectives

As mentioned previously, the safe harbor leasing provisions were designed to help distressed industries, to stimulate their investment, and in the process, to reduce the build-up of tax benefits to prevent mergers.[11] From the perspective of the first objective, the findings that 84 percent of the tax benefit went to the seller and that the "sick six" were represented as sellers, suggest that help went to distressed industries. With respect to the third objective, it is obvious that the provisions reduced the build-up of tax benefits. For example, over 80 percent of the firms selling tax benefits indicated that they were motivated to do so because of the existence of unused investment tax credit carryovers and/or unused tax loss carryforwards. However, to determine the economic effects of these results in terms of actual merger activity, investment stimuli, and the extent of help provided is difficult to measure. Rather, this section of the study analyzed the effects of the provisions as perceived by the participants.

Both purchasers and sellers were asked to respond to questions regarding the importance of safe harbor leasing rules in reducing mergers and bankruptcies. Respondents felt the rules were relatively unimportant in reducing merger activity (ten to one) and unimportant in reducing bankruptcies (two to one).[12] Concerning the investment stimulus provided by the provisions, sellers were asked about the importance of the opportunity to sell tax benefits in their property acquisition decision. Since most of the leasing transactions in the first subperiod (up through November 13, 1981), involved property purchased before enactment of the law, that subperiod was left out of the analysis. Fewer than 15 percent of the remaining tax benefit sellers felt the provisions were relatively important to their property acquisition decisions. An independent study (Arthur Andersen 1982) confirmed that most companies did not revise or plan to revise their 1981–1985 capital expenditure budgets.

The objectives were intended to help distressed firms by allowing tax benefit transfer. In the process they were also meant to promote growth through investment stimuli and reduce the trend toward greater concentration of assets in fewer corporations through mergers. The objectives, therefore, had both immediate and long-run implications, but the results suggest that management perceived investment, merger activity, and capital expenditure budgets to be little altered by the safe harbor leasing provisions. Companies appear to have taken advantage of the provisions only to the extent that prior decisions fit the conditions of the law.

Tax Policy Implications

One of the lessons learned from the safe harbor leasing provisions is that policy makers cannot afford to let what appears to be relatively minor tax legislation slip by without considerable scrutiny. As readily admitted by the Senate Finance Committee, the provisions did not have a complete airing in committee or in the Senate because both bodies reacted too quickly to White House pressure to enact tax cuts (Joint Committee on Taxation 1981; Hatch 1982). The ensuing controversy suggests that policy makers did not anticipate the public outcry against the provisions and as this study suggests, they could do little to curb the deals short of a repeal. Even if the safe harbor leasing provisions were perfectly equitable, the perception of equity is of critical concern to a tax system based on self-compliance. It may have been the perception of inequity and not necessarily the inequities themselves or the loss of revenue that caused the safe harbor repeal.

However, this study did bring to the surface several inequities in the structure of safe harbor leasing deals. *Fortune* 500 companies played a significant role in the transfer of tax benefits and were net purchasers in that role. Participating primarily as purchasers, they were not part of the target group of distressed companies. As a result of the market mechanism set-up, nondistressed companies were obtaining on average about 15 percent of the total tax benefits. Although the provisions were designed to make deals simpler and easier, this study also indicated that at least two-thirds of sellers used financial intermediaries, which diverted further tax benefits (about 1 percent) from the distressed firms.

Recognizing the weaknesses of safe harbor leasing naturally leads to an examination of possible alternatives. Although it would not be politically palatable or easy to police, a direct subsidy would eliminate many of the problems created by the back-door method to a direct subsidy that safe harbor leasing represents. In the future, should Congress deem it necessary to provide assistance to corporations in distressed industries, consideration might be given to enacting a refundable investment tax credit. With such a direct subsidy, only distressed companies would receive tax benefits, thereby avoiding the 16 percent distribution to others. The major objection to safe harbor leasing would also be eliminated by not allowing any profitable corporations access to tax benefits through deals with unprofitable companies. Also, the weaker firms would not get fewer benefits as a result of their debilitated negotiating position,which is common in the free market mechanism.[13]

However, some of the disadvantages associated with safe harbor leasing would continue were Congress to make the investment tax credit refundable. Assistance would continue to be limited to capital-intensive firms. Resources may also be allocated to unprofitable firms rather than to the most efficient and the drain on the U.S. Treasury would be significant. Although these disadvantages could be minimized by placing a ceiling on the total amount of investment tax credit to be refunded each year and on the number of years over which a company could receive such benefits, some of the basic problems would remain.

Even though a direct subsidy may be better than an indirect one, the problems mentioned above raise questions about the appropriateness of any subsidy to unprofitable firms for making capital investments. In a free market economy, the resources should be directed to the most efficient. Arbitrarily helping one segment naturally hurts others. The attempt of safe harbor leasing to generate a level playing field was limited to the capital-intensive corporate arena, but did little to help distressed service industries or individuals. Even with respect to the capital-intensive distressed companies, the attempt to stimulate growth and to reduce the concentration of corporate assets, appeared to fall short of the mark. This study suggests that the special subsidy provided by safe harbor leasing simply appeared to help finance equipment that companies had previously made commitments to purchase.

SUMMARY AND CONCLUSIONS

Congressional testimony has revealed that safe harbor leasing provisions were slipped through the legislative process without an adequate hearing. A major controversy quickly developed when several large, profitable companies were able to completely eliminate their tax liabilities as a result of buying tax benefits. The provisions were defended on the grounds that they helped distressed industries, stimulated investment, and reduced merger activity in an efficient and equitable manner.

This study of *Fortune* 500 safe harbor lease activity and perceptions, in conjunction with several other studies, suggests the following:

1. The provisions may not have been as equitable or efficient as proposed and may have fallen short of intended objectives.
2. The free market mechanism allowed a substantial portion (16 percent) of the benefits to fall outside the distressed industries target, which served to keep the playing field uneven. In addition, the more highly distressed companies received a smaller portion of the tax benefits in the negotiation process because of a weaker bargaining position.
3. The total safe harbor leasing property and benefits transferred were dominated by *Fortune* 500 firms, with their involvement primarily on the nondistressed side of the transactions.
4. Although the rules were simpler and more precise, most safe harbor participants used financial intermediaries which further diluted the benefits received by distressed industries.
5. Although safe harbor leasing was defended as an equitable adjustment to the ACRS, such an adjustment was limited to the capital intensive corporate arena.

6. The inequities and, equally important, the perceived inequities of safe harbor leasing initiated action to reduce the activity or repeal the provisions only months after its enactment. When transactions increased rather than decreased following Senator Dole's stern warning in early 1982, Congress was forced to repeal the provisions.

In addition to raising questions about equity and efficiency, this study addresses the objectives of the provisions and the extent to which they were achieved. Because the provisions were repealed in a short period of time, long-term objectives were not accomplished. Participants in safe harbor leasing did not believe that investment plans were altered or that merger activity was affected. When one considers the loss of revenue and the expensive cost of repeal, the perceived and real equity problems created, the lack of movement toward the major objectives, and the distribution of tax benefits to nondistressed companies, the safe harbor leasing example demonstrates the need for careful scrutiny and less haste in the policy making process.

NOTES

1. The targeted beneficiaries of safe harbor leasing included the "sick six"—steel, airlines, automotive, railroads, mining, and paper. These capital intensive basic industries were referenced throughout congressional testimony (see Seidman, "Statement on Safe Harbor Leasing," in Hearings before the Senate Finance Committee, 97th Cong., 2nd Sess., pt. 4 at 257 (1982) and the popular press (see Kirland 1981, p. 110).

2. Reference to the "level playing field" was introduced by Frank Borman, Chairman, President and CEO of Eastern Airlines, Inc. in hearings before Congress. (See H. R. Committee on Ways and Means, Serial 97–67, 97th Congress, 2nd Sess. pt. 2 (1982).

3. The top ten major industrial groupings that account for over 70 percent of the *Fortune* 500 companies were well represented in the sample. Nine of the ten groupings had between 30 and 56 percent of the available population present in the sample.

4. One company indicated that it bought and sold tax benefits during the same period. The reason for doing so remains unclear. One possible explanation is that the company may have been able to purchase and sell on favorable terms, i.e., not create a wash, but obtain a favorable spread by being astute or fortunate.

5. If the lessee disposed of safe harbor lease property, the agreement would generally terminate as a safe harbor lease. As a result, the lessor would have to recapture additional tax benefits to which the transferee has title.

6. Along those same lines, individuals are not permitted to buy or sell individual exemptions, medical deductions, or mortgage interest payments.

7. For example, General Electric Co., with the help of its leasing subsidiary, eliminated its 1981 tax liability and picked up $150 million in refunds for past years. See Anderson (1982, p. 36).

8. Both Chairman Dole and Senator Boren suggest that safe harbor leasing activity was reduced substantially after February 19, 1982. See "Testimony of Frank Borman" in Hearings before the Senate Finance Committee, 97th Congress, 2nd Sess., pt. 4, at 297 (1982).

9. Since the results of Table 4 represent activities for 45.8 percent of the *Fortune* 500 firms, the 1981 totals from Table 4 are multiplied by 1/.458 to approximate results for the entire group of *Fortune* 500 firms.

10. Survey results revealed that almost all available tax benefits were used to reduce current period taxes or to refund prior taxes and that most benefits were tied to transfer of equipment in the five-year property class. Computations were based on these findings.

11. One of the fears of the Reagan administration was increased merger activity caused by $10 billion in unused tax credits that would be generated annually by the mid-1980s without the safe harbor leasing provisions. See Kirkland (1981, p. 112).

12. These findings are consistent with those in an independent study by Arthur Andersen and Company (1982, p. 974), which found that repeal of safe harbor leasing would have little effect on firms' acquisition decisions.

13. It is interesting to note that former President Jimmy Carter proposed, but to no avail, a refundable tax credit.

REFERENCES

Anderson, D., ed., "A Move to Salvage 'Safe Harbor' Leasing," *Business Week* (April 12, 1982), p. 36.

Apcar, L. M., and Herman, T. "Uncertainty Cripples Tax Leasing as Lawmakers Consider Changes," *The Wall Street Journal* (April 5, 1982), pp. 25.

Arthur Andersen and Company, "Report on Survey of Selected Participants in Safe Harbor Lease Transactions," reprinted in Hearings before the Committee on Ways and Means, House of Representatives, on the Administration's Fiscal Year 1983 Economic Program, Washington, D.C.: Government Printing Office, 1982.

Chapoton, John E., "Statement on Safe Harbor Leasing" in Hearings before the Senate Finance Committee, 97th Congress, 1st Sess. (1981).

Hatch, Orrin G., "Statement of Senator Orrin G. Hatch in Hearings before the Senate Finance Committee," 97th Congress, 2nd Sess. (1982).

House of Representatives, Committee on Ways and Means, Hearings on the Administration's Fiscal Year 1983 Economic Program, (Washington, D.C.: Government Printing Office, 1982).

House of Representatives, Subcommittee on Oversight, Hearings on Safe Harbor Leasing Provisions of the Economic Recovery Tax Act of 1981 (Washington, D.C.: Government Printing Office, 1982).

Joint Committee on Taxation, "Description of Safe Harbor Leasing Provisions Under the Accelerated Cost Recovery System," in Hearings before the Senate Finance Committee, 97th Congress, 1st Sess. (1981).

Kirkland, R. "The Trade in Tax Breaks Takes Off," *Fortune* (September 21, 1981), pp. 110-112.

Pell, Clairborne, "Statement by Senator Clairborne Pell" in Hearings before the Senate Finance Committee, 97th Congress, 2nd Sess. (1982).

U.S. Senate, Committee on Finance, Hearings on Safe Harbor Leasing (Washington, D.C.: Government Printing Office, 1981).

U.S. Senate, Committee on Finance, Hearings on the Administration's Fiscal Year 1983 Budget Proposal (Washington, D.C.: Government Printing Office, 1982).

U.S. Treasury, Office of Tax Analysis, "Preliminary Report on Safe Harbor Leasing Activity in 1981," *Treasury News* (March 25, 1982).

APPENDIX: CONFIDENTIAL QUESTIONNAIRE

Safe Harbor Leasing Rules

A. What is the four-digit SIC code for the industry to which
your firm belongs? ....
    $(5-8)$

B. What is the date of your fiscal year-end? Month .... Day ....
    $(9-10)$ $(11-12)$

C. Has your firm entered into a lease agreement to "sell" tax benefits (i.e.,
depreciation deductions and/or investment tax credits)?

    (0) ☐ NO (If no, please go to question H)   (13)
    (1) ☐ YES (if yes, please answer the following questions:
       a. Did you sell the benefits ☐ direct or ☐ use a financial
                           (0)   (1)
        intermediary?   (14)
       b. What industry(s) was(were) represented by the company buying the
         tax benefits?   (15-18)
        ....
       c. Was the company buying the tax benefits a *Fortune* 500 company?
         ☐ No ☐ Yes   (19)
         (0)   (1)

D. Which of the following explains your firm's decision to sell tax benefits?
(You may check more than one box)
                                                    (GEO)
    (1) ☐ Unused tax loss carryforwards   (20)
    (2) ☐ Unused investment tax credit carryovers
    (4) ☐ Other ....

E. Please answer the following questions with respect to the tax benefit(s)
sold during each of the four time periods indicated below:

		Qualified Lease Property				Benefits Transferred		
Execution Period	Approx. Amount	Predominant Property Class (Please check one box) 3 yr. 5 yr. 10 yr. 15 yr.				Deprec. only	ITC only	Both ITC and Deprec. (Please check one box)
a. Prior to November 14, 1981 . . .		(1)	(2)	(3)	(4)	(1)	(2)	(3)
	....	☐	☐	☐	☐	☐	☐	☐
	(21-26)	(27)				(28)		

b. After November 13, 1981, but prior to January 1, 1982 . . . .

	(1)	(2)	(3)	(4)	(1)	(2)	(3)
	□	□	□	□	□	□	□
	(32-37)		(38)			(39)	

c. After December 31, 1981, but prior to February 20, 1982 . . . .

	(1)	(2)	(3)	(4)	(1)	(2)	(3)
	□	□	□	□	□	□	□
	(40-45)		(46)			(47)	

d. After February 19, 1982, but prior to July 1, 1982 . . . .

	(1)	(2)	(3)	(4)	(1)	(2)	(3)
	□	□	□	□	□	□	□
	(48-53)		(54)			(55)	

F. How important was the opportunity to sell your tax benefits in making your decision to acquire qualified lease property?

Unimportant				Important	(56)
1	2	3	4	5	

G. If the opportunity to sell your tax benefits had not been available, would your firm have acquired the qualified lease property?

Not Likely				Very Likely	(57)
1	2	3	4	5	

H. Did your firm "purchase" tax benefits (i.e., depreciation deductions and/or investment tax credits)?

(0) □ NO (If no, please go to question K)   (58)

(1) □ YES (If yes, please answer the following questions):

    a. Did you buy the benefits □ direct or □ use a financial
                           (0)   (1)
       intermediary?   (59)

    b. What industry(s) was(were) represented by the company selling the
       tax benefits?   (63-66)

       . . . .

    c. Was the company selling the tax benefits a *Fortune* 500 company?
       □ No □ Yes   (67)
       (0)   (1)

I. Which of the following best describes the use of the tax benefits purchased
by your firm? (You may check more than one box)

(GEO)

(1) □ Reduction of taxes paid in the year of the lease transaction   (68-69)

(2) □ File for refund of prior year taxes

(4) □ Creation of carryforward to be applied to taxes of future years

(8) □ Other ....

J. Please answer the following questions with respect to the tax benefit(s)
purchased during each of the four time periods indicated below:

	Execution Period	Approx. Amount	Predominant Property Class (Please check one box) 3 yr. 5 yr. 10 yr. 15 yr.				Deprec. only	ITC only	Both ITC and Deprec.
			Qualified Lease Property				Benefits Transferred		
			(1)	(2)	(3)	(4)	(1)	(2)	(3)
a.	Prior to November 14, 1981 . . .	....	□	□	□	□	□	□	□
		(70-75)	(76)				(77)		
b.	After November 13, 1981, but prior to January 1, 1982 . . .	....	□	□	□	□	□	□	□
		(78-83)	(84)				(85)		
c.	After December 31, 1981, but prior to February 20, 1982 . . .	....	□	□	□	□	□	□	□
		(86-91)	(92)				(93)		
d.	After February 19, 1982, but prior to July 1, 1982 . . .	....	□	□	□	□	□	□	□
		(94-99)	(100)				(101)		

K. In your opinion, how important are the safe harbor leasing rules in each of the following areas:

	Unimpor-tant				Important	
a. Reducing merger activity . . .	1	2	3	4	5	(102)
b. Reducing bankrupt-cies . . .	1	2	3	4	5	(103)
c. Fostering capital investment in distressed industries . . .	1	2	3	4	5	(104)

L. If your firm is currently giving consideration to the purchase or sale of tax benefits, please answer the following:
Which alternative best describes your firm's current deliberations? (You can check more than one box)
  (1) ☐ On hold—waiting to see what happens with the tax law changes (GEO)
  (2) ☐ On hold—ascertaining future tax liability situation (105-106)
  (4) ☐ Proceeding with "unwind provisions" built into contract in the event the tax law is changed
  (8) ☐ Proceeding without regard for potential tax law changes
  (16) ☐ Other ....

M. If a change in the tax laws occurs, which of the following tax results would your firm prefer?
(Please check only one box)
  (1) ☐ Repeal of the safe harbor leasing rules and no new alternative corporate minimum tax
  (2) ☐ Retention of the safe harbor leasing rules in conjunction with a new alternative corporate minimum tax (107)
  (3) ☐ Retention of the safe harbor leasing rules with a dollar limitation on the transfer of tax benefits by the seller
  (4) ☐ Retention of the safe harbor leasing rules with a dollar limitation on the transfer of tax benefits by the buyer
  (5) ☐ Other ....

N. If your firm neither bought not sold tax benefits as a result of the safe harbor leasing rules, please answer the following:
  a. My firm did not buy tax benefits primarily because (Please check only one box):
  (1) ☐ My firm has insufficient tax liability to absorb them
  (2) ☐ The cash outlay required was too large considering our present liquidity (108)
  (3) ☐ The uncertainty of future tax legislation
  (4) ☐ The return on investment was not sufficiently attractive
  (5) ☐ Other ....

b. My firm did not sell tax benefits primarily because (Please check only one box):

(1) ☐ No offers were received from potential buyers
(2) ☐ My firm has sufficient tax liability to absorb them   (109)
(3) ☐ The uncertainty of future tax legislation
(4) ☐ Unable to reach a satisfactory agreement when attempting to purchase tax benefits
(5) ☐ Other ....

THANK YOU FOR YOUR COOPERATION.

Please return in enclosed Business Reply Envelope or to the following address:

Prof. James L. Wittenbach
Professor of Accountancy
Hayes-Healy Center
College of Business Administration
University of Notre Dame
Notre Dame, IN 46556

AN EMPIRICAL STUDY OF COMPLEXITY
EXPERIENCED BY TAXPAYERS

Judith E. Watanabe, Virginia L. Bean,
and Justin D. Stolen

ABSTRACT

This study presents an empirical framework within which a quantifiable definition of tax complexity was developed. The definition permitted the measurement of complexity and its comparison between two different taxation methods. This experiment addresses the complexity experienced by selected taxpayers in handling capital gains and losses, but the methodology could be applied to any group of taxpayers and any tax provision. The Wilcoxon ranked sum test for matched pairs and an Error/Time Complexity index, expressing the relationship of complexity between two taxation methods, were used in analyzing experimental results. Generally, more relative complexity was experienced by participants under current law than under indexation. The differences were statistically significant at a 99-percent confidence level.

Advances in Taxation, Volume 1, pages 153–168.
Copyright © 1987 JAI Press Inc.
All rights of reproduction in any form reserved.
ISBN: 0–89232–782–0

Complexity in taxation affects both individuals and society. It results in high compliance costs for taxpayers andmay result in an inefficient allocation of society's resources (Browning and Browning 1979, pp. 335–368). Tax complexity may also be linked to tax evasion. According to the Federal Taxation Division of the American Institute of Certified Public Accountants (AICPA):

> The increasing complexity of the tax law can erode public confidence that the tax law is treating everyone fairly. The uneasy, perhaps even subconscious, feeling that others are escaping tax can be used as a rationalization for cutting a few corners (1983 p. 23).

The costs of evasion are significant, perhaps as high as $70 to $120 billion (American Institute of Certified Public Accountants 1983, p. 5). According to *The Wall Street Journal,* private estimates of the activity not reported to the Internal Revenue Service range from 20 to 25 percent of the measured economy (Murray 1985b).

Current complexities in tax law reflect congressional responses to dissatisfied taxpayers as well as to special interest groups. Over the years, aggressive taxpayers (and their tax advisors) have continually attempted to arrange their financial affairs in ways to minimize or avoid taxation; Congress has responded by continually modifying the law so as to restrict these ways.[1] The complexities created by the cycle of taxpayer actions and congressional reactions have resulted in a tax law that is a burden to the average taxpayer.

Since they were first adopted in 1921, provisions for capital gains and losses have been subject to continuous modifications. Over the years, a number of proposals have suggested indexing for capital gains and losses—yet another modification.[2] There has been major disagreement as to whether the proposals, if enacted, would have resulted in more or less complexity. Assistant Secretary of the Treasury Pearlman (1984), for example, stated that in general indexing would be an added complexity. The Committee on Federal Taxation of the American Accounting Association (1984, 37) and McGinley (1984) agreed. The Federal Taxation Division of the AICPA, on the other hand, stated:

> We are convinced that the complexity of indexing basis is usually overstated. It would not be difficult to have the adjusted basis of assets multiplied by an inflation factor. The newly calculated indexed basis would be used for determining gain or loss on disposition, as well as for calculating depreciation. The use of an indexed basis would result in the calculation of gain or loss on the sale of assets that would be consistent with the underlying economic effect (American Institute of Certified Public Accountants 1981, p. 13).

Previous studies have defined tax complexity in a variety of ways and have different approaches toward its measurement. The cost of taxpayer compliance is clearly related to the complexity of the tax law. Over 40 percent of U.S. households paid for professional tax assistance in 1982 (U.S. Department of Treasury 1984–1985). Total federal and state taxpayer compliance costs, including the cost of taxpayer time and costs of professional assistance, were between $17 and $27 billion (National Bureau of Economic Research, Inc. 1985). One can conjecture that compliance costs are higher for a complex law, but it is difficult to estimate how much of the cost is caused by complex financial affairs and efforts to reduce the amount of taxes and how much is caused by complexity of the tax law.

One approach to the measurement of complexity has been through an analysis of the tax law and estimation of the portion of the law due to particular provisions. Schroeder (1975) explored the issue of tax complexity by examining basic sources of tax law.[3] His stated objective was to determine the extent to which capital gain and loss provisions complicated governmental administration of income tax laws and taxpayer compliance with these laws. He concluded that over 40 percent of the code sections, 11 percent of Revenue Rulings, and 27 percent of judicial decisions were directly or indirectly affected by capital gain or loss provisions. Karlinsky measured the complexity created by capital gain and loss provisions by applying content analysis to the Internal Revenue Code and Treasury Regulations. He determined that 383 out of 584 (or 66 percent) of the income tax code sections and regulations were affected in some way by capital gain and loss provisions, and that the provisions contributed to over 15 percent of the overall complexity in the tax law (1981, p. 52). Thus, both Karlinsky and Schroeder assessed the aggregate impact of capital gain and loss provisions on the complexity of the tax law.

Koch and Karlinsky (1984) studied the effect of the reading complexity of tax law on students' task performance. They identified two tax law complexities, content complexity and reading complexity. Content complexity is the inherent level of complexity of a subject itself, while reading complexity (although not totally independent of content complexity) specifically pertains to the presentation of the subjects. In measuring reading complexity, Koch and Karlinsky presented student subjects with two explanations of Section 179 of the Internal Revenue Code. They determined reading complexity by two separate measures: the number of correct responses and the time to respond. The authors recognized and discussed the relationship of correct responses (or lack of errors) and time to respond to tax law complexity, but they did not investigate the nature of the relationship. Koch and Karlinsky concluded that the tax code was less readable (that is, more complex) than tax commentary, at least as viewed by the students for the section examined.

Two behavioral studies have examined perceptions of complexity. Milliron (1984) measured taxpayers' perceptions of complexity and analyzed the effect of perceptions on reporting positions. Long and Swingen (1985) examined tax professionals' perceptions of complexity by having the professionals assign a numerical rating to six complexity factors and identify the tax return line items for which the factors were a significant problem. Neither of these behavioral studies dealt specifically with capital gain and loss provisions.

This study differs from earlier ones in that the focus is on measurement of the difficulty taxpayers have in complying with the tax law by simulating their actual experience with the complexity of the law. A second difference arises from the base used in the measurement. Previous studies have identified complexity within the current tax law; this study compares the complexity of two alternative tax laws. This experiment addresses the complexity experienced by selected taxpayers in handling capital gains and losses, but the methodology could be applied to any group of taxpayers and any tax provision.

RESEARCH DESIGN

Overview

Here, complexity is defined as the degree to which a subject is difficult to understand or perplexing (*Webster's* 1981). The difficulty taxpayers experience in complying with the tax law was simulated through an experiment. Taxpayer subjects were provided with explanations of relevant law, a set of facts (transactions), and a set of forms for reporting the tax effects of the transactions. Since capital gain and loss provisions are generally acknowledged to be complex under current law, the transactions selected involved the disposition of capital assets. In order to measure the complexity experienced by the taxpayer subjects, an operational definition of complexity was developed whereby actions of the taxpayers were used as surrogates for complexity experienced in much the same way that actions of students on examinations are used as surrogates for students' learning or understanding. The actions measured were the time taken and the errors made in reporting the tax effects of the transactions.[4]

The complexity experienced under one tax law was compared with the complexity that would be experienced under an alternative law by a taxpayer for the same transactions. Since indexation had been proposed as an alternative to present capital gains provisions and since there was disagreement as to the amount of complexity it would add, indexation was selected as the alternative tax method. Another approach (similar to the approaches taken by Schroeder and Karlinsky) might have been to examine the degree of complexity added to the law by capital gain and loss provisions. One disadvantage would be that the measure would include two different kinds of complexity. A taxpayer with capital asset dispositions has more complex financial affairs and the measurement of income is therefore more complex than for a taxpayer without capital asset dispositions. A complexity measure developed from comparing the two taxpayers would include both complexity created by more complicated financial affairs and complexity of the relevant tax provisions.

The research question was: would indexation of capital asset transactions create more or less complexity than current capital gain and loss provisions for individual taxpayers? To answer this question, taxpayer subjects were presented with a number of transactions and a description of relevant tax law, and were asked to determine the tax reporting of the transactions (a decision frame). Half of the frames required the application of current law while half required application of indexation. A measure of relative complexity, the Error/Time Complexity index, was used to express the relationship of the complexity created by current provisions compared to the complexity created by indexation. The Wilcoxon ranked sum test for matched pairs was used for the analysis of test results.

Alternative Methods

The present method, actual tax law as of January 1, 1985, was one of the alternatives tested. In each frame, subjects were provided with the law that applied to each transaction and asked to determine the tax reporting for the transaction. Specifically, Section 1222 (determination of holding periods), Section 1202 (calculation of capital gain deduction), Section 1211 (calculation of capital loss deduction), and Sections 1245 and 1250 (determination of ordinary income from the disposition of depreciable capital assets) were involved. To make the task as clear and as easy as possible, all possible arithmetic was done for the participants,[5] some of the information was entered (in handwriting) on the test instruments, and only the information needed by the participants was provided.

The complexity inherent in an indexation method would depend upon the particular provisions enacted. The indexation method tested in the study was based on the capital asset disposition reforms described in the 1984 Treasury Department Proposal (U.S. Department of the Treasury 1984, Vol. 1, pp. 97–120; Vol 2, pp. 178–188). Real gains (inflation-adjusted realized gains) were fully includable in taxable income and subject to tax at regular rates. Real losses from dispositions of property were offset against real gains from dispositions, with any excess loss deductible up to a maximum of $3,000.

While transition to any new provision would involve additional complexity, this test was designed to measure the relative complexity of two alternatives, and not to measure the complexity of change from one law to an alternative. Thus, the indexation method did not include transition rules proposed by the U.S. Treasury.

Decisions Tested

These capital gain and loss provisions give rise to numerous questions that require tax research even by tax professionals. Given the propensity of taxpayers to arrange their affairs so as to pay the least tax possible and the propensity of Congress to "tinker" with the law in response to the actions of taxpayers and economic conditions, it seems probable that similar complexities could arise under indexation. No attempt was made here to include all complexities under current law or to anticipate all possible complexities that might be added in the future if some form of indexation were adopted. Rather, an attempt was made to compare the taxpayers' difficulties in applying the basic provisions under present law with the difficulty they might be expected to have in applying the basic provisions of indexation. An attempt was made to select common transactions, for which the law is clear, and to have the taxpayer subjects determine the tax effects. If Congress should provide for indexation based on factors other than inflation (for example, different adjustment factors for different assets) or should add indexation to present capital gain and loss provisions, indexation could clearly be more complex than present capital gain provisions.

In setting up the test instruments, every effort was made to prepare the instructions and the questionnaire for both alternatives in as clear and unambiguous a format as possible. For the present method, the authors relied heavily on existing IRS instructions and tax forms in writing the explanation of the law and the format for the participants' computations and answers. For the indexation method, the authors developed instructions and forms which paralleled the differences in the alternative laws as much as possible.

Taxpayer subjects were given four different sets of facts and were asked to make decisions and computations by applying the law to the facts. This resulted in four decision frames (see Table 1). Each frame included two subsets, the present method and the indexation method. Thus, there were four test instruments for the present method and four test instruments for the indexation method.

Each frame was designed to test a particular step in the tax-reporting process; an attempt was made to avoid testing the same step in more than one frame. The test instruments were controlled by a numbering sequence to ascertain that one-half of the subjects completed the indexation method first, while the other half did the present method first. All transactions were presented to all subjects in the same order under both methods. Since each

Table 1.   Decision Frames

	Present Method	Indexation Method
Frame 1	Determination of holding periods.	Selection of cost-adjustment factors.
Frame 2	Calculation of short-term loss, long-term gain, and application of long-term capital gain deduction.	Adjustment of cost for two capital assets, determination of the gain or loss, and combination of the results.
Frame 3	Calculation of short-term and long-term losses and application of capital loss limits.	Adjustment to cost of two capital assets, determination of real losses, and application of capital loss limits.
Frame 4	Calculation of gains on sale of residential rental property and business equipment, and application of recapture provisions.	Calculation of real gains on sale of residential rental property and business equipment.

participant completed all the frames under both methods, the result was the perfect matched pair: that is, each subject acted as his own control (Neter, Wasserman and Whitmore 1978, p. 370).

Each of the four frames encompassed capital asset transactions frequently encountered by individual taxpayers.[6] Every effort was made to make the two alternatives tested as parallel as possible given the differences in the provisions, to provide for objective measures of the results, and to minimize the arithmetic involved for the participants.

Decision frame 1 was designed to include one of the first decisions a taxpayer makes when reporting capital gains and losses: under the present method, the classification of long-term and short-term capital gains and losses; and under indexation, the selection of cost adjustment factors. A table of the cost adjustment factors provided to the participants appears in Appendix A. One of the complexities under current law is the continued and frequent modification of the law. While this study did not attempt to measure the complexity of change from current law to indexation, it did recognize that change appears to be a part of current provisions. In addition, the taxpayers completed the experiment in 1985, shortly after filing their 1984 return; accordingly, the present law encountered by the taxpayers included the change in holding period present in 1984. Under indexation, the subjects were required to determine the appropriate cost adjustment factor from tables provided.

In frame 2 under the present method the focus was the netting of a net short-term capital loss and a net long-term capital gain deduction. Under indexation, a parallel test was determined to be the application of the cost adjustment factors to the original cost of the assets to determine the real gain or loss from each transaction and combination of the gain on one asset with a loss on the other.

Frame 3 was similar to frame 2, except the net result was a loss rather than a gain. Thus, under present law the two-to-one provision relating to long-term capital losses was tested. Explanation of capital loss limitations and spaces for applying the limits were included under both alternatives, but neither the present method nor indexation required the application of the limits.

The disposition of depreciable property was addressed in frame 4, clearly the most complicated of the frames and the frame requiring the greatest number of arithmetical computations by the participants. Adjusted basis of the assets on the date of disposition was provided to the participants for both alternatives. Thus, under the present method, participants were not required to compute either declining balance depreciation or straight-line depreciation; under indexation, they were not required to multiply the beginning of the year cost adjusted-basis by the index for the year to determine the inflation-adjusted depreciation for the year. Decisions related to Section 1245 and Section 1250 depreciation recapture were required under the present method. Under indexation, the selection of the inflation-adjusted basis was required to determine the real gain from the dispositions.

Subjects

The 142 taxpayer participants in the study were selected from university faculty, staff, and students. Demographic information was collected from the subjects. Since the responses of faculty, staff, and students did not differ significantly, the findings were treated as coming from a single population of taxpayers. However, a chi-square test revealed that the sample differed significantly from the general population. While the test results are therefore not generalizable to the population as a whole, the prime concern in this study was the development of an explicit measure of complexity.

Ordinarily, motivation of test subjects is a concern in experiments using matched pairs. In this experiment, however, each subject acted as his own control. Therefore, the overall reliability of the measures should not have been biased by those subjects who were not strongly motivated.

The Simulation

The sample was divided into smaller groups for the purpose of conducting the complexity simulation because it was felt that there would be less confusion for the subjects and less chance of errors in testing with smaller groups. The test was administered in a classroom for the students and in a conference room with tables for the faculty and staff members.

The forms were divided into indexation method sets and present method sets so that the subjects could complete all the decision frames first under one method and then under the other. Because participants were not required to switch back and forth from one method to another, their confusion was minimized. The test instruments were controlled by a numbering sequence to insure that one-half of the subjects completed the indexation method first, while the other half did the present method first. The test was carefully explained and test instruments were given to the participants. To determine the amount of time used by the subjects for completion of each form, an instruction, "Record time _____," was placed at the bottom of each form. An assistant recorded the time on the blackboard at the front of the room so that there would be no confusion in interpreting the minutes on the wall clock. The test was distributed and the subjects were instructed to complete each page in order, recording the time at the bottom of each page as it was completed. They were instructed not to ask any questions about the forms or the instructions.

Scoring of Results

Completed forms were first evaluated to determine the time required for each participant to complete the test instrument. Error scores were determined using three different approaches: first, each instrument was evaluated as correct or incorrect; second, the total number of separate errors on each instrument was determined; and finally, the number of errors as a percent of the possible errors was determined for each instrument. The test results were analyzed separately for all three measures of error scores, but the results did not differ. The data analysis presented below reflects the total number of errors, but the other two measures led to the same conclusions.

DATA ANALYSIS

Descriptive statistics were used to study time taken and errors made, an index number was devised to consider the combined effect, and a ranking test based on the index measure was utilized to determine statistical significance of the differences between the two methods.

Descriptive Statistics

To determine general tendencies regarding the relative complexity of two tax methods, the means, medians, and standard deviations for errors and time were calculated (see Table 2). Smaller values of means and medians in

Table 2.   Descriptive Statistics

	Present Method			Indexation Method		
	Mean	Median	Standard Deviation	Mean	Median	Standard Deviation
Errors						
Frame 1	0.76	1	0.87	1.04	0	1.49
Frame 2	1.22	1	1.71	0.63	0	1.03
Frame 3	1.22	1	2.17	0.61	0	1.09
Frame 4	5.50	5	5.21	0.63	0	1.26
Time						
Frame 1	1.98	2	0.93	2.61	2	1.50
Frame 2	4.51	4	1.76	3.37	3	1.31
Frame 3	2.96	3	1.18	2.18	2	1.06
Frame 4	9.87	9	3.35	3.88	3	1.58

frames 2, 3, and 4 indicated less complexity under indexation, while smaller standard deviations indicated less dispersion. In frame 1, the means for errors and time were smaller under the present method. The median of errors was larger for the present method, and the median of time was the same under both methods. It appeared that the present method was more complex in frame 1, but the results were not as consistent as in the other frames. Standard deviations under the present method were less in frame 1; indicating less dispersion in the results.

Descriptive comparisons provided some insight into the relative complexity of the two methods. To combine time and errors into a single measure, the Error/Time Complexity index was derived. The index provided additional insight about the relative complexity of the two methods as well as the relative importance of errors and time.

Error/Time Complexity Index

The Error/Time Complexity index was derived using the methodology of index numbers. An index number measures the changes in magnitude from one situation to another where the situations may be time periods (for example, years or months), spatial locations (states or countries), or individuals (single or married) (Allen 1975, p. 3). In the present study, the magnitude measured by index numbers was complexity, defined as the product of errors and time, and the two situations were the present method and the indexation method of taxing capital gains and losses.

There are two potential problems associated with index numbers: the time reversal and the factor reversal conditions (Richmond 1964, pp. 495–497). The first relates to the choice of base for the index number. Within the current context, this problem was stated as follows: a complexity index calculated to compare the indexation method with the current method using the indexation method as the base was not necessarily consistent with the same protocol using the current method as the base. Because the base differed, changes from the base in percentage terms would differ. A second potential problem was the factor reversal test. From one method to the other, a ratio of the errors multiplied by a ratio of the time should equal the ratio of the product of errors and time. If one method had twice the errors and took twice as long, the relevant index of the product should be four times as large.

In his classical 1922 treatise on index numbers, Fisher (1967, pp. 220–225) developed an "ideal" index that meets both the time reversal and the factor reversal conditions. Adapting Fisher's ideal index resulted in the following formula (see Appendix B):

$$I_{et} = I_e \times I_t = \frac{\sum e_i t_i}{\sum e_p t_p} \tag{5}$$

where I = the index, e = errors made, t = time taken to complete, i = indexation method, and p = present method.

The index of the product of errors and time equals the index of errors times the index of time which equals the summation of the product of errors and time for the indexation method divided by the summation of the product of errors and time for the present method. In the first equality of Eq. (5), the respective sizes of I_e and I_t yield a comparative measure of the importance of time versus errors. The second equality indicates that index values greater than 1.0 mean that the indexation method is more complex, while index values less than 1.0 denote more complexity under the current method.

Error/Time Complexity indices were computed for each of the four frames (see Table 3). The respective components of Error/Time Complexity indices (I_e and I_t) suggested that errors and time were equally important in frames 2 and 3, while time was a greater consideration in frames 1 and 4. The combined index (I_{et}) indicated that for frames 2, 3, and 4 indexation was relatively less complex than the present method. In frame 1, the Error/Time Complexity index suggested that indexing was relatively more complex than the present method.

The indices yielded results consistent with those found using descriptive statistics: the index numbers yielded a single mathematically coherent value which described both the relative importance of errors versus time and

Table 3.   Error/Time Complexity Indices

Decision Frame	I_e	I_t	I_{et}
Frame 1	1.22	1.42	1.73
Frame 2	0.71	0.73	0.52
Frame 3	0.73	0.73	0.53
Frame 4	0.25	0.44	0.11

current law versus indexation. A ranking test, based on the Error/Time Complexity index (I_{et}), was utilized to determine statistical significance.

Wilcoxon Ranked Sum Test

Since results of chi-square tests revealed that the distributions of errors made and time taken were not normal distributions, the use of t tests was inappropriate. Therefore, the Wilcoxon ranked sum test for matched pairs, a nonparametric test, was used for testing the differences (Neter, Wasserman, and Whitmore 1978, pp. 376–382). The test statistic was found by ranking the absolute differences between the two alternatives, attaching a sign to the rank, and summing the signed ranks. If there were no difference between the alternatives, the summed ranks should have been approximately zero. If the value of the summed ranks differed significantly from zero, then one alternative was significantly different from the other.

In Eq. (5), the numerator, $\Sigma e_i t_i$, referred to the summation of the products of errors and time under the indexation method, while the denominator, $\Sigma e_p t_p$, referred to the summation of the products of errors and time under the present method. For each individual tested, products of errors and time were calculated and absolute differences were determined; the remaining steps of the Wilcoxon test were then applied.

The formal hypotheses were as follows:

H_0:   The sum of the ranks with a positive sign is equal to the sum of the ranks with a negative sign. There is no difference between the present method and the indexation method.

H_1:   The sum of the ranks with a positive sign is greater than the sum of the ranks with a negative sign, and the present method is more complex than the indexation method, or the sum of the ranks with a negative sign is greater than the sum of the ranks with a positive sign, and the indexation method is more complex than the present method.

Four separate tests were performed, one for each of the four decision

Table 4.   Wilcoxon Z Scores

Decision Frame	N	Z
Frame 1	117	−3.87
Frame 2	124	5.84
Frame 3	119	6.37
Frame 4	141	10.30

frames. Statistically, the hypotheses for the five tests were stated in the following form:

$$\mathbf{H_0}: \quad \Sigma e_p t_p - \Sigma e_i t_i = 0$$
$$\mathbf{H_1}: \quad \Sigma e_p t_p - \Sigma e_i t_i \neq 0$$

Z scores and Ns for each frame appear in Table 4. Variations in sample size resulted from including only those participants with absolute values other than zero. The results were significant at the 0.01 level ($|Z| = 2.326$) for all tests. For three of the four frames, indexation was less complex than the present method. In the case of frame 1, indexation was more complex than the present method. These results were suggested by descriptive statistics, supported by the Error/Time Complexity indices, and confirmed at a 99 percent confidence level by the Wilcoxon test.

CONCLUSIONS

The objectives of the study were achieved: a measure of relative complexity experienced by the taxpayer was developed and applied to the taxation of capital gains and losses in four separate frames. Complexity was determined by the Wilcoxon test to be significantly greater for existing law than for the indexation method in three of the four frames, supporting the notion that existing law was more complex than indexation. The study examined a simulated taxpayer experience; it added both a new way of operationally defining tax complexity and a new methodology for measuring the relative complexity of two alternative laws.

NOTES

1. One commentator, McClure (former Deputy Assistant Secretary of the Treasury, presently with the Hoover Institute, Stanford University) has accused Congress of being schizophrenic. "They want to use the tax system to encourage everything, but they don't want it to be used too much by any one person or corporation" (Murray 1985a).
2. See, for instance, U.S. Department of the Treasury (1984), and *The President's Tax Proposals to the Congress for Fairness, Growth and Simplicity* (1985).

3. Schroeder examined Sections 1 through 1399 of the Internal Revenue code, related Revenue Rulings, and relevant Federal court cases.
4. Koch and Karlinsky measured correct responses and time of completion (1984, p. 105).
5. Participants were advised, before the test simulation, that they could bring calculators and use them during the test if they wished to do so.
6. Because of time restrictions, it was necessary to limit the number of decision frames to be completed by the subjects. Six decision frames were originally developed. The six frames were evaluated by eight tax professionals and tested in a pilot study of ten taxpayers. Because of the time required by the participants in the pilot study, the number of frames was decreased from six to four for the final test. Decisions in the two omitted frames involved application of capital loss limitations (present under both alternatives) and combination of a short-term net gain with a long-term net gain. After completion of the pilot test, the test instruments were discussed individually with each of the eight tax professionals and ten taxpayers. A number of minor modifications were recommended and were incorporated into the test instruments. After viewing the modified instruments, the experts agreed that explanations of both the present and the proposed laws and the computational procedures were stated as succinctly and unambiguously as possible.

REFERENCES

Allen, R. G. D. (1975), *Index Numbers in Theory and Practice* (MacMillan Press, Ltd., 1975).

American Accounting Association, Committee on Federal Taxation (1984), *Indexing the Tax Law to Adjust for Inflation* (American Accounting Association, 1984).

American Institute of Certified Public Accountants (AICPA) (1981), *Statement of Tax Policy No. 9: Implementing Indexation of the Tax Laws* (AICPA, 1981).

American Institute of Certified Public Accountants (AICPA), Federal Tax Division (1983), *Underreported Taxable Income: The Problem and Possible Solutions* (AICPA, 1983).

Browning, E. K., and J. M. Browning (1979), *Public Finance and the Price System* (Macmillan Publishing Co., 1979).

Fisher, I. (1967), *The Making of Index Numbers* (Houghton Mifflin Co., 1922; reprinted, Augustus M. Kelley, 1967).

Karlinsky, S. S. (1981), "Complexity in the Federal Income Tax Law Attributable to the Capital Gain and Loss Preference: A Measurement Model," Ph.D. dissertation (New York University, 1981).

Koch, B. S., and S. S. Karlinsky (1984), "The Effect of Federal Income Tax Law Reading Complexity on Students' Task Performance," *Issues in Accounting Education—1984*, pp. 98–110.

Long, S. B., and J. A. Swingen (1985), "An Approach to the Measurement of Tax Law Complexity," unpublished paper (Center for Tax Studies, Syracuse University, 1985).

McGinley, L. (1984), "Indexing Proposals in Treasury's Plan Will Add Complications for Taxpayers," *The Wall Street Journal* (December 3, 1984), p. 2.

Milliron, V. C. (1984), "Taxpayer Perceptions of Complexity and the Effect of Complexity on Reporting Positions," Ph.D. dissertation (University of Southern California, 1984).

—— (1985), "An Analysis of the Relationship between Tax Equity and Tax Complexity," *Journal of the American Taxation Association*, (Fall 1985), pp. 19–33.

Murray, A. (1985a), "Simplified, More Equitable System Is No Longer a Goal of Tax Debate, Overhaul Supporters Say," *The Wall Street Journal* (November 6, 1985), p. 62.

—— (1985b), "Revised U.S. Statistics Apt to Show Bigger, More Productive Economy," *The Wall Street Journal* (November 11, 1985), p. 21.

National Bureau of Economic Research, Inc., (1985), *The NBER Digest* (April 1985), p. 1.

Neter, J., W. Wasserman, and G. A. Whitmore (1978), *Applied Statistics*, (Allyn and Bacon, Inc., 1978).

Pearlman, R. A. (1984), "The Treasury Tax Plan—Yea and Nay," *Journal of Accountancy* (February 1985), p. 86.

The President's Tax Proposals to the Congress for Fairness, Growth and Simplicity (1985) (U.S. Government Printing Office, 1985).

Richmond, S. (1964), *Statistical Analysis*, second edition, (The Ronald Press, 1964) pp. 495–497.

Schroeder, J. D. (1975), "Potential Simplification of the Federal Income Tax Law by Eliminating Special Treatment of Capital Gains and Losses," Ph.D. dissertation (Michigan State University, 1975).

U.S. Department of the Treasury (1984–1985), *SOI Bulletin*, Internal Revenue Service (U.S. Government Printing Office, Winter 1984–85).

U.S. Department of the Treasury (1984), *Tax Reform for Fairness, Simplicity, and Economic Growth*, 2 vols., (U.S. Government Printing Office, 1984).

Webster's Third New International Dictionary of the English Language Unabridged (1981), p. 465.

APPENDIX A: COST ADJUSTMENT FACTORS TABLE PROVIDED TO SUBJECTS

Adjustment Factors for Property Sold During 1984

| | Quarter Sold in 1984 | | | |
	Jan., Feb., Mar.	Apr., May, June	July, Aug., Sept.	Oct., Nov., Dec.
QUARTER PURCHASED				
1983				
Jan., Feb., Mar.	1.057	1.069	1.073	1.084
Apr., May, June	1.039	1.043	1.061	1.062
July, Aug., Sept.	1.025	1.031	1.044	1.058
Oct., Nov., Dec.	1.012	1.026	1.045	1.046
1984				
Jan., Feb., Mar.	1.000	1.013	1.027	1.032
Apr., May, June	N/A	1.000	1.014	1.028
July, Aug., Sept.	N/A	N/A	1.000	1.001
Oct., Nov., Dec.	N/A	N/A	N/A	1.000

APPENDIX B: ADAPTATION OF FISHER'S INDEX

$$I_e = \sqrt{\frac{\Sigma e_i t_p}{\Sigma e_p t_p} \times \frac{\Sigma e_i t_i}{\Sigma e_p t_i}} \tag{1}$$

and

$$I_t = \sqrt{\frac{\Sigma t_i e_p}{\Sigma t_p e_p} \times \frac{\Sigma t_i e_i}{\Sigma t_p e_i}}, \tag{2}$$

where I_e = index for errors; I_t = index for time; t = time; e = errors; p = present method; i = indexation method.

These two indexes were combined to yield the equation for the Error/Time Complexity index

$$I_{et} = I_e \times I_t. \tag{3}$$

By substituting terms from Eqs. (1) and (2) into Eq. (3), the following equation resulted:

$$I_{et} = \sqrt{\frac{\Sigma e_i t_p}{\Sigma e_p t_p} \times \frac{\Sigma e_i t_i}{e_p t_i}} \times \sqrt{\frac{\Sigma t_i e_p}{\Sigma t_p e_p} \times \frac{\Sigma t_i e_i}{\Sigma t_p e_i}}. \tag{4}$$

Equation (4) reduced to

$$I_{et} = \frac{\Sigma e_i t_i}{\Sigma e_p t_p}. \tag{5}$$

FACTORS EMPIRICALLY ASSOCIATED
WITH FEDERAL TAX TRIAL CASE LOADS

Charles E. Boynton, IV and Jack Robison

ABSTRACT

The research objective was to determine if an association existed between certain broad economic and noneconomic variables and federal tax case loads in the Tax Court and the refund courts, and to suggest the policy consequences that might follow. Two significant differences were found. First, the number of returns examined by the IRS was positively related to refund court case load and not significantly associated with Tax Court case load. Secondly, the economic climate has a significant association with changes in the Tax Court case load but is not related to changes in refund court case loads. The possibility that this relationship was merely due to the difference between government and market interest rates was investigated and rejected. This suggests that an attribute that differentiates the two types of courts accounts for this difference, namely the ability to delay payment of the tax by petitioning the Tax Court.

Advances in Taxation, Volume 1, pages 169–182.
Copyright © 1987 JAI Press Inc.
All rights of reproduction in any form reserved.
ISBN: 0–89232–782–0

Despite a decrease in both the number of returns examined and proposed adjustments over the last decade, the number of petitions filed with the Tax Court has increased markedly. By 1984 this increase in the court's case load created a backlog of over 60,000 cases awaiting trial. This backlog affects both taxpayers and the government. It has resulted in a significant delay in the resolution of taxpayer disputes which has delayed receipt of more than $12 million in potential revenue. The research presented here analyzes a suggestion of Tax Court Judge Theodore Tannewald, Jr. that the escalating backlog of Tax Court cases was due in part to pressure put on taxpayers by the "current economic situation" (Bureau of National Affairs 1983, G-4). With that statement as the starting point, this analysis seeks to determine factors that are empirically associated with the number of petitions filed with the court. The resulting evidence may provide information beneficial in alleviating the current backlog.

The research objective was accomplished by using regression analysis to determine whether a change in the economic climate as evidenced by broad economic variables was in fact associated with the number of petitions filed with the Tax Court over the last 31 years. A simple noneconomic explanation was also examined, namely that the number of returns examined by the IRS determines the number of taxpayer disputes. The analysis was then expanded to determine whether a similar relationship existed between such variables and tax refund cases filed with the U.S. District Courts and the Claims Court (refund courts). The validity of the resulting models was further tested by determining if the same model explained both the first half and the second half of the 31-year period analyzed.

This paper is divided into six sections. The first part discusses the variables analyzed. The second part describes the analysis of Tax Court petitions. The third part describes the analysis performed on tax refund cases. The results and implications of the two analyses are presented in the fourth part. Limitations of the research are presented in the fifth part, and a brief conclusion is given in the final section.

THE VARIABLES ANALYZED

Data was gathered on two types of independent variables in order to identify possible factors associated with tax trial case loads. First, a broad set of economic variables was selected to test Judge Tannewald's hypothesis that the number of Tax Court petitions filed (here generalized to tax case petitions filed) was affected by current economic conditions. The period to which he referred (1980–1982) was one of little economic growth, high interest rates, and high unemployment. The authors, therefore, chose as tentative variables the percentage change in Gross National Product (GNP), the average short-term interest rate for small business loans for the year (market interest) as computed from data reported in the *Federal Reserve Bulletin* (Federal Reserve System 1960–1985), and the unemployment rate (unemployment). GNP was selected as a measure of the general robustness of the economy. The remaining two variables were viewed as associated with conditions making delayed payment of taxes substantially more desirable to taxpayers ("tight money").

Although numerous other economic variables exist, the purpose of the research was not to search for the best economic variable but to determine if economic variables in general are associated with work load changes. Due to the intercorrelation among economic indicators, those selected can be considered sufficient to reach a conclusion as to the association between changes in the economy and court work loads.

The fourth variable was a noneconomic factor potentially related to litigation, namely the annual number of returns examined by the Internal Revenue Service (IRS). No tax case is possible unless an audit occurs first.[1] The *Annual Report of Commissioner of Internal Revenue* provided comparable data from 1954 to 1984. Data available prior to 1954 combined mathematical error cases with returns examined by auditors and thus is not comparable (U.S. Department of Treasury 1954, p. 12). The data set was therefore limited to cases for the 31-year period beginning with 1954 and ending with 1984.

In summary, four independent variables were analyzed for this research:

1. Percentage change in GNP;
2. Market interest rate;
3. Unemployment rate;
4. Number of returns examined.

The dependent variable for the first stage of the research was the number of petitions filed in the Tax Court annually. The dependent variable for the second stage of the research was the number of refund suits filed. Both variables were gathered from the *Annual Report of Commissioner of Internal Revenue* (U.S. Department of Treasury 1954-1984). Figure 1 compares the relative change in total Tax Court case load to that of the refund courts for the 31-year period under study, using 1954 as a base year of 100 for both. The Tax Court consistently receives the vast majority of the tax cases filed—an average of just over 90 percent for the period under study (U.S. Department of Treasury 1954-1984). Prior to 1970, the number of filings in each type of court appeared somewhat stable; however the number of refund suits filed does not show the dramatic increase during the 1970s that occurs in Tax Court petitions.

Figure 1.   Comparison of changes in court caseload.

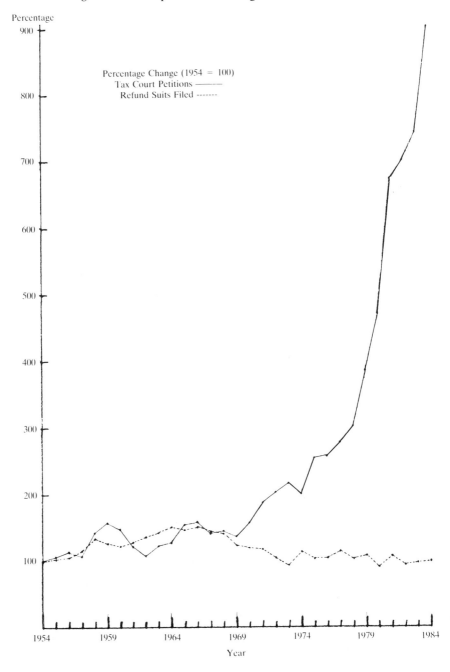

Table 1. Correlation Coefficients among the Variables

	Change in GNP	Unemployment Rate	Interest Rates
Change in GNP	1.000		
Unemployment Rate	−0.386	1.000	
Interest Rate	−0.333	0.639	1.000
Returns Examined	0.273	−0.395	−0.537

ANALYSIS OF TAX COURT PETITIONS

An initial analysis of the selected variables revealed a high degree of correlation among several of the variables (see Table 1). One of two methods are normally suggested to deal with such a situation: factor analysis or the use of a stepwise regression technique. Stepwise regression was selected because the elimination of variables from the model was not considered harmful where our goal was to confirm that economic conditions in general appear to be associated with Tax Court case loads (rather than to determine the association of one particular variable). This decision was further supported by the complexity that factor analysis adds to both the data analysis and the interpretation of results, and by the limited time period with which we were dealing.

The stepwise regression formula contained one independent variable[2] and had a R^2 of .76. Market interest was significantly positively associated with increased Tax Court case load (see Table 2 for complete details on the model). Because the data were observed over time, two further tests were performed before the model was accepted. First a Chow test was performed to test the model's stability over time. A model for each of the subperiods 1954–1968 and 1969–1984 was developed. Market interest had a positive sign in both subperiods and the Chow test revealed that, at a 95 percent confidence level, the coefficients were not different. The use of a general model covering the entire time period was therefore considered appropriate. Secondly the residuals were plotted over time to see if they were correlated. Such a correlation would violate the assumptions basic to inferential procedures and make conclusions about the model questionable. The plots showed a nonrandom weaving pattern of the residuals and their positive correlation was indicated by the Durbin-Watson *d* statistic value of 0.50 (significant at the 0.05 level). The standard errors obtained in the analysis may therefore be understated, leading to inflated *F* and *t*-values and therefore the possibility of incorrectly determining the significance of the model and/or included variables (Mendenhall and McClave 1981, pp. 470–473).

The dependent and independent variables were transformed to remove

Table 2.   Ordinary Least-Squares Regression Model for Tax Court

Variable Description		Coefficient	Standard Deviation	t score
Constant		− 5524.13	1919.61	2.88[a]
Market Interest		1955.74	200.06	9.78[b]
Summary Statistics:	R-Squared	= 0.76		
	F Statistic	= 95.6		
		signficant at .01 level		

Notes:
a. Significant at the 1 % level. Critical value for two-tail test is $t > \pm\ 2.76$.
b. Significant at the 1% level. Critical value for one-tail test is $t > 2.46$.

the correlation of the residuals over time using an autoregression technique.[3] The assumptions for regression analysis were then satisfied and the underestimation of the standard errors corrected. Thus the evaluation of the model and independent variables was possible. The results of this process are shown in Table 3.

The significance of the *t* value for the transformation confirms the results of the Durbin-Watson test: there is evidence of positive residual correlation. Furthermore, the first-order autoregressive model appears to describe this residual correlation well. A comparison between the ordinary least squares (OLS) (Table 2) and the autoregressive results (Table 3) reveals the following expected change: the mean square for error is reduced by 49 percent, resulting in slightly decreased *t* values. The conclusion that the linear relationship between Tax Court petitions and the market interest variable is of significant predictive value has not been altered.

RESULTS AND IMPLICATIONS

A variable empirically associated with the number of petitions received by the Tax Court during the 1954-to-1984 period has been identified. Economic conditions (as reflected by the inclusion of market interest) are significantly associated with the change in the Tax Court case load for the 31-year period under consideration.

The potential exists that the market interest variable was merely associated with Tax Court petitions because of its relationship to the interest charged by the government on tax deficiencies rather than because it was an indicator of the level of economic activity. The government charges interest from the time the tax was originally due to the date of payment should the taxpayer eventually lose in Tax Court. The government charged three percent on disputes governed by the Internal Revenue Code of 1939, and until the mid-1970s six percent was charged on assessments involving years

Table 3.   Autoregressive Model for Tax Court Petititions

Estimates of Autoregressive Parameters			
	Coefficient	t ratio	
	0.52	−3.42[a]	

Variable Description	Coefficient	Standard Deviation	t score
Constant	−3473.60	2738.48	−1.27
Market Interest	1789.35	275.95	6.48[a]
Summary Statistics:	R-Squared	= 0.82[b]	

Notes:
[a] Significant at the 1% level. Critical value for one-tail test is $t > 2.47$.
[b] Based on the original time-series values for court petitions.

governed by the 1954 code. Since 1975 the rate has been periodically adjusted, varying between 7 and 20 percent. Because the interest rate charged by the government was less than that charged by commercial lenders (market interest) during much of the time under examination, the potential exists that the Tax Court case load is not really affected by economic factors but instead by this potential for arbitrage. To test this theory an "interest differential" variable was created which reflected this potential gain or loss (for periods in which the government rate exceeded the market rate) accruing to taxpayers who prolonged their disputes with the government. Interest differential had a correlation with market interest of only .46, and when included in the regression equation it had a negative sign.[4] This was, of course, contrary to what would be expected and seemed to clearly support the conclusion that market interest was included in the model for reasons other than because it was a surrogate for such potential arbitrage.

The inclusion of an economic variable with a positive sign is consistent with Judge Tannewald's hypothesis that economic factors tend to influence taxpayer appeals. It should be noted that, because of the correlation among the economic variables under consideration, we are not stating that market interest is *the* sole economic variable which is related to Tax Court case load but merely that economic conditions in general appear to be related to the court's case load.

Judge Tannewald fails to explain the linkage between recession or tight money and Tax Court case loads. Two hypotheses seem appropriate:

1. During depressed economic periods taxpayers become more dissatisfied with the tax system[5] and are therefore more likely to litigate.
2. During depressed economic periods money becomes more scarce due to high interest rates and/or unemployment, and taxpayers are

therefore more likely to proceed to Tax Court since to do so delays the payment of the tax in dispute.

The study was therefore expanded to include an analysis of tax refund cases. Should a taxpayer decide to take a disagreement to either the district courts or Claims Court, it is necessary first to pay the tax and then sue for a refund. Because the tax must be paid, we would not expect recession and tight money to have any positive effect on a taxpayer's decision to sue for a refund if the second hypothesis were true. Therefore a finding that the number of refund suits is not positively related to the level of economic activity would tend to support the second hypothesis that tight money influences a taxpayer's decision to petition the Tax Court. Conversely, a significant positive relationship between the number of refund suits and the level of economic activity would tend to support hypothesis one, that recession and tight money increase taxpayer dissatisfaction or some similar factor and thus influence taxpayer appeals in general.

ANALYSIS OF REFUND SUITS FILED

The economic and returns examined variables remain the same in the refund suit analysis as in the previous Tax Court case analysis. Regression analysis was performed on these variables and the resulting equation contained only one independent variable: returns examined. Two submodels were developed to test for the stability of the model over time. The Chow test revealed that the coefficients were stable at the 95 percent confidence level. A plot of the residuals through time showed a nonrandom weaving pattern, and the Durbin-Watson d statistic of 1.12 indicated a positive correlation (at .05 significance level) among the residuals over time. The data was therefore reanalyzed using the autoregression technique discussed earlier and a first-order transformation was found to produce the most efficient results. The details of this model are shown in Table 4.

RESULTS AND IMPLICATIONS

Economic and noneconomic variables have been identified that are empirically associated with both the number of petitions received by the Tax Court from 1954 to 1984 and the number of refund suits filed with the district courts and Claims Court during the same period.

A comparison of the results for Tax Court cases with the results for refund court cases reveals two significant differences. First, the number of returns examined is positively related to the case load of refund courts and not significantly associated with Tax Court case load. Thus the tax-related

Table 4. Autoregressive Model for Tax Refund Suits

	Estimates of Autoregressive Parameters		
	Coefficient	*t ratio*	
	0.43	2.65[a]	
Variable Description	*Coefficient*	*Standard Deviation*	*t score*
Constant	633.41	94.74	6.69[b]
Returns Examined	0.21	0.04	5.81[a]
Summary Statistics:	R-Squared	= 0.71[c]	

Notes:
a. Significant at the 1% level. Critical value for one-tail test is $t > 2.47$.
b. Significant at the 1% level. Critical value for two-tail test is $t > \pm 2.76$.
c. Based on the original time-series values for court petitions.

case load of the refund courts followed the IRS case load by gradually increasing through the mid-1960s and then decreasing to its 1954 level by 1984.

Secondly, the economic climate (as reflected in the market interest variable) has a significant association with changes in the Tax Court case load but is not related to changes in the case load of the refund courts. This suggests that it is an attribute differentiating the Tax Court from the refund courts that accounts for this difference, namely the ability to delay payment of the tax by petitioning the Tax Court. When recession causes money to become a scarce resource, taxpayers are more likely to protest a proposed deficiency than during robust economic periods when money is more plentiful. This is consistent with the General Accounting Office's suggestion that taxpayers in Tax Court employ delaying tactics and their recommendation that a control of such delaying tactics may reduce the backlog at Tax Court [General Accounting Office 1984, p. 29]. It is also consistent with the rationale underlying the changes in the appeals process recently introduced by Representative Fortney H. ("Pete") Stark in HR 6125: "taxpayers increasingly have selected the judicial process hoping for a more favorable outcome and prolongation of their cases" (Bureau of National Affairs 1984, G-1). If the ability to delay is the chief attraction of Tax Court, limiting that ability should reduce that attractiveness.

LIMITATIONS

This research is based on data from cases tried over a 31-year period. Results and conclusions concerning factors associated with changing court case loads may therefore not be applicable to future (or prior) time periods.

Because this research involves a broad macro-type analysis, it is difficult to show a cause-and-effect type of relationship. In other words, it is not clear whether a change in economic activity caused a change in taxpayer actions or whether one or more other factors guided taxpayer decisions, with only a coincidental correlation of economic factors and the final decision. The correlation of the residuals over time in the models for both types of cases indicates that there is some variable affecting the number of petitions which is not considered in the model. Such a situation is not expected in a model that attempts to capture a complex relationship but contains only one of the underlying variables. An example of a missing factor might be the fact that the public's overall tendency to litigate has increased rapidly over the 31-year period under study;[6] this may actually be the primary cause of the increased Tax Court case load. However, the fact that the number of refund suits did not increase in the 1970s fails to support this conclusion.

A fundamental change in pretrial procedures does deserve examination. This involves the change from a double to a single level of pre-trial appeal process in 1978. Before October 2, 1978, the IRS provided the taxpayer with two separate levels for pre-trial review of proposed deficiencies. The first level, district conference, was handled in the office of the district director, and the second level, appellate conference, was in the Appellate Division. The appellate conference was available both to taxpayers who bypassed the district conference and to those who did not reach agreement there. The first level of review handled approximately 50,000 cases per year and the second level 20,000, (with approximately one-half that work load consisting of appeals from the district conference) (Treusch 1978, p. 499). After the change was made to a single-level appeals, activities were consolidated under the control of a regional director of appeals in each IRS region. The change was made because the IRS felt the "two-level system was a costly duplication both for the taxpayer and the service" (U.S. Department of Treasury 1979, p. 29). A former IRS Assistant Chief Counsel predicted that such a change might deter taxpayers from utilizing administrative review altogether and dump "thousands of cases that are now resolved at that stage into the already overloaded court dockets" (Treusch 1978, p. 500). Regressions were computed adding a before or after (zero or one)[7] variable to the equation to see if there was any shift in either the Tax Court or refund court case loads in 1979 and later years due to this administrative change. The variable loaded significantly for the Tax Court analysis (see Table 5) but not for the refund suit analysis. Because the previous pre-trial appeal procedure did not require any payment of tax, it is reasonable for taxpayers affected by this change to proceed to Tax Court rather than pay the tax and file a refund suit. Therefore, the difference in the outcomes appears proper. Such a result does not, of course, prove that

Table 5. Autoregressive Model for Tax Court Petitions Including a Single-Level Pre-trial Appeal Variable

	Estimates of Autoregressive Parameters			
	Coefficient	t ratio		
	0.43	2.62[a]		

Variable Description	Coefficient	Beta	Standard Deviation	t score
Constant	808.67	—	2822.43	0.29
Market Interest	1,017.11	0.45	366.42	2.78[a]
Single Level Appeal	10,807.47	.46	3659.59	2.95[a]
Summary Statistics:	R-Squared	= 0.87[b]		

Notes:
[a]Significant at the 1% level. Critical value for one-tail test is t > 2.47.
[b]Based on the original time-series data for court petitions.

the shift was caused by the change in pre-trial procedures but merely shows that the data is consistent with such a conclusion.

The increase in the Tax Court case load during the later years might be due to some fundamental change in taxpayer perception of the tax system. One possible cause might be the increased frequency of tax law changes during the 1970s, but again, one would expect any such change to affect both Tax Court and refund cases in a similar manner. Judge Tannewald suggested that "the growing dissatisfaction of citizens with the tax system" has also contributed to an increased Tax Court case load (Bureau of National Affairs 1983, G-4). Unfortunately, there is no accurate index of taxpayer dissatisfaction with the tax system.[8]

CONCLUSIONS

This paper focused on several factors associated with a large increase in the Tax Court case load during recent years. In 1982, Chief Tax Court Judge Tannewald hypothesized that the increase was due to the "current economic situation." During 1982, the United States was experiencing a recessionary economy. The interest rate for small business loans (market interest) was, in fact, found to be highly associated with the increase in Tax Court case load. A possible problem with the explanation given here is that the rapid increase in Tax Court case load during recent years tends to swamp any variance found in the 1954–1968 period. To ensure that the association between market interest and Tax Court case load was valid for the entire time period under study, separate models were developed for 1954–1968 and 1969–1984. Market interest was found to be positively significant in each period. This is consistent with the overall model.

The possibility that the Tax Court case load could be explained by the arbitrage potential available due to the difference between the interest rate charged by the government and that charged by banks was investigated. No support was found for this explanation. When the analysis was expanded to include refund suits, an explanation for the relationship between recession, tight money, and Tax Court case load became obvious.

The case load of the refund courts is associated with the number of tax returns the IRS examines, but it does not appear to be influenced by economic conditions such as changes in GNP, the market rate of interest, or unemployment. When these results are coupled with the fact that taxpayers need not pay the tax in dispute prior to proceeding to Tax Court (whereas the opposite is true in refund suits), they are consistent with the conclusion that the desire to delay payment of taxes during times of tight money may be responsible for the increased number of taxpayers choosing to litigate in Tax Court, and therefore for the increase in the Tax Court case load. The decision to delay the payment of a proposed deficiency by petitioning the Tax Court (or to eliminate payment, should the taxpayer win in Tax Court) appears to be influenced by the cost and the availability of funds to pay the assessment. The change to a single level of pretrial appeals also appears to have affected the Tax Court case load but not the refund court case load.

These findings have policy implications for the government. The attractiveness of the Tax Court appears to lie in its opportunity for delay, and, as general economic conditions make delay more desirable, more cases go to the Tax Court. The policy implications with respect to Tax Court backlog would appear to suggest procedural changes to restrict the opportunity for delay rather than an increase in the number of Tax Court judges. Congress' decision to provide a court where taxpayers may protest an assessment without the "great financial hardship and sacrifice" of having their liability determined prior to its payment (U.S. Congress, House 1924, p. 7) may impose significant costs to the government during periods of recession and tight money. It may be necessary to impose additional filing costs or to legislate new penalties (or impose existing penalties more frequently) for cases lacking in substance in order to dissuade taxpayers from filing petitions in marginal situations.[9] The General Accounting Office has suggested the need for procedural changes in the calling of cases to limit the ability of taxpayers to delay trial in the Tax Court after petitions are filed (General Accounting Office 1984, p. 29). A diminished opportunity to delay in Tax Court might lead to a lessened attractiveness of that court if delay alone were the principal objective in choosing the Tax Court.

The investigation also demonstrates the feasibility of developing empirically testable theories with policy implications which examine the process by which taxpayers decide to litigate tax assessment. Further work in the area of taxpayer decisions may lead to suggestions for changes in the tax assessment administrative system and perhaps in the design of tax laws and their required supporting documentation.

NOTES

1. Although the number of returns with audit adjustments might be a better indicator of this variable, this data is only available for 1963 to the present. Because of the high correlation between the number of returns audited and the number of returns with proposed adjustments (.84), and the fact that using the adjustment data would limit the analysis to 21 time periods, the decision was made to use the number of returns audited as the input variable.

2. The program employed was the SPSS regression analysis which uses a forward stepwise inclusion technique [Nie et al. 1975, pp. 345–347]. The drop in the sum of squares for error was analyzed using a .01 level of significance for F to determine the number of independent variables to include in the equation (Mendenhall and McClave 1981, pp. 228–229).

3. Gallant and Goebel (1976) suggest a method for estimating the parameters of a linear model whose error term is assumed to be an autoregressive process of a given order. The SAS AUTOREG program uses this method to transform the data in the following manner: First estimates of the model $Y = X + u$ using ordinary least squares are derived. Computations of the autocovariances up to lag p of the residuals from the OLS regression are then made.

The Yule-Walker equations are solved to obtain estimates $a_1, \cdots, a_p$ of the autoregressive parameters, $\alpha_1 \cdots \alpha_p$, and a preliminary estimate of σ^2. The Yule Walker equations are of the form:

Toep $(r_0, \cdots, r_{p-1})$ a $= (r_1, \cdots, r_p)'$ where $(r_1, \cdots, r_p)'$ is the pxl vector of autocovariances and Toep is the Toeplitz operator.

All the variables from the original data are transformed. The first p observations are transformed using:

$$z = SPx$$

where P is a Choleski root of Toep $(r_0, \cdots, r_{p-1})^{-1}$. The transformation is different if a subset model is used. The remaining observations are transformed by the autoregressive model:

$$z_t = x_t + a_1 x_{t-1} + \cdots + a_p x_{t-p}$$

Then, using the transformed data, β is re-estimated by an OLS regression. This is equivalent to a generalized least squares estimate with appropriate weights. (SAS Institute Inc. 1982, p. 191).

This technique was used employing a first-through third-order transformation. A first-order transformation produced the most efficient results.

4. An alternative method of specifying this variable was also explored. In situations where the government rate exceeded the market rate (situations originally coded as negative values), zero was used. The rationale for this coding was that there would be no advantage in not paying the tax in such a situation. When the interest differential variable was coded in this manner it again loaded with a counterintuitive negative sign.

5.   Attitudes toward taxes have been shown to be associated with economic indicators in past research (Citrin 1979, p. 115).

6.   The number of U.S. civil nontax cases filed was used as an indicator of the overall tendency to litigate (Administrative Office of U.S. Courts).

7.   Although the use of such an ordinal variable violates the assumptions underlying analysis, past research has shown that regression is robust enough to be insensitive to such violations (Harris 1975, p. 7).

8.   Opinion polls have asked taxpayers: "Do you consider the amount of income tax you (your husband) have (had) to pay as too high, too low, or about right?" (*Public Opinion* 1978, p. 31). However, these polls have been conducted at sporadic intervals, and there is some question as to whether such surveys provide an accurate index of taxpaper dissatisfaction.

9.   Although Sec. 6673, which provides for penalties of up to $5,000 against taxpayers instituting proceedings merely for delay, has been applied with increasing frequency by the Tax Court, it tends to be applied only in extreme situations (e.g., tax protestors). A possible sign that the Tax Court will be taking a more stringent position is its new rule with respect to filings. Per a February, 1986 news announcement every paper filed with the Court must now be signed. One purpose of such signature is to certify that the document "is not interposed for any improper purpose, such as harassment or delay" (Research Institute 1986, p. 43).

REFERENCES

Administrative Office of U.S. Courts (1965–1984), *Annual Report of the Director* (1965–1984).

Bureau of National Affairs (1983), "No Reduction in Tax Court Backlog Seen by Chief Judge," *Daily Tax Report* (March 7, 1983), pp. A, G-4, G-5.

_____ (1984), "Stark Bill Would Limit Tax Litigation," *Daily Tax Report* (August 15, 1984), pp. A-1, A-2, G-1.

Citrin, J. (1979), "Do People Want Something for Nothing: Public Opinion on Taxes and Government Spending," *National Tax Journal* (June 1979), pp. 113–119.

Federal Reserve System (1960–1985), Board of Governors, *Federal Reserve Bulletin* (Board of Governors of Federal Reserve System, 1960–1985).

Gallant, A. R., and J. J. Goebel (1976), "Nonlinear Regression with Autoregressive Errors," *Journal of the American Statistical Association* (December 1976), pp. 961–967.

General Accounting Office (1984), *Report to the Chief Judge United States Tax Court* (General Accounting Office, 1984).

Harris, R. J. (1975), *A Primer of Multivariate Statistics* (Academic Press, 1975).

Mendenhall, W., and J. T. McClave (1981), *A Second Course in Business Statistics Regression Analysis* (Dellen Publishing Company, 1981).

Nie, N. H., C. H. Hall, J. G. Jenkins, K. Steinbrenner and D. H. Bent (1975), *Statistical Package for the Social Sciences* (McGraw-Hill, 1975).

Public Opinion (1978), "Opinion Roundup" (July–August 1978), pp. 30–31.

Research Institute of America (1986) *Weekly Alert* (Research Institute of America, February 13, 1986).

SAS Institute Inc. (1982), *SAS/ETS User's Guide* (SAS Institute, 1982).

Treusch, P. E. (1978), "The District Conference—Can It Be Saved and Is It Worth Saving? *Taxes* (August 1978), pp. 498–503.

U.S. Congress, House, H. Rept. No. 179, 68th Cong. (1924), 1st Sess. (February 11,1924).

U.S. Department of Treasury, Internal Revenue Service (1954–1984), *Annual Report of Commissioner of Internal Revenue* (1954–1984).

QUALIFICATIONS FOR A TAX SPECIALIST:

SOME TAX PARTNERS' VIEWS

Peggy A. Hite

ABSTRACT

Specialization is becoming more and more evident in the accounting arena. Whether or not specialization will be formalized by a certification process remains to be seen. In the present study, tax partners of randomly selected CPA (Certified Public Accountants) firms completed questionnaires voicing their opinions about qualifications for a tax specialization. The importance of education, experience, a qualifying exam, periodic exams, and letters of reference were examined.

The issue of recognized specializations for the Certified Public Accountant has been discussed time and time again, but attempts to designate such specialists have repeatedly failed on the national level (Olson 1982). Recently however, the Colorado Society of Certified Public Accountants began a program for designating specialists. The first type of specialist

Advances in Taxation, Volume 1, pages 183–198.
Copyright © 1987 JAI Press Inc.
All rights of reproduction in any form reserved.
ISBN: 0–89232–782–0

designated was the Accredited Financial Planning Specialist. In the near future, two more specializations are to be formalized: the Governmental Audit Specialist and Computer Systems Specialist. These specialties were created to help the users of the CPA services become more informed about the advice they are purchasing.

A call to help potential buyers of tax accounting services has also been expressed by Johnson (1984). To assist the buyers of tax services, the information perspective has frequently been advocated. An information perspective views occupational licensing and certification arrangements as screening/signaling mechanisms. Screening mechanisms help potential buyers to differentiate between high- and low-quality services. Signaling mechanisms enable competent sellers to certify the quality of their services to the market. According to Akerlof (1970), an uncorrected asymmetry between buyers and sellers is a type of market failure called "adverse selection" which he explains as follows:

> There are many markets in which buyers use some market statistic to judge the quality of prospective purchases, e.g., average quality. In this case, there is incentive for sellers to market poor quality merchandise since the returns for good quality accrue mainly to the entire group whose statistic is affected rather than to the individual seller. As a result, there tends to be a reduction in the average quality of goods and also in the size of the market (p. 492).

The two primary mechanisms by which high-quality sellers differentiate their services from low-quality services are mandatory licensing and voluntary licensing arrangements. In mandatory or occupational licensing, certain minimum entry and/or retention requirements are imposed by law on all individuals desiring to sell a particular type of service. By contrast, voluntary or occupational certification does not legally restrict the sellers, but it provides them an opportunity voluntarily to obtain evidence of their competency (Johnson 1984). The American Taxation Association (ATA) has voiced support of the occupational certification mechanism. In 1982, the ATA's Committee on Certification of Tax Specialists recommended a voluntary arrangement that would be open to CPAs and non-CPAs. Thus, tax practitioners who could satisfy certain minimum educational and experience requirements and who could pass a specially designed competency examination could earn the designation as a Certified Tax Specialist (CTS). While that recommendation has not yet been implemented, such action may be fast approaching if other states begin to copy Colorado's specialization programs.

Another factor leading to specialization is the withdrawal of Interpretation 502–4 by the Ethics Executive Committee of the American Institute of CPAs (AICPA). Thus, as long as a claim is not false or deceptive, a claim of specialization is no longer prohibited. It is this freedom to claim to be a specialist that may lead to controlled requirements for accreditation in specific areas.

One of the major concerns with any specialization program is the determination of requirements for obtaining and maintaining certification in a given specialty. As the AICPA membership has long opposed the designation of specialists (Olson 1982), it is imperative that the opinions of CPAs be considered prior to establishing such programs. The present study surveyed some tax partners in CPA firms to gain insights into the appropriate prerequisites for obtaining designation as a tax specialist and requirements for maintaining this type of accreditation.

METHODOLOGY

Surveys were sent to tax partners of certified public accountant firms. The firms were randomly selected from a membership roster of CPA firms. The study utilized two separate surveys—one on opinions about prerequisites for obtaining and requirements for maintaining a tax specialization, and second to examine the importance of education and experience when determining salaries for new tax employees. One hundred tax specialization surveys were mailed to tax partners and thirty-six completed surveys were returned (a 36% response rate). The response rate for the survey on salaries for new tax hirees was 23%. Fifteen firms responded with the salaries and pertinent data of 91 employees.

Task

The opinions of tax partners in CPA firms were solicited to examine the importance of qualities that may be used in establishing criteria for tax specialization. Likert statements were used to seek agreement or disagreement on various statements (1 = "strongly agree", and 5 = "strongly disagree"). The questionnaire began by investigating opinions on education, experience, and references when hiring tax employees. Next, subjects responded to statements about education, experience, and references for becoming a tax specialist. The last section concerned requirements on education, experience, and references for maintaining certification as a tax specialist. The questionnaire was designed with three settings to examine whether the criteria differed when applied to different purposes. Consistent responses in all three settings strengthens the results. In addition, responses that differ among the settings could indicate self-interested responses. For instance, if experience is valued when judging which tax employee to hire, then experience should be an important characteristic when judging firms and their employees as tax specialists. Thus, this study posed the following two questions:

1. What are the qualities that are perceived as important when hiring tax employees, when certifying tax specialists, and when maintaining a tax specialization?
2. Is the relative importance of job qualities such as experience and education consistent in decisions involving the hiring of tax employees, the certifying of tax specialists and the maintaining of a tax specialty certification?

A separate survey was sent to a different group of randomly selected CPA firms to examine how education and experience affected the salaries paid to new tax employees. The purpose of this part of the study was to serve as a check on the perceived importance of education and experience as reported in the Likert-type responses. If the opinions indicated that experience was important, then experience should have been an important factor for determining salaries. The following question was examined:

3. Is the relative importance of education and experience reflected in the salaries of new tax employees?

This second survey was sent to an independent group of CPA firms. Segregation of the two surveys was necessary so that respondents did not purposefully coordinate the responses on the two instruments.

RESULTS

Descriptive statistics (means, standard deviations, and frequency of responses) for each item in the first survey are presented in Appendix A. The first twelve survey questions deal with the hiring process for tax employees. Questions 13–24 involve the process of certification as a tax specialist, and questions 25–30 concern the requirements for maintaining certification as a tax specialist. The results are discussed in the same order.

When hiring tax employees, the strongest opinion was that sex of the applicant was unimportant (94 percent disagreed that sex was important). The next demographic factor was age. Respondents (73 percent of them) disagreed that age was important.

Education was important for hiring tax employees, but note that 77 percent agreed accounting education was important, compared to 65 percent who agreed tax education was important. A master's degree in taxation was more important (36 percent) than a master's degree in accounting (18

Table 1. Average Responses to Important Characteristics for Hiring Tax Employees*

Characteristic	Mean	Standard Deviation
Tax Education	2.06	0.89
Accounting Education	2.09	0.97
Employer References	2.35	1.10
Tax Experience	2.56	1.19
Accounting Experience	2.77	1.13
Institution	2.82	1.17
Master's Degree in Taxation	3.06	1.18
Faculty references	3.27	0.99
Master's Degree in Accounting	3.77	0.99
Age	4.03	0.90
Sex	4.53	0.71

Notes:
*1 = Very Important; 5 = Very Unimportant.

percent), but neither received much support as being important. The institution providing the education was rather important (53 percent agreed). Tax experience was important (50 percent) and accounting experience was less important (44 percent agreed). Note, however, that there was a larger percentage of respondents agreeing to the importance of education than to the importance of experience (65 percent and 77 percent for tax and accounting education versus 50 percent and 44 percent for tax and accounting experience). Only 21 percent agreed that faculty references were important but 74 percent agreed that previous employer references were important. Table 1 summarizes the relative importance on these questions according to mean responses. The results indicate that more respondents agreed education was important than were agreed on the importance of employer references or work experience.

The next group of questions investigated similar characteristics as to their importance for receiving certification as a tax specialist. First, subjects were asked if CPAs should encourage specialization without specific certification. Most respondents (67 percent) agreed. Conversely, when asked if certification should be required, 60 percent disagreed. If a tax specialization were approved, 70 percent thought it should be for a general tax specialist and not categorized by designations such as corporate or estate tax specialist.

Respondents were asked to respond to the level of importance of certain characteristics as prerequisites if a program for tax specialization were adopted. The qualities that were examined concerned education, experience, references, and a qualifying exam. The mean responses for these items are presented in Table 2.

Table 2.   Average Responses to Important Characteristics for Becoming a
Tax Specialist*

Characteristic	Mean	Standard Deviation
Tax Experience	1.59	0.86
Education	2.21	1.08
References	2.88	1.12
Qualifying Exam	4.24	1.05

Notes:
*1 = Strongly agree as to importance;
 5 = Strongly disagree.

Table 3.   Responses to Important Characteristics for Maintaining
a Tax Certification*

Characteristic	Mean	Standard Deviation
Tax Experience	2.09	0.93
Experience over Education	2.65	1.01
Education over Experience	3.47	0.99
Periodic Exam	3.53	1.24
References	4.09	0.75

Notes:
*1 = Strongly agree to importance; 5 = Strongly disagree.

Table 4.   Significant Results for One-Way ANOVA on Survey Responses
by Size of Tax Staff

Variable	F Statistic	Value
For hiring tax department employees how important is:		
Prior accounting education	9.945	.004
Prior tax experience	13.218	.001
Prior accounting experience	20.332	.000
Under 30 years of age	5.816	.023

Experience was the most important prerequisite, with 91 percent agreeing, followed by education, references, and a qualifying exam. To be more precise, two comparative questions were asked about the relative importance of education and experience. Experience was more important than education according to 70 percent of the respondents. A comparative question was also asked concerning education versus the qualifying exam. When asked if education itself should eliminate the need for a qualifying exam, 82 percent disagreed. Likewise, 76 percent disagreed that experience alone should eliminate the need for a qualifying exam. When asked if a qualifying exam was sufficient by itself (see Table 2), 88 percent disagreed. In short, subjects believed some combination of the three—experience, education, and qualifying exam—was important, and most agreed that experience was important.

The last group of questions examined requirements for maintaining a tax certification. The mean scores are presented in Table 3. The results indicate that annual tax experience is most important for maintaining a certification in the tax area (74 percent agreed). To examine the relative importance of education and experience, two comparative statements were presented. In both statements experience was more important than education, with at least 50 percent agreeing. The majority (59 percent) disagreed that periodic exams were important, and 81 percent disagreed that periodic letters of reference were important.

To insure that the results were representative of both large and small firms, the respondents were divided into two groups according to the size of their tax staffs. Those with 6 or fewer tax staff were assigned to one group while those with more than 6 (up to 200) were in the second group. One-way analyses of variances were then performed to see if responses to statements on the survey differed according to the size of the tax staffs. Variables that significantly differed ($p < .05$) on the size factor are presented in Table 4. The size factor did not affect responses concerning the prerequisites for becoming and requirements for being a tax specialist. Differences were found, however, on some characteristics for hiring tax employees. The perceived importance of prior accounting education differed significantly ($p = .004$) between the large and small tax staffs. Firms with small tax staffs reported that accounting education was important (mean 1.78, standard deviation .67) while large firms were more neutral as to the importance of prior accounting education (mean 3.00, standard deviation 1.22). Opinions also differed significantly on tax experience ($p = .001$). Small firms thought experience was more important (mean 2.26, standard deviation 1.01) than did the large firms (mean 4.00, standard deviation .71). Likewise, accounting experience was more important to small firms (mean 2.35, standard deviation .83) than to large firms (mean 4.20, standard deviation .84). The other significant difference ($p = .023$) involved an age variable. Being under 30 years of age for an entry-level position was neither important nor unimportant to large firms (mean 3.00, standard deviation 1.58), but age was definitely unimportant to the small firms (mean 4.17, standard deviation .83). One other factor, master's degree in taxation, was significantly different ($p = .060$). Large firms tended to agree that the master's in

Table 5. Stepwise Regression for Factors Related to
Salary when Hiring Tax Employees

Significant Variables	Beta Coefficient	
Degree	0.580**	
Tax Experience	0.274*	
Years of Tax Experience	0.257*	
Adjusted R^2 = 0.484**		

Nonsignificant Variables	Beta Coefficient	Value
Year Hired	0.049	0.555
Sex	0.007	0.948
Accounting Education	0.209	0.063
Tax Education	0.145	0.199
Accounting Experience	0.086	0.449
Years of Accounting Experience	0.160	0.156

Notes:
  *p <0.05
  **p <0.001

taxation was important (mean 2.20, standard deviation .84) while small firms did not (mean 3.30, standard deviation 1.18).

In the second part of this study, salary information along with education and experience data were requested on new tax employees. A stepwise regression analysis was performed to see what variables best explained salary. Table 5 presents the results, which indicate that the educational degree was the most important variable (ρ < .001). In other words, a master's degree resulted in more salary than did an undergraduate degree. Tax experience as a dichotomous (yes or no) response was significantly related to salary as was the interval response for years of tax experience. To insure that certain large firms were not driving the results, firm size was statistically controlled. The regression model was still significant with degree and tax experience as significant factors (ρ < .01). In this case, however, tax experience (beta coefficient .448) was more important than educational degree (beta coefficient .264). In addition, years of accounting experience was a significant variable (ρ < .01) in this model with a .205 beta coefficient.

CONCLUSIONS

Specialization is becoming more and more evident in the accounting arena. Whether or not the specialization should be formalized by a certification process remains to be seen. In the present study, tax partners of randomly selected CPA firms completed questionnaires voicing their opinions about qualifications for a tax specialization.

The first point to be emphasized is that respondents did agree that specialization should be encouraged. Assuming that specialization did occur, experience was important both for becoming a tax specialist and for maintaining that tax specialty. Most agreed that experience was more important than education, but education was also considered important for the prerequisites and requirements of a tax specialist. A qualifying exam was considered important for becoming certified but not for maintaining the certification. Similarly, letters of reference were perceived as important for prerequisites but not for requirements to maintain the certification. It is interesting to note that these findings did not differ according to the size of the firm.

In the hiring of tax employees, education was reported as more important than experience. This is in contrast to the certification statements that indicated experience was the more important factor. The issue then becomes whether the results are inconsistent or whether the different situations necessitated different priorities. A second survey also analyzed the qualifications for hiring by requesting data on new tax employees. In this study, salary was explained by level of educational degree, and by tax experience. Thus, those with a master's degree and those with previous tax experience tended to receive more salary. The results from the regression analysis indicated that degree was important but education per se was not. Analysis of variance results indicated that preference for a master's degree in taxation was dependent on firm size. When results were controlled for firm size, tax experience was more important in determining salary. It is interesting to note that education was more important on the opinion survey for hiring characteristics but in the salary survey experience was linked to a higher salary. To explain this apparent inconsistency, it may be conjectured that experience is not generally expected of new employees and so is not a major factor at that stage.

This study is limited by the generalizability of the results as it involved CPAs from one state only. That state was chosen due to its recent designations of targeted specialties. Another limitation is suggested by the nature of the study. Since the survey asked for opinions, those opinions could be based on motives that reflect self-interest rather than concern about the users of the CPA's tax services. Nonetheless, the opinions of constituents must be considered prior to implementation of certification programs.

Future research should examine how the amount of experience and education could be measured to insure that adequate levels of both characteristics are considered in any certification process. For instance, tax experience may be measured in billable hours, but depending on the nature of the work those hours may not reflect sufficient levels of expertise. Hours of education may also not be a proper surrogate for expertise. Perhaps continuing education credits should include tests at the end of each course. Research should also focus on the proper balance between education and experience. Another area of future research is to seek opinions from users and potential users of the services. Secondary resources such as lawsuits against tax preparers may provide insight to qualifications that need to be enforced.

This study indicates that informal specialization should be encouraged but specific certification should not. If certification in the tax area becomes a reality, experience and education are the primary qualifications to be considered. A qualifying exam is important as a prerequisite but not as a periodic requirement. Letters of reference were marginally important for certification, and they were very unimportant for maintaining the certification. Since experience and education are vital to the certification process, the profession should begin to examine how the quality—and not just the quantity—of these characteristics can be monitored.

REFERENCES

Akerlof, G. A. (1970), "The Market for Lemons: Quality Uncertainty and the Market Mechanism," *Quarterly Journal of Economics*, (August 1970), pp. 488–500.

Johnson, S. B. (1984), "An Economic Perspective on the Certification of Specialists in Tax Accounting," *The Journal of the American Taxation Association*, (Spring 1984) pp. 27–39).

Olson, W. E. (1982), "Specialization: Search for a Solution," *Journal of Accountancy*, (September 1982), pp. 70–79.

APPENDIX A: DESCRIPTIVE STATISTICS BY QUESTIONNAIRE ITEM*

	Very Impor- tant	Impor- tant	Some- what Impor- tant	Un- Impor- tant	Very Unim- por- tant
1. How important is the amount of prior tax education for hiring tax department employees?	1	2	3	4	5
[$\overline{X}$ 2.06, S.D. .89]	(32)	(33)	(32)	(3)	(0)

	1	2	3	4	5
2. How important is the amount of prior accounting education for hiring tax department employees? [$\overline{X}$ 2.09, S.D. .97]	(27)	(50)	(15)	(6)	(2)
3. How important is the amount of prior tax experience for hiring tax department employees? [$\overline{X}$ 2.56, S.D. 1.19]	(24)	(26)	(24)	(24)	(2)
4. How important is the amount of prior accounting experience for hiring tax department employees? [$\overline{X}$ 2.77, S.D. 1.13]	(12)	(32)	(32)	(15)	(9)
5. How important is the institution (that grants an educational degree to the applicant) for hiring tax department employees? [$\overline{X}$ 2.82, S.D. 1.17]	(6)	(47)	(18)	(18)	(11)
6. How important is a master's degree in taxation for hiring tax department employees? [$\overline{X}$ 3.06, S.D. 1.18]	(9)	(27)	(26)	(27)	(11)
7. How important is a master's degree in accounting for hiring tax department employees? [$\overline{X}$ 3.77, S.D. .99]	(0)	(18)	(9)	(53)	(20)
8. How important is the sex of the applicant for hiring tax department employees? [$\overline{X}$ 4.53, S.D. .71]	(0)	(3)	(3)	(32)	(62)

9. How important is it that the applicant be less than 30 years of age for an entry level position?

	1	2	3	4	5
[$\overline{X}$ 4.03, S.D. 1.06]	(3)	(6)	(18)	(32)	(41)

10. How important is the age of the applicant for hiring tax department employees?

	1	2	3	4	5
[$\overline{X}$ 4.03, S.D. .90]	(0)	(6)	(21)	(38)	(35)

11. How important are faculty references for hiring tax department employees?

	1	2	3	4	5
[$\overline{X}$ 3.27, S.D. .99]	(0)	(21)	(50)	(11)	(18)

12. How important are previous employer references for hiring tax department employees?

	1	2	3	4	5
[$\overline{X}$ 2.35, S.D. 1.10]	(32)	(33)	(32)	(3)	(0)

	Strongly Agree	Agree	Uncertain	Disagree	Strongly Disagree

13. As CPAs, we should encourage specialization without specific certification.

	1	2	3	4	5
[$\overline{X}$ 2.46, S.D. 1.18]	(18)	(49)	(9)	(18)	(6)

14. As CPAs, we should encourage specialization by requiring special certification.

	1	2	3	4	5
[$\overline{X}$ 3.61, S.D. 1.22]	(6)	(16)	(18)	(33)	(27)

15. If certification were to occur in the tax area, there should be a specialist designation for each area (i.e., Individual, Corporate, Estate)

	1	2	3	4	5
[$\overline{X}$ 3.73, S.D. 1.38]	(12)	(9)	(9)	(33)	(37)

16. If certification were to occur in the tax area, there should be only one designation and that should be the tax specialist.

	1	2	3	4	5
[$\overline{X}$ 2.44, S.D. 1.16]	(18)	(50)	(9)	(18)	(5)

17. In the tax area some amount of educational tax training should be a prerequisite for certification.

	1	2	3	4	5
[$\overline{X}$ 2.21, S.D. 1.08]	(24)	(49)	(15)	(6)	(6)

18. In the tax area some amount of work experience should be a prerequisite for certification.

	1	2	3	4	5
[$\overline{X}$ 1.59, S.D. .86]	(56)	(35)	(6)	(0)	(3)

19. In the tax area experience and education are not an issue for certification as long as the applicant can pass an initial certifying exam.

	1	2	3	4	5
[$\overline{X}$ 4.24, S.D. 1.05]	(32)	(33)	(32)	(3)	(0)

20. In the tax area experience should be more important than education as a prerequisite to certification.

	1	2	3	4	5
[$\overline{X}$ 2.15, S.D. 1.05]	(29)	(41)	(18)	(9)	(3)

21. To be certified in the tax area, applicants should supply letters of reference to document their experience.

	1	2	3	4	5
[$\overline{X}$ 2.88, S.D. 1.12]	(3)	(50)	(12)	(27)	(8)

22. In the tax area education should be more important than experience as a prerequisite for certification.

	1	2	3	4	5
[$\overline{X}$ 3.91, S.D. .79]	(3)	(0)	(18)	(62)	(17)

23. To be certified as a tax spe- 1 2 3 4 5
cialist, experience should
speak for itself, thus eliminating the need for a qualifying exam.
[$\overline{X}$ 4.09, S.D. 1.00]   (3)   (6)   (9) (44) (38)

24. To be certified as a tax spe- 1 2 3 4 5
cialist, experience should
speak for itself, thus eliminating the need for a qualifying exam.
[$\overline{X}$ 3.85, S.D. 1.05]   (3) (12)   (9) (50) (26)

25. If tax certification were to 1 2 3 4 5
occur, annual continuing education requirements in the
tax area are imperative.
[$\overline{X}$ 1.88, S.D. .88]   (35) (50)   (6)   (9)   (0)

26. If tax certification were to 1 2 3 4 5
occur, annual continuing tax
work experience require-
ments are imperative.
[$\overline{X}$ 2.09, S.D. .93]   (27) (47) (21)   (3)   (2)

27. For maintaining a tax certi- 1 2 3 4 5
fication, education should be
more important than experience.
[$\overline{X}$ 3.47, S.D. .99]   (3) (15) (26) (44) (12)

28. For maintaining a tax certi- 1 2 3 4 5
fication, tax accountants
should supply periodic letters
of reference.
[$\overline{X}$ 4.09, S.D. .75]   (0)   (3) (15) (53) (29)

29. For maintaining a tax certi- 1 2 3 4 5
fication, experience should
be more important than education.
[$\overline{X}$ 2.65, S.D. 1.01]   (12) (38) (24) (26)   (0)

30. For maintaining a tax certi- 1   2   3   4   5
    fication, tax accountants
    should be required to pass a
    periodic exam.
    [X̄ 3.53, S.D. 1.24.89]   (3)   (26)   (12)   (32)   (27)

31. Please feel free to comment
    on any aspect of the ques-
    tionnaire.
*[ ] denotes mean response (X̄) and standard deviation (S.D.).
 ( ) provides percentage responses.

Appendix B follows

APPENDIX B: NEW EMPLOYEE DEMOGRAPHICS

Tax Department New Employee Since 1981	Date Hired	Degree (BS/MS/MBA)	Major	Institution Granting Latest Degree	Annual Starting Salary	Sex (M/F)	Previous Work Experience Accounting (Yes No #Yrs)	Previous Work Experience Taxation (Yes No #Yrs)	Previous Education Accounting (Very Weak 1 2 3 4 5 Very Strong)	Previous Education Taxation (Very Weak 1 2 3 4 5 Very Strong)	Other Comments
1.									1 2 3 4 5	1 2 3 4 5	
2.									1 2 3 4 5	1 2 3 4 5	
3.									1 2 3 4 5	1 2 3 4 5	
4.									1 2 3 4 5	1 2 3 4 5	
5.									1 2 3 4 5	1 2 3 4 5	
6.									1 2 3 4 5	1 2 3 4 5	
7.									1 2 3 4 5	1 2 3 4 5	
8.									1 2 3 4 5	1 2 3 4 5	
9.									1 2 3 4 5	1 2 3 4 5	
10.									1 2 3 4 5	1 2 3 4 5	
11.									1 2 3 4 5	1 2 3 4 5	
12.									1 2 3 4 5	1 2 3 4 5	
13.									1 2 3 4 5	1 2 3 4 5	
14.									1 2 3 4 5	1 2 3 4 5	
15.									1 2 3 4 5	1 2 3 4 5	
16.									1 2 3 4 5	1 2 3 4 5	
17.									1 2 3 4 5	1 2 3 4 5	
18.									1 2 3 4 5	1 2 3 4 5	
19.									1 2 3 4 5	1 2 3 4 5	
20.									1 2 3 4 5	1 2 3 4 5	

CAUTION:

TEACHING AND RESEARCH AWARDS AHEAD

William H. Bassichis, D. Larry Crumbley, and
Carlton D. Stolle

ABSTRACT

The adverse effects that may accompany various awards to faculty members
are enumerated. Proper planning is critical because avoiding tax liability on
those awards has become more difficult in recent years. Suggestions are
presented which could minimize undesirable tax consequences.

The practice of rewarding outstanding educators has a long history. Student
groups, alumni organizations, or university administrations choose worthy
recipients and honor their accomplishments with plaques and watches and
sometimes with cash awards. Generally awards are taxable, but certain
types of awards given for specific types of achievement may avoid taxation.

Advances in Taxation, Volume 1, pages 199–210.
Copyright © 1987 JAI Press Inc.
All rights of reproduction in any form reserved.
ISBN: 0–89232–782–0

However, care must be used in designing the selection process and choosing the recipient; otherwise, the award will be considered nothing more than another form of compensation.

Awards can be, and probably have been, given for almost every kind of human endeavor—from the heroic to the frivolous, for the greatest of altruistic acts to the blatantly ridiculous, for achievement in sport and for achievement of the intellect. Section 74 of the Internal Revenue Code and Section 1.74 of the Regulations clearly make most awards taxable.

Awards to faculty members take on special characteristics. Most often the recipient is an employee of the honoring institution involved in teaching, research, service, or administration and the award is generally given in recognition for noteworthy accomplishment.

AWARDS AS TAXABLE COMPENSATION

On the surface, if an award is in recognition of some achievement connected with the employment of the recipient, the award is merely additional compensation, and the fair market value of the award is to be included in gross income of the recipient. (Sec. 74(a); Reg. Sec. 1.74–(a)(1)) Also, awards that are no more than incentive bonuses are also another form of compensation and are taxable (LTR 8228112). Care must be taken in structuring the award because the appearance of an award as additional compensation will defeat any tax advantage. Thus, in absence of the special characteristics which render an award nontaxable, an award by a college or university to its exceptional faculty is generally considered additional compensation. Preserving tax deductibility of an award under tax reform will become even more difficult. We shall examine the recent evaluation of the law affecting these awards.

Prior to the enactment of the Internal Revenue Code of 1954, tax treatment of prizes was determined by case law, and awards were generally treated as tax-free gifts (Rev. Rul. 54–110, 1954–1 C.B. 28). Winners of well-known prestigious awards like the Nobel and Pulitzer Prizes have always found those awards to be tax-free. However, even though a faculty member may have received a less prestigious award than than the two mentioned, Section 74(b) enacted as part of the Internal Revenue Code of 1954, provided an avenue to avoid taxation. The manner in which the awards are structured, including the way in which recipients are chosen and conditions under which the award are granted, are crucial. The teacher receiving an award for distinguished teaching or research may find such award either taxable or nontaxable. This has been neither an easy nor clear area of law; nonetheless a long list of regulations, letter rulings, and court cases do provide a pattern which help determine the taxability of such awards.

RECENT CONDITIONS FOR NONTAXABILITY

In recent years three statutory conditions had to be satisfied in order for an award to be nontaxable. First, it must have been made primarily for religious, charitable, scientific, educational, artistic, literary, or civic achievement. Second, the recipient must not have placed his or her own name into nomination for the award. Third, the recipient must have no future obligation to the grantor after the award is given (Sec 74(b)). Each of these conditions requires further elaboration.

Condition 1: The Limited Fields Qualifying for Tax-Free Awards

There are a limited number of fields of achievement in which awards may escape taxation. The fields listed in Section 74(b) are the following: religious, charitable, scientific, educational, artistic, literary, and civic. Awards are definitely taxable if given for achievement in a field other than those listed above [*Simmons* v. *U.S.*, 308 F.2d 160 (CA–4, 1962)], but even if achievement is in one of the listed fields, the award may still be taxed unless other conditions are satisfied (Rev. Rul. 57–460, 1957–2, C.B. 69). For example, awards to athletes recognizing exceptional prowess in a sport are taxable because the first test is not met—sports is not one of the explicitly mentioned categories for which exclusion can be granted [*Paul Hornung*, 47 TC 428 (1967) and *Wills* v. *Commissioner,* 411 F.2d 537 (CA–9, 1969)].

Awards made to faculty members can generally meet this first test because their work is normally for an educational institution and typically represents achievement in the educational area. If the award is given to honor activities not of an educational nature the award cannot escape taxation. For example, if a faculty member receives an award for exemplary support of his university's athletic program, the first test for exclusion is not met because the awarded activity is not educational.

Whether one's honored activities fall into one of the favored fields is not clear in all situations. The argument for nontaxability of an award failed in two court cases involving government employees when the courts decided that their "scientific" achievement was really "technical" achievement [*Frederick W. Denniston*, 343 F.2d 312 (CA–4, 1964), and *Griggs* v. *U.S.*, 314 F.2d 515 (Ct.Cl., 1963)].

A more recent case decided in favor of the award's recipient was that of Robert Jones. In the *Jones* case the award was made to this NASA scientist based on his overall scientific achievements. The award was not given for any particular scientific achievement nor for any specific activity connected with his employment. Furthermore, Jones was not required to release any claims or compensation or to execute any licenses to the government as a condition for receiving the award. Instead, Jones' achievements were considered valuable to aeronautical and space activities and to the advancement of scientific knowledge in general.

The Ninth Circuit ruled that the Jones award was nontaxable. If the award had been made for a specific achievement related to his work with NASA, the implication of the decision is that the award would have been taxable [*Jones* v. *U.S.*, 743 F.2d (CA–9, 1984)]. The key to the taxpayer's victory was that an exchange of services for the award did not take place. The IRS indicated in Rev. Rul. 86–31 that the IRS does not agree with the *Jones* decision. The IRS will continue to follow Reg. Sec. 1.74–1(b) which states that Section 74(b) does not exclude from gross income prizes or awards from an employer to an employee in recognition of some achievement connected with the employee's employment.

Contrast the Jones award with another award made by NASA. In the *Rogallo* case, a license was granted to the government to use a specific invention which was the subject of the award. Rogallo's award was taxed because it was argued that his activities were for the benefit of NASA and the award was an extension of compensation to him (that is, an exchange services for the award occured) [*Rogallo* v. *U.S.*, 475 F.2d (Ca-4 1973)].

The award must be given to honor rather than to compensate, but the distinction between an honor and compensation is sometimes difficult to discern. When an employer makes an award out of a desire to honor or show respect or admiration for an employee, and the award is not compensation for acts which primarily benefit the employer, the award should be excludible under Section 74. When the facts suggest that the employer's purpose in making the award was to compensate the employee, the award may be included in the employee's income.

Clearly an award made by an employer to an employee carries the appearance of compensation. It is perhaps a stronger case for nontaxability when the grantor is an entity separate from the employer such as in the case when an alumni group selects the faculty member and grants the award. However, the source of award funding from other than the employer is in itself no guarantee of nontaxability. In Rev. Rul. 57–460 (1957–2 C.B. 69) an individual gave a substantial gift to a university with the stipulation that the funds were to be used to reward outstanding performance through a salary supplement. The IRS ruled that these awards, as salary supplements, were added compensation regardless of the source, and the amounts were taxable.

Condition 2: The Faculty Member May Do Nothing to Enter the Contest or Proceeding

Faculty member X has for years been known to friends, colleagues, students, and former students as an outstanding educator. It is time once again for an award to be given to honor an outstanding educator. Students of X convince her to submit her name for consideration. If X wins the award the IRS will probably declare the award taxable (even if all other tests for nontaxable status are met) because of X's role in "entering" herself for consideration. A winner of a government service award was taxed because he submitted his name and qualifications for the award [*Max Isenbergh*, 31 TC 1046 (1959)].

It is unclear at what point the actions of a person cause him or her to be considered for an award and whether those actions constitute "entering" the proceedings. Clearly, if the recipient took no action to place his or her name in nomination and was unaware that he or she was even being considered, the rule has not been violated. On the other hand, suppose a potential recipient was asked to provide a resume to a selection committee after the individual was nominated by others. The person is aware of the nomination and now has become an active participant in the selection process. Has the award been tainted by providing a resume? Perhaps not, but one can see that the differentiation becomes less clear and is more subject to dispute. Awards to high school students for academic and civic achievements were tax-free even though the students had to fill out forms and appear for personal interviews. However, the students had previously been nominated by faculty members (Rev. Rul. 57–67, 1957–1 C.B. 33). On the other hand, if a faculty member influences her students to nomininate her for an award, the tax-free status of the award may be jeopardized. Clearly, the less involvement a recipient has with the nomination and selection process, the better the chance of the tax-free status being upheld.

Condition 3: No Required Substantial Future Service

Satisfaction of a third statutory condition is also necessary for favorable tax treatment. If the award requires any future service, the tax-free status will be lost. Letter Ruling 8211080 describes an award which clearly meets the third condition. An award recipient was granted tax-free treatment in part because the grantor required that the award be paid even if the recipient died, became disabled, or left the faculty of the institution. The award was not conditioned upon the future employment of the recipient.

As a second example, amounts paid to scientists by a muscle research institute were not excludible. The awards were not primarily made in recognition of past achievement, and substantial future services were required [*Mueller* v. *Commissioner*, 338 F.2d 1015 (CA–1, 1964)]. In Rev. Rul. 68–20 (1968–1 C.B. 55), a manufacturer provided a beauty contest winner with a wardrobe, shoes, perfume, and cosmetics. Because the recipient was expected to perform services for the manufacturer, the fair market value of these items was taxable. Contrast this ruling with a scholarship award to a beauty contest winner. Because her public appearances following the contest were not necessary in order to receive the award, it was not taxable [*Wilson* v. *U.S.*, 322 F. Supp. 830 (DC Kan. 1971)]. See also *Benjamin Taylor, Jr.* (TCMemo 1982–163) where payments from the National Institute of Health to a Ph.D. were held to be taxable.

Rev. Rul 84–9 (1984–1, C.B. 22) provide two examples where awards were nontaxable because neither placed a continuing obligation on the recipient. In the first, annual payments were to continue for ten years, with the amount of the payments dependent on the recipient's age. In the second, annual payments were to continue for the lifetime of the recipient, who was at or near retirement, in the amount of $100 per year less the person's annual retirement income.

Recognition of Achievement of Employment

Aside from the above three statutory requirements, the regulations impose a fourth condition for nontaxable treatment. Reg. Sec. 1.74–1(a)(1) indicates that a payment by an employer to an employee is taxable if the payment is in recognition of some achievement in connection with employment. In other words, if the award is work-related *and* paid by the employer, then the award is taxable income. Because a teaching or research award would seem both to qualify for exclusion according to the educational criteria and not to quality because teaching is connected with a teacher's employment, confusion results.

The courts have not completely accepted this condition suggested by the regulation. However, the amount of awards to employees made because of successful sales effort is taxable income [*Bell Electric Co*, 45 TC 158 (1965)]. The Ninth Circuit [*Rogallo* v. *U.S.* 475 F.2d 1 (CA–4 1973)] indicates that legislative history only partially supports this condition in the regulations. "Prizes and awards for scientific or other pro bono achievements, however, are not disguised compensation."

If prizes or awards are incentive bonuses or disguised compensation such payments are taxable income. For example, the fair market value of a trip to Japan awarded to a merchant was taxable. This trip was furnished by his suppliers and was based upon meeting certain production quotas (*Claud E. Lynch*, TCMemo 1983–173).

The Ninth Circuit has refused to follow Reg. Sec. 1.74–1(a)(1) to the extent it requires all awards from employers to employees to be included in gross income [*Jones* v. *U.S.*, 743 F.2d 1429 (CA—9, 1984)]. Instead, the Court adopted the rule that awards made by an employer to an employee to show honor, respect, or admiration, and not made in compensation for a specific benefit accruing to the employer, are excludible from gross income.

IMPORTANCE OF PROPER PLANNING

The strongest case for a teaching or research award being held nontaxable exists when the following conditions are present:

1. The recipient's outstanding past contributions are honored.
2. The award is made for the purpose of honor alone with no intention to supplement salary or provide an incentive.
3. The employee did nothing to enter the proceedings for nomination and selection. An employee should avoid the taint of self-nomination or nomination by someone else who the employee may have influenced in fact or appearance.
4. The award does not obligate the employee to the employer in the future in any manner.

Many universities or departments require that any faculty member wishing to be considered for an award submit biographical data and suggestions of names of former students and present students and colleagues to be contacted for letters of recommendation. This approach clearly violates the IRS criteria that no self-nominations be allowed. Also, since the university administration is in a sense "the employer," this relationship raises the issue of indirect compensation.

The best planning approach would be to let an outside source (for example, an alumni group) select the recipient. While the organization wishing to award faculty members would have the task of soliciting names of possible candidates and deciding on the recipients, this process could be facilitated by using faculty members previously awarded for teaching excellence or student committees. Biographical data are available from sources other than the candidates themselves, such as the departmental personnel records. Letters of recommendation could be solicited through organization newsletters or university newspapers. Any restrictions the granting organization wished to impose would be independent of the employer and could not constitute violation of IRS criteria. Finally, since the granting organization is not the employer it would be difficult to argue that the award was "disguised compensation." Obviously, university and departmental administrations may not wish to divorce themselves from the selection process, but the risks of losing tax incentives are great when the employer retains too much control over the selection process.

SABBATICALS AND PAID LEAVES

In the minds of some, paid faculty development leaves are closely associated with awards and honors. However, the IRS is not so benevolent. Paid faculty development leaves are generally undertaken to increase the usefulness or professional effectiveness of the faculty member to the institution. The act of increasing one's usefulness carries a future obligation to the institution, so the intent behind sabbaticals and similar leaves of absence violates the conditions which makes certain honors and awards tax-free (*Joseph Werganz*, TCMemo 1981–403). Do not forget, however, that if the faculty member moves to a new temporary location, many living expenses become deductible as travel expenses.

PROFESSORSHIPS AND CHAIRS

The use of the terms "professorships" and "chairs" carries various meanings, and implies a wide array of purposes and funding arrangements. When a faculty member is awarded either a professorship or a chair and the monetary amount is clearly intended as a salary or a salary supplement, the amount is taxable to the recipient. However, in specialized cases, amounts paid in connection with a professorship or chair may be considered a nontaxable award.

Avoiding taxation of payments from professorships and chairs is complicated because such payments generally are designated as salary supplements intended to attract superior faculty members or to award past accomplishments and spur superior efforts in the future. Such intentions make the amount taxable. In addition, the amounts involved are also significant, are paid over a long duration, are paid by an employer, and are used to determine other job-related employee benefits (such as retirement benefits).

Consider the following form of professorship. A large energy company has funded a professorship "for the purpose of awarding past achievements in teaching, research, and service, and to encourage future exemplary performance." The amount involved is $500 per month to be paid over 48 months to the recipient with payments continuing as long as the faculty member remains an employee in good standing with the university. The payments are used to compute the fringe benefits of the employee. While the situation is hypothetical, the IRS would undoubtedly consider the $6,000 per year fully taxable.

Contrast the above example with the following facts described in Letter Ruling 8211080. A charitable organization accepted gifts from alumni and friends. Gifts were given with the intention that they be used to recognize outstanding faculty accomplishments. A special committee recommended nominees to an independent board of trustees which selected the recipient. The recipient was to receive the award in five annual installments and the amount was not used to compute fringe benefits or retirement benefits. Also, the amount would be paid even if the faculty members died, became disabled, retired, or left the institution. The IRS recognized this "chair" as a tax-free award. Ltr. Rul. 8211080 determined this professorship to be a nontaxable award (See also Ltr. Rul. 7948023).

FELLOWSHIPS AND SCHOLARSHIP GRANTS

Grants to faculty members may also be made to encourage continued study and research in their specialized areas. These grants may carry the designation of scholarships or fellowships which offer certain tax incentives if they qualify under Section 117.

While the distinction between scholarships and fellowships is not always clear, scholarships are usually given to deserving students pursuing college study, whereas fellowships are given to aid individuals in study or research (Reg. Sec. 1.117–3). Generally, the term scholarship is the designation commonly used when the recipient is a degree-seeking graduate or undergraduate student, while the designation of fellowship is used when the recipient is a faculty member and not a candidate for a degree (Reg. Sec. 1.117–3(a) and (c). The name by which the grant is called is not critical from a tax standpoint. What is critical is whether the recipient is a degree-seeking student.

A grant received by a degree candidate will be allowed certain exclusions for the portion of the receipts that are not payments for teaching, research, or other services that are in effect conditions of employment [Sec. 117(b)(1)]. However, our focus will remain on grants to faculty, that is, individuals who are not degree candidates.

Fellowships generally allow for two types of exclusions from gross income: a $300 per month exclusion for educational costs and an exclusion for payments which reimburse certain other study and research costs.

The $300 per Month Exclusion

Fellowship funding is normally provided in the form of monies or as direct reduction to educational registration fees. Fellowship fees which qualify for an exclusion of $300 per month [Sec. 117 (b)(2)(B)] are tuition fees, including other required fees for registration, fees to buy required books, supplies, and equipment, and fees to pay for services and housing costs of the recipient and family. These latter fees may include costs for room, food, and laundry services [Reg. Sec. 1.117–3(c)(d)].

The law provides that up to $300 per month can be excluded from gross income if fellowship funds are received to cover the aforementioned costs. Furthermore, the $300 exclusion can be claimed for up to 36 months or the period of time covered by the fellowship, whichever is shorter [Sec. 117(2)(B)].

An *award* excludable under Section 74(b) honors past achievements of the recipient and has no connection with future activities [Reg. Sec. 1.74–1(b)]. A fellowship contemplates future activities by furthering the recipient's study or research [Reg. Sec. 1.117–3(c)]. Certain exclusions are available for fellowships and scholarships. Although these are not as potentially advantageous as in the case of an award under Section 74(b), the facts of the situation will determine whether the payment may be classified as an award or as a fellowship. This is a mutually exclusive determination [*Cass* v. *Commissioner*, 86 TC No. 75 (1986)].

Other Fellowship Exclusions

In addition to the fees above (which qualify for the $300 per month exclusion), a fellowship may provide funding to cover other costs necessary for study or research. If fellowship funds are received to pay for travel in connection with the studies, other out-of-pocket research costs, clerical help or equipment, the taxpayer may exclude from income that part of the funds which were actually expended by the recipient [Sec. 117(a)].

The recipient must include in gross income the amount of any fellowship funds received above the actual expenditure for any of the four types of costs specifically covered. Any fellowship funds received to cover costs not includable in the four conditions listed above, must be included in gross income [Reg. Sec. 117–1(a)]. Reimbursable travel expenses which qualify for the exclusion include the cost of meals, lodging, and an allowance for the recipient's family [Reg. Sec. 117–1(b)].

Timing and the Fellowship Grant

The timing of the payments during the period of the fellowship grant is important in determining when income is to be reported. A brief example will show the effects of the timing of the payments.

Assume Dr. Scholar is awarded a post-doctorate fellowship grant in the amount of $8,400 which will cover the grant period September 1, 1986 to May 31, 1988 (21 months). Dr. Scholar's university has given him the option of receiving grant income on one of two payment schedules: (a) the entire $8,400 may be received on September 1, 1986 or (b) it may be received at $400 per month, beginning in September 1986 and ending in May 1988.

If Dr. Scholar, a calendar year taxpayer, chooses option (a), he may exclude $6,300 ($300 x 21 months) of the $8,400 from income in 1986 and exclude nothing in 1987 or 1988. While he would be allowed the total available exclusion in 1986, he would include $2,100 in gross income in 1986.

If (b) is the choice, in 1986 Dr. Scholar may exclude $1,200 ($300 x 4) from gross income while $400, the excess of the $400 per month received over the exclusion limit, would be included in gross income. In 1987 he will exclude from gross income $3,600 ($300 x 12) while including $1,200. In 1988, he will exclude $1,500 ($300 x 5) while including $500 that year [Reg. Sec. 1.117–2(b)(3)].

Source of the Fellowship

We normally think of the grantor of a fellowship as being the employing college or university of the recipient. While this is usually the case, other fellowship grantors will be recognized by the IRS without jeopardizing the tax incentives of the grant. Other than colleges and universities or other tax-exempt organizations recognized in Reg. Sec. 501(c)(3)–1, the following are also qualified grantors of fellowships:

1. foreign governments,
2. international, binational, or multinational cultural foundations created under the Mutual Educational and Cultural Exchange Act of 1961, or
3. the Federal government, its instrumentalities or agencies, including a state, territory or the District of Columbia [IRC Sec. 117(2)(A)].

Importance of Compensation and Fellowship Distinction

As in most transactions, the IRS will look beyond a transaction to its substance to determine its tax consequences [Reg. Sec. 1.117–4]. Any fellowship which is given as additional compensation to the recipient rather than for the legitimate pursuit of education or research will be taxed as income. Any time the grant is intended to pay for study or research primarily to benefit the grantor, the grant will be considered compensation and will be taxable, but if the grant is primarily to aid the recipient in study and research without compensation as the motive, the grant may qualify as a fellowship and enjoy the associated tax benefits [Reg. Sec. 1.117–4(c)(2)].

CONCLUSION

There is a split between the Fourth Circuit and Ninth Circuit with respect to awards given to employees to recognize lifetime rather than single achievements. Until this issue is settled by the Supreme Court or by new legislation, adverse effects may accompany various research and teaching awards made to faculty members.

A second source of uncertainty is the fact that at the time of this writing, tax reform legislation is still being debated. Unfortunately, it seems certain that the outcome will be less favorable to award recipients than current law.